A Kinder, Gentler America

A Kinder, Gentler America

Melancholia and the Mythical 1950s

Mary Caputi

University of Minnesota Press
Minneapolis • London

Excerpts from *The Arcades Project,* by Walter Benjamin, translated by Howard Eiland and Kevin McLaughlin and published by the Belknap Press of Harvard University Press, reprinted by permission of Harvard University Press. Copyright 1999 by the President and Fellows of Harvard College.

Excerpts from *The Origin of German Tragic Drama,* by Walter Benjamin, translated by John Osborne, reprinted by permission of Verso Press.

Excerpts from *Black Sun: Depression and Melancholia,* by Julia Kristeva, translated by Leon Roudiez, reprinted by permission of Columbia University Press.

Published by the University of Minnesota Press
111 Third Avenue South, Suite 290
Minneapolis, MN 55401-2520
http://www.upress.umn.edu

Library of Congress Cataloging-in-Publication Data

Caputi, Mary, 1957–
    A kinder, gentler America : melancholia and the mythical 1950s / Mary Caputi.
        p. cm.
    Includes bibliographical references and index.
    ISBN 0-8166-4407-1 (hc : alk. paper) — ISBN 0-8166-4408-X (pb : alk. paper)
    1. United States—Civilization—1945-. 2. Nineteen fifties. 3. National characteristics, American. 4. Popular culture—United States. 5. Nostalgia—United States.
6. Depression, Mental—Political aspects—United States. 7. United States—Politics and government—1945-1989. 8. United States—Politics and government—1989-.
9. Political culture—United States. 10. Conservatism—United States. I. Title.
    E169.12.C274 2005
    973.921—dc22
                                                        2005012921

Printed in the United States of America on acid-free paper

The University of Minnesota is an equal-opportunity educator and employer.

12 11 10 09 08 07 06 05   10 9 8 7 6 5 4 3 2 1

For my parents

Contents

ACKNOWLEDGMENTS

Many people helped me with this project in its various stages of completion, and I'm grateful for the confidence they expressed in it and the guidance they gave me. Clark Dougan and Marlie Wasserman helped me in the earliest days by assuring me that it was a feasible project of interest, and their encouragement and editorial advice were much needed at the time. Friends and colleagues who also read early drafts or who discussed the manuscript with me in its more embryonic stages include Fred Alford, Elyse Blankley, Susan Buck-Morss, Cynthia Burack, Larry George, Jim Glass, Chuck Noble, Edwin Roberts, Ron Schmidt, and Victor Wolfenstein. I am also grateful for the valuable input of Dan O'Connor later. Among the most influential of those who read the manuscript in its entirety is Bill Chaloupka, whose invaluable insights helped shape the book into its current form. He provided useful references and offered superb commentary that helped strengthen the manuscript as a piece of theoretical writing and as an interpretation of American politics, culture, and history. The final outcome is very indebted to his contributions. I am also grateful for the input of my anonymous reviewers, who gave me excellent feedback and advice.

My deepest thanks go to Carrie Mullen for her sustained and sustaining confidence in the project's worth, and for her professional savvy in steering it through some narrow straits. Her knowledge and experience helped guide the book, and her confidence was always appreciated. I'm also grateful to Jason Weidemann for his careful attention to the text and artwork, and to Judy Selhorst for her fine copyediting.

My family and friends also gave me much help and support along the way. I am especially grateful to my parents, my sisters and their families, Beth Lau, and of course my husband, Richard, and daughter, Rahael, for listening to my endless commentary on this project and for offering encouragement, caring, and laughs when they were needed.

CHAPTER 1

"The Fifties," an American Metaphor

Neoconservatism and the 1950s

Since the Reagan administration, the decade of the 1950s has loomed
large in American political culture. Thanks to the neoconservative ideology that Reagan proclaimed at the national level, it is a time span
that has acquired a dense layering of mythological meanings and metaphoric overtones, an era freighted with encoded references that play
on America's self-understanding. Indeed, by now, "the 1950s" no longer
refers to a mere ten-year interval whose significance can be captured
in historical narrative, for its impact reaches beyond chronology. For
Americans, the 1950s bristle with an array of ideological connotations, a swirl of aesthetic resonances, a battery of moral implications
so highly charged and emotionally laden that any mention of the
decade in the current context far exceeds literal, historical references.
The surplus of meaning surrounding this decade causes it to operate
as a richly endowed American metaphor: today, the 1950s is a figure
of speech, a trope that highlights the profound anxieties surrounding
our self-definition.

The flurry of associations that now accompany this decade have thus come to play a special role in America's culture since the Reagan Revolution. For it was then that the neoconservative groundswell sought to combat at the national level the free fall of meaning under way in the United States since the 1960s and 1970s, tapping into Americans' angst concerning our faltering, floundering identity. Now at the national helm, neoconservatism promised to return to a simpler, clearer American identity, which two decades of hang-loose liberals had, in its opinion, nearly destroyed. Hippie values, feminism, gay pride, multiculturalism—these cultural forces had caused us to lose our innocence and to stray from the reputedly safe, self-referencing world of Ozzie and Harriet into the darker reaches of arbitrary meaning. Both the fun and the anxiety of postmodern uncertainty had come to replace the would-be stability and cultural cohesion that rabbit-eared TV sets and kids in striped T-shirts recalled. If the 1960s and 1970s had sought to subvert our American heritage—if they had cast doubt on the Founding Fathers and Christopher Columbus, on Lewis and Clark and Daniel Boone—neoconservatism was here to reaffirm these, proclaiming that the old was new again and that our nation could again ride tall in the saddle.

Above all, the neoconservative episteme insisted that our embattled nation needed to reconnect with its true foundations.[1] It needed to recall our past, revive our cultural heroes, and consider anew the principles that had made our nation great. Thus, in his fatherly fashion, Reagan often spoke of "restoring" our nation, of "returning" us to older values, of "regaining" an anterior mission that had been lost during (what he and others deemed) the turbulent, crazy years. "Let us begin an era of national renewal," he proclaimed in his 1981 inaugural address. "And as we renew ourselves here in our own land . . . [w]e will again be the exemplar of freedom."[2] Neoconservatism would be the road home to a safety and an innocence, an Eden, that had long been the mythical substrate of America. This movement's mission was thus to reconnect us to a past that would then be projected onto the future, to return us to an innocence that would become the innocence of our future. In the words of George H. W. Bush, America under neoconservative direction was in search of a "kinder, gentler" version of itself. Intuitively, we understood this as a search for a 1950s version of America to be replayed in the present, like an old-time movie in which we would all play a part, with a golden oldie as its theme song.[3]

With neoconservatism's rise to the national helm in the early 1980s, it is perhaps not accidental that Ruby's Diner, a blast-from-the-past old-fashioned American eatery, opened just about then, in December 1982.

This 1940s-style restaurant exudes nostalgia, as its decor, furniture, glassware, and, to some extent, menu are reminiscent of the 1940s. Old-timey advertisements for Coca-Cola cover the diner's walls, and gum ball machines, vintage black telephones, and nostalgic, post–World War II signs take customers back half a century. Even the waiters and waitresses dress in 1940s attire. Here, the ramped-up hyperexcitement of contemporary rock 'n' roll seems out of place, as we expect some crooner's soothing melody to be heard from the old-style jukebox. All of this allows Americans to enjoy postwar anachronisms as though they were a living reality, to sit and drink Maxwell House coffee from heavy china cups just as easily as they might enjoy a Frappuccino at the local Starbuck's.

Although Ruby's celebrates the 1940s, it is especially the 1950s that sets in motion the thematics of America's self-definition. The 1950s are that robust, expansive decade announcing that good times had returned to America after wartime deprivations. It designates—mendaciously, many feel—an era of prosperity, family, and fun such that many use it as the benchmark against which to measure other time periods. For this reason, the decade touches a nerve in us all, neoconservative or not. Indeed, even those who deplored Bush's quest for a kinder, gentler

The interior of Ruby's Diner, a blast-from-the-past eatery that opened in Balboa, California, in 1982.

nation, insisting the 1950s *weren't* so wonderful,[4] nevertheless knew instantly how he proposed to fulfill his longing: he wanted to bring back 1950s culture within the contemporary setting, to make the current, confused melee of shifting signifiers and destabilized meanings resemble an episode of *Father Knows Best*. To be sure, even Americans who never experienced the historical 1950s seem to understand that this time frame somehow correlates with America's interpretation of itself, and that the decade's defining attributes partake of a narrative about who we are and what we stand for.

Hence, at this writing, Target department stores across the country feature a line of products for the home that are collectively titled Swell, an unmistakably 1950s expression. Swell's insignia is that of happy housewives, some of whom obviously fit a 1950s profile. They wear fitted, full-skirted dresses, and some have flip hairstyles. As they help advertise housewares, they strike poses that suggest joy and fulfillment in the home: life is grand in America, and Target is here to let the good times roll. The simple lettering and pink coloring of this line of merchandise also invoke 1950s styles as they appear on items ranging from patio dinnerware to bath towels, from hair accessories to hardware. Bath towels and towel hooks further suggest a 1950s mind-set by promoting "Good Clean Fun."

Surely not all the Target shoppers who consume these items in the early twenty-first century lived through the 1950s. Many of them are only vaguely aware, if not entirely ignorant, of Donna Reed's serene smile and Howdy Doody's silliness, of Joe McCarthy's witch hunt and of the box of Jell-O so crucial to the Rosenberg trial.[5] Nevertheless, allusions to the time span set off something other than literal meanings. Indeed, the presence of Swell products in Targets across the country suggests that reference to the decade carries deep metaphoric power. At issue is the *mythical* 1950s, that "kinder, gentler" time by now saturated with meaning whose tremendous spiritual force jettisons the need for historical accuracy.

This spiritual force is, of course, variously received in American culture, for not everyone endorses the mythmaking activity that the decade inspires. Persons of varying and often contrasting political opinions and professional interests have engaged the decade's myriad connotations differently. But, importantly, they all engage it. Although disagreement over the 1950s lived experience abounds, such interpretive variety does not preclude consensus as to the set of meanings invariably put into play by any mention of our nation at midcentury. There is consensus, even if unspoken, over what the 1950s invoke and how exactly the decade's florid mythological powers might contravene our multicultural, globalizing, postmodern sensibilities. The briefest glance at Ike's crew cut and happy grin, the faintest allusion to Mamie's pert bangs and whimsical charm bracelet, suffices to set in motion a panoply of consistent associations that now cling to the expansive, exhilarating, communist-bashing 1950s, a decade whose homeward orientation ironically fueled the engine of its manifestly powerful forward drive.

In the contemporary setting, there is of course disagreement regarding the credibility of our kinder, gentler potential and regarding whether the 1950s really are America's blueprint. Such disagreements divide along clear ideological lines. Neoconservatives and others of traditional orientation endorse the time span enthusiastically, often viewing it as the seminal, originary site of our nation's identity. They concur that the 1950s performed the crucial, obligatory task of reengaging our nation's anointed mission established with the pilgrims and made paramount during the Founding. This was a mission whose aim was to reaffirm the bond between earthly ambition and God's intention, to align the weighty history of human chronology—time as we know it—with the blessed register of cairology: the redeemed, messianic time whose

Swell products at Target are designed to recall a 1950s lifestyle.

severance from God had been healed. In other words, they share the vision of such early American authors as James Fenimore Cooper and Herman Melville, who argued that, in many ways, America saw itself as the New Garden of Eden located outside of chronological time, a nation of pioneers on a spiritual journey unlike that traveled by Europe.[6] America for them has always been the New Jerusalem, a nation blessed unlike any other whose time and mission therefore occupy a register radically different from other countries' experience of time. This understanding of America as the New Jerusalem, a culture less mired than others in chronological time, is crucial to the neoconservative mission, even if it remains unstated, for it explains the desire to escape from a bewildering, fractious present and recover a happier, more innocent time in the past when our national purpose seemed clearer.

Neoconservatives are persuaded that a true, foundational identity — an identity begun with the pilgrims and revitalized during the 1950s — exists in America's lived history and can be projected onto the future. For them, the 1950s are not a mythological construct or a mythical departure from reality. There is virtually no slippage between what *actually* happened and what they *wish* had happened, between the television version of 1950s reality and everyday life during the decade. Many argue that the Norman Rockwell vision of American life for the most part records life as it was, illustrating the paradisiacal attributes of our political, cultural mission. The happy families and safe neighborhoods, the homespun quality of simple American virtues, the innocence and predictability of it all: the minutest detail of Rockwell's charmed vision reaffirms America's greater purpose.

Rockwell himself stated that "even if it wasn't an ideal world, it should be."[7] Subsequently, especially in his earlier years, he often painted those aspects of the world that seemed ideal, insisting, "I will not disturb my audience."[8] And indeed, many Americans choose along with him to focus only on our nation's friendly familiarity, the cozy sense of being at home, the warmth that accompanies the fact of being known in a safe environment. They wish to see an idealized 1950s environment as America's true environment while lamenting the violence and uncertainties of the present as aberrations. Eager to revive a 1950s ethos while searching for this kinder, gentler country, former Speaker of the House Newt Gingrich therefore urges Americans to peruse carefully the Rockwell illustrations that graced the covers of the *Saturday Evening Post* throughout the 1940s and 1950s. "Go and look at . . . *The Saturday Evening Post* from around 1955," he writes, insisting that in "the Norman Rockwell paintings of the 1940s and 1950s, there was a clear sense of what it meant to be an American."[9]

In specifying the Norman Rockwell of the 1940s and 1950s, Gingrich offers a quite selective account of the painter's repertoire, for in later decades Rockwell's art displayed less of the earlier, signature coziness and ceded to a more painful glimpse at our nation's uglier realities. To be sure, American poverty, crime, and racial conflict made for a less euphemistic interpretation of what goes on within our borders as the artist seemed far more willing to disturb his audience. Yet Gingrich's ability to read these paintings selectively, along with a tendency to condemn the 1960s and 1970s, exemplifies neoconservatism's mythical reconstruction of America's true foundation located at midcentury. Mythmaking occurs when the belief in a missing substrate is made credible; it occurs when the search for a missing foundation seems a worthy and credible endeavor.

How starkly Gingrich's desideratum—the desire that we might share "a clear sense of what it means to be an American"—contrasts with the undeniable spiritual angst and welter of postmodern confusion that now characterize America. If only Americans could successfully overcome such profound malaise merely by reading magazines. If only our nation's classrooms—to pick one out of many American battlegrounds—could embody less confusion simply by appreciating the charm of Rockwell's *Teacher's Birthday* (1956). Little wonder, then, that George W. Bush, who follows in his father's footsteps and hopes to revive a 1950s sensibility, has been described as "a throwback," "Eisenhower with hair."[10] Little wonder that William H. Rehnquist's Supreme Court has been interpreted as taking us "back to the future."[11] In a way, then, Ike and Mamie still inhabit the White House, thus allowing us to forget about the troubled, intervening years that threw open the question of American identity and cast doubt on our cairological mission. In a way, a brush cut and pert bangs can still be seen by those who discern an effort to go backward as the younger Bush and wife Laura pursue their vision of the future.[12] Thus on the death of Reagan, the *Los Angeles Times* noted that "Republican spokesmen again look . . . for polite ways to remind [people] that Bush is, in many ways, Reagan's ideological heir."[13]

The conservator of an anterior culture, neoconservatism thus sees itself as the remnant, the "relic," that holds out hope for uncovering the Eden that is a substrate of the contemporary confusion.[14] This conservatorship is seen in nearly every aspect of its political agenda—for example, in its trumpeting of "family values" and passage of the Defense of Marriage Act (1996); in its opposition to progressive politics organized around feminism, gay pride, and racial relations; in its targeting first of an "evil empire" and subsequently of an "axis of evil"; in its support of the USA Patriot Act. It is seen in the claim that America experienced an internal cohesion that was latent if not manifest from its earliest days until the disruptive, disloyal, insane 1960s. Gingrich writes, "From the arrival of the English-speaking colonists in 1607 until 1965, there was one continuous civilization built around a set of

Norman Rockwell, *Teacher's Birthday*, cover, *Saturday Evening Post*, March 17, 1956. Printed by permission of the Norman Rockwell Family Agency. Copyright 2005 the Norman Rockwell Family Entities.

commonly accepted legal and cultural principles."[15] The political success of the neoconservative agenda subsequently relies on the mythico-poetic associations that surround our "continuous civilization" whose tenets were so beautifully captured in everyday life at midcentury. Contemporary references to the 1950s—to the happy nuclear family out for a ride in a shiny new convertible, Dad in a double-breasted blazer, Mom in pearls; to the malevolent Russian Bear drunk on vodka; to an energized Elvis Presley whose twitching, gyrating gestures were deemed egregiously salacious—deliver profound statements about America's

Norman Rockwell, *After the Prom*, cover, *Saturday Evening Post*, May 25, 1957.
Printed by permission of the Norman Rockwell Family Agency. Copyright 2005 the
Norman Rockwell Family Entities.

self-understanding both then and now, both at midcentury and today, amid a maelstrom of postmodern, multicultural indeterminacies. Thus, at the 2004 Republican National Convention, Governor Schwarzenegger of California could proclaim that "America is back," which of course assumes that it was temporarily gone.

In many ways, the 1950s probably *were* a kinder, gentler time. For many Americans—provided they were white, middle-class, Christian, and heterosexual—the decade probably *does* recall an innocent past. "The distorted sugar-coated nostalgia for this period is not all distorted and sugar-coated," writes Barbara Norfleet, whose collection of photographs titled *When We Liked Ike* illustrates the health and prosperity of the decade.[16] And Steven Spielberg admits that although he grew up in America, his first memories of Norman Rockwell were "almost subliminal," for the painter's vision was "already becoming part of the American fabric."[17] Yet we all know that extremely racist, sexist, and heterosexist prejudices were rampant in 1950s America, and that the safety and innocence that many knew was paid for by the segregation and discrimination imposed on others. Most recently, the film *Far from Heaven* (2002) has dramatized the tenuousness of 1950s mythology and the emotional pain that the pretense of safety and innocence in fact caused. It portrays an apparent dreamscape of 1950s conformity as the central characters cling as best they can to the white mainstream's lexicon of family values. The film's protagonist is a married, middle-class woman at midcentury who so epitomizes the joys of hearth and home that she is celebrated in the newspaper society pages. A paragon of 1950s etiquette, Cathy Whitaker is the perfect wife and mother; she dresses immaculately, lives in an impeccable home, and enjoys a color-coordinated world of cocktail parties, gallery openings, and vacations.[18] Her life seems so meticulously ordered that when her son says, "Ah geez," she reprimands him for his use of foul language.

Yet underneath, a different reality mars this beautiful tableau, as racial prejudice, class distinctions, and sexual taboos disrupt a seemingly perfect world. Cathy is ultimately forced to confront her husband's homosexuality as well as her own attraction to an African American man. She learns to accept that desires deemed illicit are nevertheless impossible to restructure. Moreover, she is troubled to learn that her closest friend is more accepting of her husband's proclivities than of her own attraction to a black. Thus behind the look, the veneer of contentment within white, mainstream 1950s America, there resides a jarring dissonance between social conventions and human desires. It is perhaps for this reason that *Far from Heaven*'s exquisite high color—its magnificent purples, oranges, reds, and greens that fill the screen—contrasts so sharply with the black-and-white palette we often associate with the decade. The rich hues make the film a series of stunning panoramic vistas and opulent interiors, implying that the decade knew an emotional and intellectual richness that is often overlooked: figuratively speaking, the 1950s were not as black-and-white, as ordered and predictable, as we tend to think. And if the forces that mar cultural integration were no less present then than they are now, then a mythico-poetic, *Ozzie and Harriet* version of the decade *is* dishonest. The 1950s did not revive an older, cairological mission, the film implies, but witnessed many fierce human dramas that were located not in Eden, but "far from heaven." Hence the film's title, color, and story line all contravene the neoconservative assurance that the 1950s offer a "clear sense of what it means to be an American." They suggest a different reality that was, with its racism, homophobia, and general prejudice, quite confused and unhappy.

Why the 1950s?

What in the lived history of the 1950s, when viewed with hindsight, confers on that decade a mythological status? Why might neoconservatism choose this decade to function as its mythically charged blueprint, thus participating in what Derrida terms "the complicity of origins"?[19] Surely the various successes of the postwar decade play a large role in answering this question. After 1945, the nation's emergence as a leading player in the international arena, our rise to superpower status along with our rebounding postwar economy, conferred an ideological self-certainty on our mission that surely resonated with the earlier thematics of America's unique and blessed status. Against the backdrop of success and prosperity, here had to be a deliberate confidence to our political profile, a discourse of self-assurance that affirmed that our identity was God given. With our recent military success, our emerging status as a superpower, and our ongoing economic growth, a blessed, Edenic status conceived since our inception (but often in abeyance) now seemed resuscitated, more alive than ever.

The paranoid, Manichaean politics of the Cold War years further allowed us to revive these cairological dimensions of our identity and to exaggerate the biblical thematics that many deemed implicit in our identity. For many, the Soviet Union provided ample and perfect contrast against which to measure our rewarded benevolence. Communism was atheistic and state-worshipping; it sought self-aggrandizement (which, presumably, we didn't) and resorted to evil tactics (which, presumably, we avoided). Whereas the Soviet Union embodied humanity's fall from grace, the United States enacted a redemptive politics that could cause cairological time to stand in alignment with chronology: it could reenter human history and make Eden real. Our extensive efforts to combat the Soviet Union's perverse secularism and evil political ideology were themselves a sign of America's ordained mission and Edenic

Norman Rockwell, *Before the Shot*, cover, *Saturday Evening Post*, March 15, 1958. Printed by permission of the Norman Rockwell Family Agency. Copyright 2005 the Norman Rockwell Family Entities.

status. Having an enemy thus clarified our state of grace by allowing our purity to stand out in relief: the more demonic our adversary appeared, the closer we seemed to Eden.

The copious supply of 1950s science fiction films, which a contemporary audience struggles *not* to read as parody, amply documents the consuming, ubiquitous paranoia of a clearly defined American goodness under attack by a foreign enemy. Indeed, these films recount an allegory of enemy invasion that animated the decade, an allegory of malevolent forces so beguiling that their ability to penetrate American

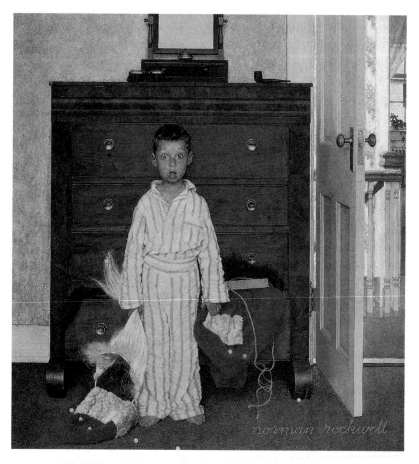

Norman Rockwell, *The Discovery*, cover, *Saturday Evening Post*, December 29, 1956. Printed by permission of the Norman Rockwell Family Agency. Copyright 2005 the Norman Rockwell Family Entities.

boundaries exceeds our ability to stand guard. In so doing, they promote the mythology of a benign, ordained American identity whose
moral decay comes strictly from outside its boundaries. American goodness knows no internal dissension, the allegory implies, but suffers disintegration and moral decay only from nefarious forces originating
outside the nation's boundaries.

In this way, we might interpret the wonderfully imaginative science
fiction tale *Invasion of the Body Snatchers* (1956) as paradigmatic
of this biblically charged reading of Cold War America wherein our
ordained status becomes corrupted by sinister foreign agents. The film
is a densely figurative account of the 1950s conviction that discord
could originate only outside of American borders in places such as the
Soviet Union. The film depicts the town of Santa Mira, California,
being skillfully overtaken by an evil foreign influence in the mid-1950s.
The enemy's sinister strategy is truly ingenious: rather than mount a
bloody takeover that will stir up commotion, it resorts to quietly hatch-
ing giant pods that produce life-size look-alikes of the persons abducted.
Although these look-alikes closely resemble the persons they have
replaced, they are in fact unemotional ersatz simulacra, big dummies
devoted only to the party line that have no feelings for anyone. This
sneaky pod-hatching strategy utterly confounds the town natives, for
they find it impossible to control something so wickedly clever. Soon
the calm, ordered quality of life in Santa Mira gives way to chaos and
confusion as the community loses control over its boundaries, for there
is no outwitting this evil force. "Stop acting like a fool, Miles, and
accept us." These horrifying words convey to the protagonist that his
girlfriend is now one of them, just another zombie with steely eyes and
a hardened face for whom "there's no need for love."

Invasion of the Body Snatchers counts among a preponderance of
similarly imaginative films made during the 1950s. Recounting alle-
gories of communist takeover, these films artfully dramatize enemy
invasion, landing spaceships, abduction by aliens, scary monsters, and
the terrorizing of American life. They play on fears that something
loved and familiar might soon change irrevocably and that the mind
and heart of our culture will be taken away by evil impulses, leaving
only the shell of what was. Thus the gently bemused question that
Miles puts to a concerned Santa Miran—"Well, is he Uncle Ira or isn't
he Uncle Ira?"—answers to a deeper fear that the United States itself
might lose its way. It reveals an anxiety that our ordained mission and

exceptional status might be lost amid the heavy weight of chronological time and unredeemed, ungodly ideologies.

It has been estimated that no fewer than five hundred science fiction movies were made between 1948 and 1962, many of which fall into the category of "alien invasion film."[20] And with titles such as *Earth vs. the Flying Saucers* (1956), *It Came from Beneath the Sea* (1955), *The Creeping Unknown* (1956), and *Them!* (1954), who could miss the bloodcurdling message? Hand in hand with such terror, however, these films always contained a reminder of America's Cold War mission and the nation's special ability thereby to partake of both cairology and chronology. For the degree to which the Soviets were demonic and bound by chronology was the degree to which we were cairologically blessed: their wretchedness had its counterpart in our exceptionalism.

I vividly remember watching cartoons featuring spies Boris and Natasha that helped convince my impressionable young mind that America's international mission was indeed God ordained. Cross-legged in front of the TV, I watched these cartoons in the sixties, although they clearly dramatized a 1950s Cold War archeplot. The hilarious episodes centered on bungled espionage carried out by two grossly inept Soviet agents. Boris and Natasha were clownish and clumsy, forever mishandling their assignments in ways that made children laugh even when the ideological resonances escaped them. Boris was shifty-eyed, nervous, and wore concealing black garments. His frenetic energy got in the way of his performance. Conversely, Natasha always seemed tired or under the influence of some mood-altering substance, for she was lethargic and had dark circles under her eyes. She wore a strapless black dress, and a cigarette often dangled from her lips. Her appearance and manner suggested a busy night life. Together, these partners in espionage were enough to convince me that sinister elements abounded in their atheist, vodka-soaked, furry-hatted culture.

Thanks to Boris and Natasha, whose story lines were part of the adventures of Rocky the flying squirrel and his friend Bullwinkle the moose, I associated proper hygiene, a teetotaling work ethic, and technological savvy with American qualities imitated by friends and allies, but not shared by sinister foreign powers.[21] Indeed, many of the cartoon episodes were concerned with the development of technology and its ability to change the world, illustrating how good guys always possess advanced technology while scoundrels, in their wickedness, get left behind. Thus Rocky and Bullwinkle, the cheerful squirrel and unassuming moose, embarked on a host of space-age adventures that showcased the measure of America's scientific advancement. They flew to the moon using their secret formula for lunar propulsion, took control of an antigravity metal called upsidaisium, and discovered an underwater city called Submergia that featured a wailing whale, Maybe Dick. Bullwinkle also swallowed a formula for a secret explosive called Hushaboom. Hushaboom's formula had been written on the side of a banana, and its disappearance caused panic. Yet the moose's uncanny ability to remember everything he ever ate set things straight, ensuring that America would retain control over this form of armament.

Indeed, it was not only the development of technology that was at issue in the Rocky and Bullwinkle cartoons. Echoing the Rosenberg trial, these amusing episodes also conveyed anxiety concerning the struggle to control technology as it changed hands, crossed borders, and served differing ideological purposes. In contrast to Rocky and Bullwinkle, then, Boris and Natasha could be ruthless in their use of technology for evil intent. In several related episodes, for instance, they brought on a widespread epidemic of stupidity through their use of a secret weapon called goof gas. In several others, Boris feigned a kind deed when he offered Rocky and Bullwinkle a bean to be sprouted and subsequently entered into a flower show. The evil Russian's gift of a "Pottsylvania creeper" turned out to be a disaster, for although it soon flourished, it had the nasty habit of eating everything in sight.

As a child, I was a devotee of these cartoons that instilled fear and loathing toward the Soviet Union. No wonder I urged my parents to build a bomb shelter and stock it with canned food and bottled water, as my teacher advised. No wonder I practiced "duck and cover" so willingly, learning to crouch under my desk and then leap from the classroom window in case of an air raid. It was not until Mikhail Baryshnikov sprang upon the American cultural scene with breathtaking grandeur that I thought differently about the Soviet people. Here was gracefulness and sophistication in a young Soviet man not much older than myself. True, he later chose to defect. But if his native land were as utterly depraved and morally corrupt as I had been taught, how could it produce one of the world's greatest dancers, willing to devote his life to artistic expression? And if the Soviet Union was in fact neither Sodom nor Gomorrah, was the United States really Eden?

Yet the mythico-poetic version of 1950s America to which neoconservatism adheres does not emanate solely from *political* sources. Economic factors also play a large role in casting the 1950s as that movement's Edenic blueprint. This is because the historical reality of the 1950s economic boom has, by now, similarly acquired a set of larger, metaphoric associations that factor into our reading of the decade. As before the Fall, an innocent state of moral rectitude is believed to have gone hand in hand with a lavish material generosity: in paradisiacal fashion, being good and enjoying earthly delights coincided. Indeed, the economic largesse of the 1950s carries with it cairological overtones as it raised the standard of living and showered America with a barrage of new and exciting consumer goods. The average white American family experienced a steady rise in the standard of living during the period, as the net expendable weekly earnings for a worker with three dependents rose by 41 percent.[22] This aids in creating a picture of cultural health and vitality, of an economic groundswell that radiated good vibrations and lavish prosperity. An abundance of consumer goods, many of them genuinely new, thus presented themselves to middle-class Americans. Vacuum cleaners, washers, dryers, kitchen appliances, television sets, air conditioners, frozen foods, Barbie dolls, hula hoops—all of these were part of the consumer abundance and expanding media culture of the decade. This rise in the standard of living generated new ideas in family homes and new possibilities for fun-filled vacations—Disneyland opened in 1955—all of them keynoting the themes of convenience, practicality, and good times. Indeed, the explosion in consumer goods assured Americans that the drudgery, privations, and self-sacrifice of the 1930s and 1940s were now a thing of the past. The 1950s were about consuming, enjoying, and celebrating the American way of life.[23]

For white, middle-class America—but not persons of color or the poor—the standard of living was thus on a delightful upswing during the 1950s.[24] In 1948, 54 percent of American families owned a car; by 1956, the figure was 73 percent. Whereas only 2.9 percent of American families had a television in 1948, by 1956 this item was nearly ubiquitous, providing viewing pleasure in 81 percent of our households.[25] America was up and coming, a prosperous country eager to enjoy the fruits of its labor, a land flowing with milk and honey:

> By the late 1940s . . . Americans were the richest people on the globe—indeed, the richest in recorded history. In merely five years, after 1940, their gross national product . . . doubled. . . . With 6 percent of the world's population, the United States produced 50 percent of the world's goods.[26]

Needless to say, this ability to produce so many goods and to have so much materially further contributes to a self-understanding that stands aligned with paradise. A crucial characteristic of Eden is of course its opulent self-sufficiency, which leaves no room for hunger's lack or desire's longing. The garden of earthly delights needn't import anything, and this grandeur offers further testimony to the presence of God in its midst. America's thematics of plenty, further witnessed in such things as the Marshall Plan, surely fuels an identity that is self-confident, an identity believed to be on a path radically different from that of other needy, lacking nations mired in the weight of chronology.

Hence the God-ordained Cold Warrior mission and economic largesse of the 1950s contribute greatly to the decade's current mythological attributes within the logic of neoconservative ideology, for the dual purposes of battling evil and enjoying earthly opulence necessarily invoke an exceptional dimension outside the conventional, chronological register of time. Importantly, however, Eden also combines the thematics of cairology and of wealth with that of a *place,* a situated, annointed locale that one inhabits. And without question, 1950s America is a spiritual place housed in our past, an imagined dwelling space where neoconservatism would like us to live in the future. It is an idealized locale created by a longing in the present, a painful awareness of our current lack. This spiritual place performs the crucial political task of regaining control over American identity amid the despair that, for some, accompanies meaning's free fall, the despair that the 1960s and 1970s ushered in thanks to their critique of the American tradition, their moral and intellectual relativism, and their openness toward rewriting the narrative that sustains us. Neoconservatism seeks to regain control over the meaning that has subsequently been destabilized. It seeks to reaffirm "a clear sense of what it means to be an American" and thus to parry the painful indeterminacies of our nation's floundering, globalizing, multicultural identity.

The American Right's Longing for Control

Within the logic of this argument concerning the Edenic status of the 1950s, the opposite of a paradisiacal richness that is central to American exceptionalism would be not only poverty but the inability to locate a true origin in the present. It would be a sense of exile amid a contemporary confusion, a destabilized disinheritance that studies charming, old-timey Rockwellian scenes in search of an identity. Such spiritual exile in present-day America seems to be the plight of David, the protagonist of the 1998 film *Pleasantville*. A high school student in the late 1990s, David is a devotee of a 1950s sitcom, also titled *Pleasantville,* that dramatizes the many delights of a kinder, gentler time in 1950s America. David watches this show every day, for he is deeply attracted to its portrayal of the stable, predictable, lighthearted world of forty years prior, an economically prosperous world diametrically opposed to the one he inhabits. Indeed, the 1990s America in which David lives is characterized by crazed conflict, profound social fragmentation, and pervasive despair. It is frenetic and loud, a restless place where life is unpredictable, human relationships are uncertain, and the economic forecast is dim. In school, he is warned about the dangers, the despair, and the hopelessness of modern-day life. Entry-level jobs and real income are falling in America. Worldwide, the AIDS epidemic looms ominously on the horizon, as do global warming and ozone depletion. There will be famine and drought everywhere as governments become increasingly incapable of addressing such crises. Overall, it is a very bleak picture. Hence, for David and other teenagers, education seems tantamount to accepting a litany of awful truths, to living a routine nightmare that is indeed far removed from Eden's tranquility and pleasure. Loneliness, despair, senseless violence, and rage keynote the dismal contemporary American landscape. Educators offer no hope; rather, they understand their mission to be that of helping students accept the world's harsh realities.

Is it any wonder, then, that when David returns home from school each day, he wants to "flash back to kinder, gentler times"? Every day, he looks forward to enjoying another lighthearted episode of *Pleasantville,* a 1950s sitcom about a city by the same name. David finds great solace in the ever-repeating, ever-predictable reruns of his favorite television show, which he watches religiously. His tuning in has the attributes of a sacred ritual, for the show seems to nourish his soul in ways that his daily routine in 1990s America cannot. Indeed, for David *Pleasantville* operates as a soothing antidote, reassuring him that a lost cultural cohesion—a kinder, gentler America—is truly lodged in our collective memory as his mind and heart escape to the cheerful episodes about everyday occurrences at midcentury. Using memory and myth, fiction and metaphor, David leaves behind the 1990s maelstrom, which is neither gentle nor kind, and goes to live in a time when innocence, orderliness, and predictability prevail (or, at least, seem to on television). "Honey, I'm home!" shouts an upbeat George, a *Pleasantville* sitcom character, as he returns from work and hangs up his hat. Clean-cut George is greeted by his smiling wife, Betty. Prim, composed, the keeper of an immaculate house, Betty, with her carefully arranged curls and full-skirted dress, resembles the housewives included in the Swell insignia currently at Target. George is also greeted by their two cheerful children, Bud and Mary Sue, who show nothing but respect and deference toward their parents. "Hey, Pumpkin, what's that I smell? Is that your meatloaf?" George asks. After a warm greeting, he announces that he probably will get that raise he was promised, and Bud speaks proudly of an award he won at school.

David knows the *Pleasantville* episodes by heart. With eyes glued to the television set, he recites their lines, anticipates their plots, and sings their jingles. He has seen each episode many times. He loves their predictability, and he looks forward to reruns as though they were brand-new to him, for his need for their familiar charm never diminishes. He will be a formidable contender in the upcoming "*Pleasantville* Marathon."

In similar fashion, Americans know how to read midcentury's vast array of encoded meanings along with him. We know the deeper meanings of the newspaper delivery boy and the friendly repairman, the malt shop and haberdashery, the impeccably tended homes with geometric furniture and flowered drapes. We know how each episode of *Pleasantville* will play: the dramatic buildup, the mishaps and misunderstandings, the comic denouement, the essential innocence of life. Most important, we understand the larger message being conveyed as the sitcom unfolds, for today, for some, these episodes forever announce home sweet home, a haven that counters the enraged, embattled scene of contemporary America. Throughout these episodes, we rarely see—but never really expect to see—many blacks, and we remain unsurprised by the complete absence of Jews, gays and lesbians, social misfits, and delinquents. "There are no homeless people in Pleasantville," David tells a friend. In fact, every source of harshness, tragedy, and irrationality has been extracted from this locale, such that it never rains in Pleasantville, the basketball team always wins, and the fire department knows only how to rescue cats from trees.

Because they call into question the Edenic attributes of 1950s America, *Pleasantville*'s episodes stand juxtaposed to the painful sense of indeterminacy that we all, left and right, experience along with David in the contemporary setting. Whether we agree with the show's representation of 1950s life or not, the sitcom's lighthearted episodes succeed in highlighting the cultural fragmentation and shifting signifiers that typify life in postmodern America, along with the pain and rage that these so often induce. Thus we quickly identify with David, whether we enjoy the show's cheerful rendition of small town-life or not.

One afternoon, as David and his sister, Jennifer, argue over the television's remote control while David is watching *Pleasantville,* they are mysteriously catapulted into the TV show itself. Clearly, the cheerful, eccentric TV repairman has a hand in orchestrating this strange maneuver, which allows 1990s America to suddenly *become* a 1950s sitcom. There, in the world of imagination and longing, David and Jennifer assume the roles of Bud and Mary Sue, part of *Pleasantville*'s regular cast. They are now living through the sitcom's episodes every day, and, at least for a while, Rockwellian America *is* America. As they mysteriously partake of the "kinder, gentler" world of TV-land, they are exhorted to keep the episodes exactly as they are, word for word, line for line, with 1950s' lingo intact. Nothing should ever change, they are told, in this safe, happy place, even though they themselves are from the loud, fractious 1990s, where high school is dominated by sex, drugs, and rock 'n' roll. For a time, David and Jennifer acquiesce in life-as-a-sitcom, and can thus live out the neoconservative dream of reliving the 1950s amid the present postmodern disarray.

Similarly, some Americans enjoy seeing the well-worn stories of life in 1950s America play over and over again like a rondo theme, a catchy refrain or advertisement jingle that you can't get out of your mind. They are like David, whose emotional investment in *Pleasantville* reveals the desire for a shared origin that might still be discovered amid the present-day turmoil brought on by arbitrary meaning. Like David, Americans finding solace in 1950s certitude long for reassurance that contemporary America—fragmented, raging, cacophonous—might claim some deeper, abiding meaning that ensures its stable foundation. Dreaming about this foundation is surely easier and more fun than confronting the divisions that preclude such a foundation. Imagining a singular, Edenic purpose is more enjoyable than admitting that we are overwhelmingly a nation of immigrants, a mixed bag of different ancestries, customs, and beliefs whose demographics scarcely resemble those of Pleasantville in the 1950s. Once the shock of being catapulted into TV-land is over, then, David finds sitcom "reality" to be more fun than real life in 1990s America.

The strength, richness, and cohesion of midcentury America as dramatized on *Pleasantville* thus carries a battery of literal and metaphoric meanings, all lending a magical, mythical quality to the brilliance of its luminous past. As opposed to the sometimes bewildering fragmentation and vaunted diversity highlighted in contemporary American life, this era invokes the homogeneity, the accord, the like-mindedness that are frequently the by-products of cultural cohesion. It suggests the orderliness and predictability of many a 1950s sitcom rerun, wherein Dad proclaims "Honey, I'm home!" and hangs up his hat. Above all, it implies *control:* self-controlled individuals, controlled families and neighborhoods, controlled conversations, a controlled foreign policy. It is a control that emanates from the fact that our culture's definitions are stable and intact, for we are, in this decade, at home in the spiritual space where we belong.[27]

Some call such a longing for lost origins melancholia, which I will discuss presently. And if such a melancholia permeates the contemporary American spiritual landscape, it especially permeates neoconservatism. Neoconservatism identifies itself as our connection to a severed past, our ability to locate Pleasantville amid the contemporary confusion, and allows us to cast aside the destabilizing impact of the 1960s

Fact and fiction are blurred when David and Jennifer, catapulted back in time against their wishes, are forced to be part of a 1950s sitcom in *Pleasantville* (1998).

and 1970s. Thus Garry Wills wrote in the 1980s that the Reagan Revolution "offers not only a path of entry into such an America, a relic of its reality, but a guarantee of its continued existence into our time." This guarantee ensures that we can regain control over what we thought we had lost. Reagan "renews our past by resuming it," as does George W. Bush today.[28] Just as David can feel renewed by retaining power over the remote control—the remote control over which he fought with Jennifer—so can we experience a sense of renewal by engaging this decade's narrative. So can we experience a sense of reconnection to America's true meanings, neoconservatism suggests, when we relocate ourselves in the past and discover that, chronologically and figuratively, "America is back."

The Left's Insistence on "the Fifties"

Persons to the left of the American political spectrum decry the metaphoric 1950s that neoconservatism has created and insist that the mythmaking about kinder, gentler times displays a large dose of unreality. In an effort to counter this relic's spiritual force within the reality of present-day American society, they dismiss the claim that this decade succeeded in bringing Rockwellian reveries to life, or that the American family truly experienced life as on a well-loved TV show. Everyday life during the 1950s resembled neither a magazine cover nor a sitcom (although many may have wanted it to). Rather, the left would agree that *Far from Heaven,* with its portrayal of illicit desire, racism, and homophobia, presents a much truer picture of the postwar era, wracked as it was by well-maintained secrets, paranoia, and a pervasive angst about maintaining appearances. Unconvinced that predictable sitcoms truly dramatized lived reality, the left perceives heroes of "the fifties" as make-believe role models and dismisses the decade's putative success story as exaggerated folklore. It sees only hypocrisy and self-deceit in the gesture of casting the Ike-and-Mamie decade as hugely successful and consequently deplores the neoconservative effort to "revive" family values and "restore" American greatness. The 1950s cum glory days amounts to a *mythical* re-creation of the postwar era, a desire to regain lost innocence amid the diversity, fractiousness, and dissonance *that in fact are more genuinely American.*

It is well-known that, in terms of historical narrative, the left's version of the 1950s differs radically from that offered by the right. First, the left highlights the censorious manner in which that decade sought to erase the very existence of the left in America. This was the decade of the Rosenberg trial and executions, of the McCarthy hearings and Smith Act persecutions, the decade that blacklisted American talent and censored American entertainment. It was the decade of Jim Crow laws and the Arkansas nine, which restricted civil liberties and for many encouraged an apolitical disinterest in society at large. Certainly, its censorious nature discouraged young people from being attached to a social movement. For instance, in her memoir *Previous Convictions: A Journey through the 1950s*, Nora Sayre explains how, in 1956, a group of Harvard and Radcliffe undergraduates sought to oppose the Soviet invasion of Hungary in some public fashion and planned to stand on the steps of Widener Library. On further reflection, however, they decided that the best form of protest was no action at all. "So the broad flight of steps remained empty in defiance of the Russians," Sayre writes, "and in tribute to the Hungarian invasion."[29] Sayre also tells of a classmate who rose early in order to read the *New York Times* before it disappeared into the dormitory. Soon enough, however, the young woman realized there was no reason to rise early—no one else was reading the newspaper.

The left also underscores the degree to which the 1950s mainstream was subject to cultural censorship. This was not for lack of talent, for despite the intimidating climate there was an abundance of literary, musical, and dramatic energy during the decade. It was the decade of abstract expressionism and of existentialist literature, of Jackson Pollock, Marc Rothko, Truman Capote, Mary McCarthy, Norman Mailer, Henry Miller, Jack Kerouac, Paul Goodman, Allen Ginsberg, and marijuana.[30] Nor could the decade's cultural bankruptcy be blamed on the lack of a counterculture's critical edge. Rather, various voices within the mainstream were so devoted to a feel-good expression of American life that they excelled at domesticating some of the more maverick sensibilities. Thus, while serious art and literature surely explored the darker reaches of the decade's experience, the sunnier side of 1950s culture helped curb the expression of a renegade contingent. "The big victims of that time were the American people," states Fred Hellerman, a charter member of the folk group the Weavers, for Americans had to "suffer all the movies that were never made, all the books that were never written, all the songs that were never sung, all the thoughts that were never thought." According to Hellerman, this explains why the early days of rock 'n' roll—the days of Elvis Presley, Buddy Holly, the Spinners, and the Platters—coincided with the practice of blacklisting.

These artists produced music that, in Hellerman's view, was utterly vacuous and lacking in all cultural commentary. It prospered because it
was nonthreatening, upbeat, and superficial; it was wholly domesticated. Artistically, however, it was "nothing." "Shoo bap bee doo bap
bee doo wap: you just don't get anything more nothing than that."[31]
   The left draws attention to the renegade elements of 1950s culture,
elements constituting what many have termed "the 'other' fifties." These
elements sought to resist the dominant paradigm, which was neither
as charming nor as rewarding as the right contends. Instead of Main
Street, USA, the left draws attention to those who sought refuge in the
beat culture of Greenwich Village and other havens of the counterculture. For many women and men, the strictures of the dominant culture spelled a spiritual death from which it was necessary to escape.
Thus, in her discussion of beats and "bad girls," Wini Breines recounts
how for some women only the Village felt like home, with its late nights,
its parties, its lifestyle so diametrically opposed to that seen on *The
Donna Reed Show*.[32] Without question, there were dissenting, disaffected voices that were taken seriously during the decade, voices whose
anger and incredulity made an impact. Consequently, a small enclave
within the mainstream identified itself in opposition to the white, clean-
cut paradigm. "There was a barely visible cultural rebellion of some
white middle-class girls and young women in the 1950s," writes Breines,
"a number of whom flirted with or lived a bohemian life. . . . the 1950s
were not good years for women because we learned to understand our
lives as a flight from that time."[33]
   Hence an oppositional force embedded within the illusion of Rockwellian charm fed the mainstream's angst. And although it was overshadowed by the feel-good culture of "nothing," it was never eclipsed.
Even *Peggy Sue Got Married* (1986), a mainstream Hollywood film,
takes pains to portray a renegade beat who despises the decade's mainstream. When Peggy Sue, like *Pleasantville*'s David and Jennifer, is catapulted back into the 1950s, she revisits her high school and encounters
Michael Fitzsimmons. Fitzsimmons is an unconventional, independent
young man who steers clear of the regular high school crowd. He rides
a motorcycle, keeps late hours in coffee shops, reads voraciously, and
loves Peggy Sue's "pilgrim soul." He sings the praises of Jack Kerouac,
who is "out there burning, feeling, grooving on life." He also predicts
that he will one day "check out of this bourgeois motel, push myself
away from the dinner table and say, 'No more Jell-O for me, ma!'"
   Those who share Fitzsimmons's disaffection for the decade often

refer to it as "the fifties." The deliberate use of quotation marks introduces irony into the time span's received meanings and thus expresses
opposition to the right's more credulous embrace of the decade's significance.[34] Most important, these ironic markings highlight the left's
utter rejection of the claim that 1950s America offers a foundation for
our nation's identity. They rebut the assertion that the decade can
function as an origin or blueprint meant to direct us toward our cairological mission. Incredulous toward America's Edenic century, Fredric
Jameson thus writes not of the 1950s, but of "that rather different
thing, the 'fifties,'" something constructed by the era's own television
shows and cultural mainstream.[35]

In these pages, I concern myself especially with what has been termed
the *cultural left*—that is, the intellectual strain within the American
left that is especially critical of any "complicity of origins"[36] and that,
subsequently, is especially incredulous toward authentic foundations.
As Richard Feldstein carefully explains, it is a position whose indebtedness to deconstructive and psychoanalytic premises causes it to dis-
believe in foundational assumptions and first principles.[37] Its embrace
of deconstructive premises fuels its larger critique of paternalistic and
Eurocentric epistemologies in the West, causing it to analyze race, class,
gender, and other politically relevant categories in ways that render our
"true" foundations untenable.

This refutation of origins creates a position that is hostile toward
"the belief in a unified field [that] grounds the certainty of neoconservatives who believe they know the incontrovertible Truth."[38] It gener-
ates an incredulity wholly oppositional toward those who "consider
themselves purists at heart [and] are forced to disidentify with any
rebellious counteridentification" regarding the status quo.[39] Because so
much of the cultural left's intellectual commitment emanates from a
disbelief in true foundations—be they historical, cultural, theological,
or intellectual—it highlights the unreality of the *Father Knows Best*
ethos to which American neoconservatism clings. Its commitment to
deconstructing such mythologies as American exceptionalism pits it
squarely against the right's nostalgic stance, as it deliberately replaces
the longing for a lost cultural unity with a commitment to an unrooted,
deliberately destabilized performative politics located in the present.

This is not to say, however, that the cultural left does not acknowledge that a longing for foundations is part of the human psyche and
that a nostalgic orientation toward something that never existed may
well be part of an overarching cultural narrative. On the contrary, a

defining component of this position is its acknowledgment of the impossible structure of desire, the desire that longs for something that, by definition, cannot be fulfilled. This assumption, which marks the point of overlap in the work of Julia Kristeva and Walter Benjamin, produces a theory of melancholia that is central to this study.[40] It grounds this examination of neoconservatives' invocation of the mythical 1950s and the cultural left's criticism of the same. The difference between these two positions is that, for the right, the 1950s—historical, metaphoric, or somewhere in between—are truly America's point of origin in modern times (in that the decade revived the cairological promises of America-as-New-Jerusalem). Conversely, the cultural left, with its insistence on performativity, acknowledges that such an origin contributes to the structure of American desire yet refutes the claim that such desire can ever be fulfilled. By analyzing these divergent responses to the 1950s, I aim to reveal the melancholy that has animated American political culture for more than twenty years. If we can understand this melancholy better, we can begin to accept that America's true identity is not located in some mythological register of time, but in the here and now amid chaos and confusion. We can take a more performative approach to things and let go of the worries and sadness that drive the need for foundations in the first place.

A Theory of Melancholia

In *Black Sun: Depression and Melancholia,* Julia Kristeva writes of how she and Walter Benjamin share a common theory of melancholia.[41] This theory posits the modern subject as one who longs for an anterior richness missing from the present, a person driven by an internalized desire that, by definition, can never be fulfilled. Albeit from different disciplines, both Kristeva and Benjamin understand the contemporary consciousness as one that sees in the surrounding world the imprimatur of a former union that never really existed, for which the present is filled with glimpses of a cohesion that has now been displaced. The modern subject experiences an "imagination that has been deprived of . . . stability but is still anxious to give itself a new meaning."[42] Thus the present world, filled though it might be with material richness and noise, is characterized by a spiritual flatness, an evisceration that nevertheless bears the traces of a previous connection. This deep connection means that time's movement forward always contains a longing to recapture or re-create something that went before: linear "progress" is thus an illusion that conceals the desire to go back and rediscover a former love. Although chronological time seems to suggest such progress, then, the movement forward is in fact animated by a longing to unveil something that is withheld or missing from the present, an occulted substrate pregnant with meaning.

Melancholia is defined as an existence in the present that forever seeks to uncover an anterior connection, a saturnine quality embedded in chronology that hopes to enter a different, fulfilled register of time. Although the trappings of progress abound, chronological time within the (post)modern world is something from which the melancholic seeks release. The enmeshment within chronology contains an often disguised effort to rekindle a different, withheld understanding of time, one inherently connected to a spiritual purpose that endows life with a unifying substrate. Thus, despite appearances, a present abundance soon becomes overabundance, bewilderment, despair, too many choices and too much noise, nothing of which connects to a singular purpose. For both Kristeva and Benjamin, the heavy weight of modernity's freedom is the search for an anterior union, a different register of time that, encoded within the fragmentation, never lost sight of life's deeper purpose.

As stated, these authors differ somewhat in their reading of this alternative approach to time. Yet both perceive time's other register, its fulfilled version, as a form of repressed conscience. This repressed conscience is the typically unmanifested companion of our experience of historical time. It shadows the belabored chronology we know, whose investment in progress, performance, and cultural engagement in fact emanates from our sense of lack. Melancholia occupies the space between these two registers of time: enmeshed within chronology, it always perceives the trace of a former redemption, the lingering mark of an experience not predicated on lack. Melancholia is thus the by-product of the impossible structure of desire that, by definition, can never be fulfilled.

The sadness of melancholia, then, does not derive from a sense of the world's utter meaninglessness. The emptiness that the melancholic perceives is not absolute, leaving the modern subject alone to impose purpose on an otherwise senseless world. On the contrary, the melancholic is one who *has felt* deep connection at an earlier time, or at least believes on some level that he or she has done so. Whether real or perceived, there has been a connection to sources that now feel out of reach; therefore, life's deeper purpose now seems occulted by surface reality. Yet this potential for a deeper world abides as a latent possibility

within the everyday occurrences that we know. It is this latent quality, this buried connection, that produces melancholic insight into the
present: the discerning eye perceives the connection yet feels its tenuousness within the weight of the present. This anxiety ensures a constant
wandering, a spiritual hunger, amid life's manifest abundances. Like
David, it wants to flash back to kinder, gentler times and once again be
charmed by a well-known, well-loved episode whose meanings remain
stable.

The Ambiguities of Kristevan Transposition

Kristeva interprets this characteristic of modernity largely from the discipline of psychoanalysis. She views the temporary failure of object
relations as the cause for the crushing disconnection between our deeply
felt desires and the reality we confront every day. "The failure of object
relations" refers to the failure of the external, temporal world to recoup an inner reality, to re-create meaningfully an inner world that
answers to the terrifying, joyful bonds of infancy. It is the failure of
the individual to consistently identify correspondences that confer deep
meaning on surface reality, the failure to re-create amid adult relationships the richness of the mother-child dyad that endowed life with a
(however counterfeit and unreal) sense of foundation. The disappearance of that richness accounts for the flatness that overwhelms the
melancholic, a flatness that disallows deep correspondences and makes
all of life seem haphazard, temporary, and therefore unreal.

Kristeva's theory of melancholia posits infancy as the time during
which a saturnine foundation is laid thanks to the workings of desire.
She posits the loss of the maternal body experienced in infancy as that
which ensures our unending search for a loved, irretrievable object, for
that body was the source of life, love, food, and warmth as well as terror, rage, and despair. It was the first encounter with a loving object
whose remoteness ensures that it will always retain an erotic quality.
This female body and the horrifying, cherished union that it forever
designates comes to denote an ineffable realm anterior to culture, a
remembered, idealized space that precedes language. It is Kristeva's
argument that our inauguration into culture, marked as it is by the
acquisition of language, always retains an unspeakable underside, an
"asubjective lining" that longs for union with the reviled, revered maternal body whose loss is essential to our identity. This is true even though
our memory of that union may be retroactively imposed, something

arrived at later in time such that its mirage registers our longing far more than it invokes a lived, historical experience.

The maternal body assumes an unattainable, ineffable quality once our inscription within culture is complete. Once our access to her has seemingly been denied, her status becomes dangerous and contrapuntal, none of which diminishes our desire for reunion with the realm preceding language. In fact, the severance of this bond only exalts its erotic value. Being lost to us as it evades the grasp of speech, the maternal body nevertheless appears all the more powerful as the mother-child union assumes an elusive quality outside of culture. Indeed, it retains an erotically charged, retroactively imposed aura despite the more horrifying, death-dealing aspects of maternal power. Because the union with mother remains tied to a realm that predates culture, because it necessarily precedes our existence within language and logic, it assumes the quality of something whose powers can never be spoken and whose meaning can never be contained. It retains an ineffable quality outside of chronology's range, conforming to the logic of time's different register.

Thus, in "Women's Time," Kristeva writes that a female, maternal register "becomes a problem with respect to a certain conception of time: time as project, teleology, linear and prospective unfolding: time as departure, progression and arrival—in other words, the time of history." Maternity always carries with it the attributes of a cherished space, "nourishing, unnameable," a space that is longed for yet also unattainable.[43] In that space, there exists no concept of progress or linearity, because fulfillment has already arrived. Our overwhelming erotic bond to a terrifying, asubjective space thereby subverts our own inscription within chronological time, causing the latter to be animated by the dream of returning elsewhere. Like "the fifties," it unveils a current longing but does not reference a lived experience. In "Motherhood According to Bellini," Kristeva writes:

> As long as there is language-symbolism-paternity, there will never be any other way to represent, to objectify, and to explain this unsettling of the symbolic stratum, this nature/culture threshold, this instilling the subjectless biological program into the very body of a symbolizing subject, this event called motherhood.[44]

Still, the very desire that animates culture holds out hope for the possibility of reviving that erotic bond, for our cultural encasement breeds the desire to find a lost connection. Indeed, our desire for reconnection to the maternal body preceding language prevails despite the fact that this pre-oedipal space carries with it terrifying connotations. Because this space so countervails against the cultural forces that otherwise define us, the maternal subversion of symbolic meanings is not solely pleasurable. It is above all ambivalent—"a fluid haze, an elusive clamminess"—that is both "unapproachable and intimate," something that attracts and repels at the same time.[45] The space that precedes culture denotes a loss of subjectivity resonating with the death drive, the absorption into an asubjectivity that annihilates and terrifies, yet that also implies union. For the death drive's trajectory toward the inorganic stages of life implies a conservative impulse that revives "an earlier state of things," an impulse that wards off future expenditures of energy and instead seeks union with a former terrain.[46] Hence the pre-oedipal union with the maternal body, now retroactively imagined by desiring subjects, truly marks an ineffable experience that defies our acculturated sensibilities. It marks "the absolute because primeval seat of the impossible—of the excluded, the outside-of-meaning, the abject."[47]

Because abjection stands outside of chronological time, then, its memory inspires both desire and dread as it suggests our ability to step outside of our acculturated identities, spiritually if not intellectually. Importantly, then, Kristeva's understanding of the lost maternal body revolves around a terrifying reality whose promise of wholeness implies a loss of boundaries. The lost maternal body, whose space anterior to culture subverts symbolic time, thus parallels the Lacanian real, the Thing, which is "my imaginary wholeness" prior to culture,[48] and its pronounced abjection nevertheless holds out the promise of an undisputed foundation. "The abject is the violence of mourning for an 'object' that has always already been lost."[49] "Always already" because it cannot be conceived of until it is missing. "Always already" because, like "the fifties," it registers a lack within the present by appealing to the past.[50]

Yet it is possible to experience some semblance of reconnection to an ineffable past, thanks to the subtle power of language. *Transposition* describes the ability of speech, with all its beauty and nuance, its instrumental purpose and emotional, poetic force, to recoup the connection to an anterior richness and thereby unleash a spiritual repression. It describes the power of language to contain within culture, in however brief and tenuous a fashion, that which eludes its grasp. For language works against itself whenever attempts at rational discourse are ironically undermined by the sheer impact of language's beautifully evocative materiality. Transposing the lost maternal body, connecting with Eden, parallels those moments in which chronological time seems imbued with cairological purpose and our atomized encasement within culture feels connected to the world's deeper meanings. In this way, contingent, fleeting reality reveals a heady transcendence as the power of human speech within the chronological register succeeds in invoking a buried cairological dimension. David's serene, happy face as he sits in front of yet another episode of *Pleasantville* might be read as the experience of transposition. The heavy weight of chronology's absurdity seems lifted when, mesmerized by television, he flashes back to kinder, gentler times. As David enjoys beloved reruns *exactly* as he remembers them, what seemed ineffable is now, temporarily, within reach, and chronology's angst is relieved by the beauty of cairological promise. Indeed, David seems relaxed and happy as he recites an episode's lines while eating potato chips. The beauty of Kristevan transposition thus resonates with Gingrich's claim that, for him, America is "a series of romantic folktales that just happen to be true," a signifier filled with erotic resonance and romantic meaning.[51]

This power, which Kristeva describes as typical of poetic language (but why not American television?), is nevertheless elusive. The delights of "women's time" can be experienced only within the confines of chronology and thus always remain contrapuntal. None of us can fathom why at times the world seems full of meaning and at others it is marked by "the absurdity of bonds and beings."[52] The cycles of mental life are such that the temporary, fleeting joys of transposition, which deeply animate everyday life, give way to a world painfully bereft of any such connection. Melancholia ensues when surface reality stands alone and there is no spiritual antecedent to ground it. The burden of chronological time does not know the refreshment of redeemed time, only the weight and monotony of passing days and unfulfilled desire. The melancholic thus constantly searches for a missing antecedent amid the absurdity of the chaotic, overabundant present whose former richness has disappeared.

Yet the now missing antecedent ensures that this absurdity finds itself enmeshed within a world of abundant yet arbitrary meaning. In these pages, the "meaning" I refer to is the meaning of America, the geopolitical entity that, like other leading nations, struggles in the globalizing, postmodern context to ascertain its identity and redefine its mission. Without question, America's meanings have changed radically since the nation's earliest days; they surely have changed drastically since the 1950s. I propose a melancholic matrix through which to read America's current state, for I see neoconservatism as a political movement searching above all for a clear antecedent that will countervail against the spectacular collapse of meaning that characterizes postmodernity. This search tells us that the movement's longing for a stable antecedent gives rise to "the dead language they speak [that] conceals a Thing buried alive."[53]

Walter Benjamin: Overnaming as Melancholy

Kristeva's melancholic world too full of signifiers yet seemingly devoid of an antecedent shares points of overlap with Walter Benjamin's reading of modernity. Benjamin interprets modernity's spiritual anxiety from a different angle than Kristeva, yet shares in her general reading of a continuum between a withheld richness buried in human consciousness and a current vacuity. The severance he acknowledges does not involve the immediacy of maternal flesh, nor does it give rise to desire exactly as Kristeva understands it. Nevertheless, Benjamin's understanding of an imagination deprived of stability and in search of an antecedent indeed shares in Kristeva's belief that modernity engenders a longing for an anterior cohesion located more in the unconscious than in human history.[54] For according to Benjamin, modernity's logic reveals the desire for a spiritual substrate partaking of cairological time; its furibund drive toward "progress" and self-improvement unmasks a stored-away wish for messianic completion hidden within the logic of capitalism and the larger dynamics of (post)modernity. It conceals a stored-away wish for a changed reality that—although not fully utopian—reflects a more just social order.

The weight of theology, as Benjamin understands it, has had a great impact on the modern imagination such that even the most secular, chronological axis of history bears relationship to cairological time.[55] Indeed, he argues that his work forever carries the trace of a spiritual knowledge that has been overshadowed by, and yet still informs, the modern age. The latter in fact remains "saturated" with theology, given that the imprimatur of a fulfilled humanity is retained in the collective unconscious.[56] Chronological time thus always holds an occulted, shadow relationship to redeemed time and can be apprehended by the knowing critic who reads modernity's "progress" deeply and against itself. Just as Kristeva maintains that all desire within the register of everyday time bears a relation to the Thing buried alive, so does

Benjamin believe that in the West, human history retains a relationship
to theological, redeemed meanings. "My thinking is related to theology as blotting pad is related to ink. It is saturated with it," he wrote
in his unfinished study of the Parisian arcades.[57]

Even in an early essay titled "On Language as Such and on the Language of Man" (1916), Benjamin offers a theological reading of how
the world's profusion of signifiers in fact delivers severed, arbitrary
meaning that denotes not abundance, but lack. In the essay, he employs
a theological base to construct an argument similar to Kristeva's observation regarding the absurdity of bonds and beings. Benjamin argues
that language itself encapsulates our enslavement in a world of haphazard meanings, an overabundance of signifiers whose profusion points
nowhere. For the story of language's severance from God's immediate
intention offers us in allegorical form the origins of our own melancholy as we confront a world of overabundant, arbitrary meaning, a
world that is absurdly enslaved within folly in the ways Kristeva describes. Indeed, the cacophonous prattle that Benjamin identifies in
language's mournful overabundance—too many signifiers, too much
noise, too many choices, too much contingent reality—is none other
than the prattle induced by the Fall, the arbitrariness of meaning that
ensued once the cohesion of an originary, Adamic language, *Ursprache,*
was lost. This theological narrative thus offers us Benjamin's linguistic
source of melancholy, for an overnamed world is heavy with conflicting meanings, all of which at first blush seemingly disclaim the existence of a unifying antecedent.

Ursprache points to a now lost union between the radically contingent world of matter and the eternal, transcendent existence of God.
This union between material contingency and spiritual essence contained in Adamic language precludes any marring disjuncture between
immanent reality's stark existence and God's eternal, unchanging being.
Ursprache signals human contingency's union with a spiritual essence
given that such contingency emanates from God. The logic of this language is thus that the very existence of material things gives witness
to a transcendent being, and there follows a necessary union between
nature and spirituality, between the contingency of fleeting life and the
eternity of God. Hence within the pronouncement of Adamic language,
concrete, material phenomena reveal the spiritual source that produced
them, as everything refers back to the creative purpose of God's work.
"With the creative omnipotence of language it begins, and at the end

language, as it were, assimilates the created, names it. Language is therefore both creative and the finished creation; it is word and name."[58]

Importantly, such referencing was contained in Adam's ability to name the immanent reality he found. Once named, the things around him simultaneously referred back to God; their expression always led home to an antecedent. Adam's extending gesture was thus also one of return, and *Ursprache* revealed its theological source. This ability to contain the ineffable within sound, to bring a transcendent dimension into human speech, allows for "the nameless in the name . . . the translation of the language of things into that of man."[59] This act of naming, which announces the essential fusion of immanent and transcendent meanings, alone constitutes "true" knowledge, for the resultant Adamic language was not mediated by concepts. Instead, God's creativity was immediately present in the name chosen by Adam, and language registered no distance. "Man is the namer; by this we recognize that through him pure language speaks."[60]

Hence culturally determined conventions and private, self-referential terms play no role in this original language, whose purity disallows the equivocating hesitations brought on by critical distance or self-reflection. Thanks to the unity between cognitive moment and named reality, language instead succeeds in communicating the authentic, spiritual essence of created being. Rather than being conventional or arbitrary, it is unified. It reveals dimensions of God's creative efforts and identifies the world's participation in that effort. Adamic language, not unlike the poetic language of the German romantics, is thus "blissful" and noninstrumental. It speaks of an original union between immanent, historical reality and God's eternal purpose. In this, *Ursprache* reveals no exile for contingent reality, but allows for an untrammeled foundation, a seamless union between Creator and creation that is manifestly logocentric.

The exile that keynotes the Fall entails the loss of this spiritual communication whose ability to convey unity now gives way to the deafening prattle of numerous languages. *Ursprache* is replaced by the instrumental, conventional medium we employ, in which name and idea are forever mediated by concepts, culture, and history. In a world inhabited by thousands of languages, the union between God and word is now lost, and the resultant, belabored speech is incapable of revealing spiritual reality. Rather, in its conventional, variegated guise, speech now implies distance from God and is thus deemed "ignorant." Its ignorance carries a confused, chaotic disarray, an "enslavement of things in folly almost as an inevitable consequence."[61] To be sure, language's "vanished capacity for absolute disclosure"[62] breeds only a chaotic prattle ensnared in an exhaustive effort to make sense of our radical contingency, whose spiritual underpinnings are now uncertain. The world is too full of potential meaning, too variegated and confused, too full of unstable signifiers. It reveals "overnaming as the linguistic being of melancholy."[63]

This overnaming, with its attendant sadness, was later conjoined to Benjamin's interest in Marxian theory and hope for a classless society. The interfusion between theological and Marxian poles, to be developed in chapter 2, is what allows Benjamin to perceive *modernity* as particularly melancholic, for Marx offers a reading of socioeconomic reality that understands capitalist relations as equally beset by arbitrary meaning. Benjamin's insight into modernity's melancholy directly parallels the Kristevan concept of failed transposition, for surely the absurdity of bonds and beings that she identifies parallels the "enslavement within folly" that Benjamin describes.

It is on this intellectual terrain shared by Kristeva and Benjamin that my own theory of melancholia in contemporary America rests. Although these theorists are both European, their reading of a depressive mindset in search of a loss antecedent is pertinent to the United States today, where rage and despair keynote our struggle for self-definition. If this inquiry into melancholia can suggest how we might live in the present, amid America's overwhelming cultural diversity, and not conclude that the latter is overnamed and absurd, it will have been worthwhile. If it can help us live within chronology's register and dwell only in the present, it might help us uncover a kinder, gentler identity located not in TV-land, but in the here and now.

CHAPTER 2

A Vertiginous Languor:
Modernity and Melancholia

Fado, Modernity's Theme

In greeting workers at the American embassy in Lisbon during the summer of 2000, President Bill Clinton revealed his newfound enthusiasm for fado, the melancholic Portuguese music that longs for a past that never was and perhaps never will be. Fado is a hauntingly beautiful style of music that, in treating the themes of longing, fate, and acceptance, helps the listener "discover . . . the lost chord."[1] Mr. Clinton admitted that, thanks to his European trip that summer, he had fallen in love with this musical expression of melancholy, so much so that he was now eager to promote it worldwide. "I think fado has now become my major passion in life," he explained.[2] Surely Mr. Clinton's enthusiasm for this music is largely aesthetic, owing itself to the beauty of the songs' rhythm, melody, tone, and instruments. Yet it is perhaps not coincidental that the meaning of fado lyrics, which concern themselves with unfulfilled longing and "a graceful acceptance of one's destiny,"[3] might resonate so meaningfully for the American head of state on the threshold of the twenty-first century.

There is much in the broader Western tradition that engages the concept of lost origins, keynoting in numerous ways such themes as exile and diaspora, odyssey, and banishment. This motif of lost origins is concurrently biblical and futuristic, mythic and science fictional as it reaches backward and forward in a doubled gesture that imposes the past on the future or that travels forward in an effort to reconnect with the past. Lost origins find ample expression in both the high and low cultures of the Western world, from the lost tribes of Israel to *The Wizard of Oz*, from Proust's madeleine dipped in lime tea to *Mad Max beyond Thunderdome*. And because originary sites are so densely layered with meaning, because they are so often alloyed to claims to truth and authenticity, the search itself can be an exquisite pleasure, for it "unleashes the vast structure of recollection."[4]

By its very nature, modernity engages lost origins in an especially poignant way. This is because, in the West, modernity's self-definitions are the result of a deliberate break, a rupture from the old world order and worldview whose most basic premises modern society repudiates. In many ways, the modern world constitutes a reaction against several older schools of thought, for its philosophical first principles deliberately counter the ethos that predated the seventeenth century. Indeed, the far-reaching intellectual and moral disenchantment so championed by the modern sensibility, grounded as the latter is in the scientism and empirical methods of the Enlightenment, disdains the perceived superstitions and ideological infantilism of the premodern world, whose normative outlook it felt could not sever fact from value. The premodern world, steeped in a host of now-repudiated assumptions about order and authority, had been "enchanted" in that it denied human hands the control of their destiny, locating it instead in places exceeding human potential: in God's Great Chain of Being, in Platonic forms, in teleology, in nature. Yet modernity's efficiency and empiricism broke with this preordained arrangement of things and instead gave far greater status to our powers of inductive and deductive reasoning, to our ingenuity and creativity, and to our ability to make "progress."

The project of modernity, then, was to "disenchant" this world by affirming human control over what had previously been relegated to the hands of fate. It was to dispel the supposedly mythical quality of a universe whose essential working principle was not rational, or at least was not always discernible to the human faculty of reason. The enlightened modern mentality, having its origins in such thinkers as Hobbes and Locke, Bacon and Descartes, stressed the great potential in logic and empiricism, such that strict reliance on faith, philosophy, or folklore gradually became associated with an older, less reliable worldview. The reliance on empirical data now translated everything into human terms, and, although not all of modern philosophy dismisses a priori categories out of hand, it gave greater status to the five senses' role in verification of cognitive assumptions.

Disenchantment especially sought to make human beings the masters of their fate, thanks to the cognitive skills that allowed them to control nature: now, they could be self-determining and self-reliant rather than beholden to an already prescribed worldview. The scientific inroads originally made by such thinkers as Copernicus, Galileo, and Newton encouraged a radical break from the older way of thinking, and science contributed to the larger project of disenchantment in ways their experimentation could not have foreseen. Thus committed to demystification, the scientism especially promoted in Francis Bacon's *New Atlantis* (1627) made possible a larger degree of freedom and a newfound mobility. By exalting the positivist, reasoned deduction that accompanies scientism's outlook, the enlightened sensibility claimed to leave behind what it believed to be the immature, superstitious mentality that still saw God in nature, an enchanted mentality mired in the ancient and medieval obscurities of the Greek, Roman, and Judeo-Christian worlds. The enlightened, modern world was to dispel such anachronisms and instead glory in the power of rational calculation. At the extreme, it took science as the model for every form of critique in a gesture that was supposed to establish human sovereignty. "The human mind, which overcomes superstition, is to hold sway over a disenchanted nature," write Horkheimer and Adorno of the Enlightenment's project. "There is to be no mystery—which means, too, no wish to reveal mystery."[5]

As it sought to overthrow the obscurities of an old order, the modern sensibility promoted what for some constituted a mature outlook. Because science had made authoritative discoveries into such comprehensive issues as the structure of the universe and the movement of heavenly bodies, a newly disenchanted, enlightened world understood itself as one that asked mature, comprehensive questions in many disciplines. Thus, in his celebrated 1783 essay "What Is Enlightenment?" Kant equated enlightenment with maturity, and the historical process for many seemed linked to undisputed progress. Kant interpreted a modern episteme as one that is responsible and intellectually curious, no longer intimidated by antiquated principles. For him, modernity urges the individual to emerge from a former timidity, as its worldliness carries with it a sense of responsibility toward the public sphere. This intellectual and spiritual break with the past thus ushered in a disenchanted outlook that fostered humanity's coming of age, for the premodern world was now accused of a sort of intellectual infantilism and puerile religious faith. The hallmark of this enlightened maturity, Kant argued, was self-reliance and a daring to know:

> Enlightenment is man's emergence from his self-imposed nonage.
> Nonage is the inability to use one's own understanding without
> another's guidance. This nonage is self-imposed if its cause lies not
> in lack of understanding but in indecision and lack of courage to
> use one's own mind without another's guidance. Dare to know.
> (Sapere aude).[6]

In this way, the modern world was to be a mature world, a world whose scientific methods, rational outlook, and belief in progress garnered humankind a magnificent recovery of nerve.[7] Its scientism was to let go of the quietism of spiritual life and allow human achievement to make its mark on the world.[8]

Contained in modernity's essential makeup, its daring to know, are thus rupture and repudiation, the act of building on the superstitious, God- and nature-centered past while simultaneously discarding and denying so many of the latter's theoretical tenets. In eschewing those aspects of the Western cultural heritage that made us mere stewards of creation, modernity relies on what has gone before while also foregrounding the need to take control, to have a significant impact on the world by demonstrating a belief in the ever-growing maxim of change-as-progress. Human agency is augmented as the mysteries of a God-centered world no longer hold our attention.

Thanks to this maxim of change-as-progress, modernity has increasingly engendered an agitated, excited pace whose profound restlessness proves both rewarding and daunting. Such an investment in the dynamism of change-as-progress surely means that the vast energies unleashed in the modern world's recovery of nerve must always be rethinking and re-creating themselves. They can never rest, but must supersede the benchmarks and standards that, often, they themselves have only recently established. In daring to know, one must remain forever curious and explorative, trying new things, testing new hypotheses. Indeed, by definition, daring to know cannot accommodate restfulness or a quietism that calms the will; rather, it fuels an unending search for the new and the many promises that lie buried in newness. *Sapere aude* constantly rethinks the received wisdom, lest even the latest idea be accused of puerility.

To be sure, restlessness is a hallmark of modernity, for to seek repose in the competitive, expansive modern world—in science and economics, in agriculture and industry—is to bring about one's ruin. The modern world is a Faustian world that necessitates, engenders, and in some ways revels in lost connections.[9] Modernity thus adheres to a feeling of rootlessness, an inability to stand still given the focus on invention, discovery, and the allure of novelty. Indeed, the fundamental rupture that characterized modernity's inception in the seventeenth century has increasingly augmented this commitment to discovery. For any measure of quietism in a world devoted to secular, progressive forces—a world currently enamored of technology's new frontiers—risks being at odds with the prevailing ethos and marshaling its energies in the wrong direction. Thus to submit if not extinguish one's will to forces beyond human control hardly meshes with modernity's signature—namely, the recovery of nerve and subsequent belief in the promise of exploration.

The emergence from nonage that Kant encouraged in the late eighteenth century cannot be understood apart from the important rise in bourgeois individualism and middle-class culture that eventually replaced Europe's ancien régime. The many political and economic changes that allowed for modernity's disenchantment had bred a far more individualist, egalitarian society that conferred new freedoms, a new social mobility, and new responsibilities on the emergent middle class. The enchantment of the premodern universe, with its comprehensive theological and philosophical underpinnings, gave way to an enlightened world whose new ethos and class structure could rewrite an antiquarian vision of a preconceived, preordained universe. If, according to modern political thought, rights were inalienable, if established rankings could in fact be leveled, then social mobility could replace the static hierarchy that preceded it. To be sure, the middle-class values central to bourgeois individualism defended an *economic* self-determinism just as strongly as they did a political one.

The freedoms contained in this abolition of the medieval order were not without their own anxieties, however. Now one's social standing was to be determined not by birthright or conferred rank, but increasingly by one's own performance in the economic sphere. Although social mobility and self-determination were modern possibilities, achieving these dreams depended entirely on an enterprising, competitive spirit capable of delivering a fine performance. Performing, *being able to* perform, being able to *outperform* one's coworker or competitor—these became the concerns of an emergent bourgeois individualism supported by the ideology of the Protestant work ethic.[10] The ethos of change-as-progress was indeed committed to a constant forward motion as the human body became an instrument of labor, an agent of production and competition. The work ethic of modernity thus denies the body its previously held status as a repository for larger theological designs. Now tied to performance and production, it could not reveal an innate value, nor could it evince a world whose deeper meanings are unrelated to the ebb and flow of commerce. Rather, it had to point forward thanks to its enmeshment within market relations and to its role in facilitating change-as-progress.

Thus Isaac Kramnick argues that within the logic of bourgeois individualism, the prescribed social ordering of earlier regimes, "ascription," gave way to a modern meritocracy that allowed the individual room for maneuver. Importantly, the marketplace was now the arena in which one proved one's self-worth. Kramnick writes: "Ascription, the assignment to some preordained rank in life, came more and more to be replaced by achievement as the major definer of personal identity. . . . what one did in this world came soon to be understood primarily as what one did economically."[11] A competitive economy constantly in search of new opportunities only encouraged the Faustian restlessness and anxiety so pronounced in a world that had let go of a belief in quietism or pregiven values.

Constant motion thus accompanied the modern world's economic growth and social mobility as this world encouraged new discoveries and an eagerness to improve on tradition. Yet the frenetic quality of constant motion is also the root of modern pathology, and of the anxieties that surround performance. When the human body is an instrument of labor, a means to an end, when it must do something in order to prove its worth, it can never rest. Change-as-progress necessitates an investment in movement and in outward result begun with the erosion of an organic vision. To seek repose is to perish in a world that looks only for results. It follows, then, that a culture increasingly marked by the Protestant work ethic is less troubled by the guilt of sin or the fear of God's punishment than it is by an anxiety regarding a failed economic performance. "Anxiety forever haunts bourgeois man," writes Kramnick, who adds that within the logic of bourgeois individualism, "only success in the marketplace brings the notice and valuation of others."[12]

Thus, if the ancient and medieval worlds honed a guilt-ridden sense of duty or an acquiescent resignation regarding one's station in life, modernity harbors a deep anxiety emanating from one's efforts to go it alone. Although the experience of modernity fosters great creative potential, the exhilaration of the creative process necessarily engenders a pathological restlessness, an uprootedness, an apprehensive need to stay ahead of others. For unlike the more organic, cohesive worldview that had prevailed in any number of premodern settings, the ethos characteristic of the modern West denies any comprehensive normative purpose. Radical contingency no longer reveals a profound yielding to God's purpose or to nature's design; instead, the immanent realm merely offers the raw materials to be used for human ends.

The many benefits of bourgeois individualism—its creativity and spark, its energy and innovation—might therefore be countered by a growing sense of meaninglessness and, at the extreme, of the absurdity of life. The importance placed on individualized performance and profession induces a shift, it has been argued, away from an organic, maternal world order toward one more aligned with paternal demands and the chastising superego.[13] For the freedom that comes with the ability to assign meaning, to confer one's own interpretation on things in a now secular world, is likely to yield the anxious suspicion that life, at bottom, is meaningless.[14] This suspicion yields melancholia, for the connection between a creaturely immanence and a transcendent purpose has been hidden from view. The melancholic matrix through which the modern Western world operates knows no correspondence between immediate givens and a larger, spiritual purpose. Although it necessarily bears the traces of such correspondences thanks to the older tradition it has repudiated, its own self-definitions must bypass these in order to allow bourgeois culture's radical individualism to be operative.

Thus one specific reading of modernity, the reading that equates with my reading of melancholia, argues that the more modern life offers a preponderance of material goods, the more immanent reality appears bereft of intrinsic, embedded value. The more filled with noise, activity, and change, the less meaningful this commotion appears—at least to the melancholic, whose position amid such commotion painfully heightens his or her awareness of how shallow the immanent world really is. Indeed, this dialectic between success and despair, abundance and vacuity, constitutes the modern world's inherent, fascinating pathology. This is the pathology of a mind that lacks a firm substrate yet travels in search of one, a mind painfully aware of an overabundant, overnamed reality whose manifold of signifiers nevertheless lack an antecedent. It offers the matrix of melancholia shared by Kristeva and Benjamin, conducive to a depressive mind-set that keynotes contemporary Western society.

This emphasis on performance and ever-changing output in many ways reaches its theoretical conclusion in the postmodern emphasis on simulacrum and pastiche. Much postmodernist theory insists that virtually every form of identity is performative, an effect or by-product of another performance in an endless chain of culturally created simulacra that claims no origin. Neither pregiven nor preordained, certainly not natural, all claims to an identity exist as the by-products of imitation and continually deferred reinterpretation. Because there are no true origins that exist as foundational moments, there can be no charge of falsehood, only the ironic ruse of feigned imitation. Thus not only are foundations themselves dishonest, but so are the "imitations" that follow, because to imitate is to imply a proper origin. An incredulity toward origins renders all identities suspect and all philosophical systems insincere, as the ontological statements that work to ground an origin have now been discredited. If ontology rests solely on mythology and metaphor, on the *desire* for a foundation rather than the reality of one, then the simulacrum contained in performance is all we have.

Within a postmodern episteme, all forms of identity politics thus give way to the logic of performativity, which insists on the impossibility of identity's truth. The postmodern attention to simulacrum and pastiche delivers a profound incredulity that can be at once playful and despairing, for all previously revered social narratives—religion, philosophy, even secular humanism itself—lose their authoritative claims. An incredulous mind attuned to the signifier's open-ended possibilities recognizes an inauthenticity and endless chain of performative gestures even amid the most ardent claims to ontology.

This sustained attention to the performative nature of social and political life, aware of the biases implicit in the Western tradition's gendered, racial, and sexual normativities, questions such normativity at its core. In postmodernist theory, what passes as "natural" and "logical" in keeping with common sense is exposed as politically motivated, for the erosion of Western culture's traditional narratives disallows assumptions from going unquestioned. Performativity turns the "natural" into an act; it reduces the "original" to the status of an imitation in ways that can meaningfully discredit harmful assumptions about race and gender, about sexual identity and class dynamics, about what constitutes a family, and about what "America" in fact represents. Judith Butler thus argues that feminism, as a form of identity politics, stands to gain much from realizing that all identities are provisional and performatively constituted: "Perhaps, paradoxically, 'representation' will be shown to make sense for feminism only when the subject of 'women' is nowhere presumed."[15]

Yet the progressive dimension of this position, forcing us to rethink our most basic political categories, is also tied to melancholia. The postmodern focus on pastiche and simulacrum could induce the state of melancholia described here just as easily as it encourages a progressive position subversive of identity. Given that it disallows a stated antecedent, it can induce a desolate spiritual landscape that goes hand in hand with its political promise of instigating real change. For indeed, a universe lacking stable referents, causing consensus and community to at least *appear* untenable, can be as spiritually ruinous as it is intellectually probing.[16] Performativity's logic can induce the melancholic outlook at the same time that it challenges the intellect, for in meaning's wake there is spiritual desolation.

Hence the forward motion of modernity and the performativity of postmodern incredulity both contribute to the melancholic matrix described here. The endless energy of a (post)modern world delivers not merely a sense of creativity and accomplishment but a sense of a chaotic universe whose furibund quality seems senseless. It sets in motion a forward drive that seemingly goes nowhere and, in detaching surface reality from deeper meanings, throws open the larger organizing principles. Hence, ironically, the fury that ensues once a former cultural matrix has been abandoned delivers a sense of purposelessness, and the greater the fury, the more overwhelming the void. Within the melancholic landscape, a world too full of meaning and possibilities whose signifying potential is not confined to an established lexicon ultimately produces a sense of absurdity. The flip side of postmodern creativity is thus the traditional vice of acedia, the taedium vitae of melancholia, which, weary of life, sees no point in it all. Acedia is the state of languor that cannot see God's presence in the world and views life as a meaningless journey. Within its logic, immanent reality holds no possibility for erotic connection, and our energies are spent in a futile manner amid noise, confusion, and strife.

Recall that Benjamin's linguistic origins of melancholy posit precisely such an overnamed, overextended exhaustion as central to the modern imagination. Deprived of the deeper correspondences that it itself rejected, this imagination searches for a stable substrate despite its apparent fascination with change-as-progress. Thus a modern acedia may well hide behind the outward commitment to invention, innovation, and forward drive. Two examples of this acedia to which Benjamin gives attention in his work are the taedium vitae characteristic of baroque tragic drama and the fascination with the "new" that is central to the poetry of Charles Baudelaire. Indeed, Benjamin's interest in these two forms of artistic expression emanates directly from their allegorical exploration of an overnamed world and the impossible structure of a desire that longs to end such overnaming. For despite the radically different cultural settings in which these forms of art were conceived, they share a modern, melancholic sensibility. They exemplify for us the same modern pathology that drives David to watch reruns of *Pleasantville* every day after school. For it is clear that part of him longs to end the overnaming in late-1990s America in favor of the stable cultural substrate he sees on television. With endless repetitions of "Honey, I'm home!" he hopes to project the past onto the future and thereby bestow on the current abeyance a sense of cultural moorings.

For this reason, (post)modernity's meanings create a context in which the leitmotif of reconnection becomes highly charged, fraught with special significance given the centrality of rupture and fragmentation to the modern cultural experience. For if our epoch is characterized by constant motion and unchecked energies, "the sense of being caught in a vortex where all facts and values are whirled, exploded, decomposed, recombined,"[17] the very idea of a past in which life knew more correspondence and more embedded meaning appears desirable and even exotic (although it may be only an idea). The freedom and vitality of the new world notwithstanding, the impossible structure of desire gravitates toward an earlier time—even an imagined earlier time—in which immanent reality carried a deeper substrate. Hence in melancholia we see the doubled gesture of reaching forward and backward, of projecting the past onto the future and of moving forward in order to regain the past.

It must be said that the dichotomy presented here between a stable premodern world heavy with correspondence and an agitated (post)modern one longing for reconnection is oversimplified. In many ways, this polarized characterization of things premodern and (post)modern does not ring true. For despite fado's beautiful melancholy, not all readings of the past result in a longing for reconnection, or in a certainty that there even exists a vital origin that must be rediscovered. However, the thematics of Ruby's Diner, of Target's Swell, of fado, all ponder how things might have been different had 1950s America not been radically changed by the 1960s and 1970s, by changes at the bottom and at the top, changes in the American family, in American education, in American attitudes. How would our culture be different if sex, drugs, and rock 'n' roll had never sullied our sensibilities? Where would America be today if the New Frontier, the Great Society, détente, and Jimmy Carter's compassion had never been at the helm? Against the backdrop of our forever changing, increasingly diverse, frenetic national culture, both left and right of the political spectrum can appreciate these questions, even as they disagree on the answers. "I'm going to promote *fado* music all over the world!" Mr. Clinton exclaimed while in Lisbon.[18]

Trauer, a World Overripe with Meaning

To experience meaning's overabundance is, of course, a principal ingredient in melancholia as I have defined it. It is an overabundance that, far from satisfying intellectual curiosity or simply widening one's horizons, proves bewildering in the vast array of possibilities it extends. The sadness that accompanies this bewilderment is, for Benjamin, especially poignant in the experience of modernity, which searches for an antecedent amid an otherwise overwhelming sense of disarray. As mentioned, this search for an antecedent explains Benjamin's interest in two inquiries into the modern condition: the tragedy particular to *Trauerspiel,* or baroque mourning play, and Charles Baudelaire's understanding of modernity's obsession with the new.

In *The Origins of German Tragic Drama,* Benjamin explores the significance of *Trauerspiel,* as this genre of seventeenth-century baroque tragic drama differs from a more conventional understanding of tragedy.[19] First published in 1928, this essay especially details how the baroque concept of *Trauer* differs from a more conventional understanding of tragedy. This is because *Trauerspiel* dramatizes a melancholy that comments on much more than a series of events that end unhappily. In truth, it is a genre concerned less with how events unfold than with observing a fundamental rupture at the center of the European baroque. *Trauer* refers to a privileged insight capable of discerning a larger cultural sadness while also recognizing that such sadness is endemic to Reformation culture. The chaos and confusion of this genre point to an essential lack of fulfillment in the culture at large, a sadness that accompanies a world deprived of a stable substrate now reflected in the dramaturge's storytelling.

The tragic dimension particular to *Trauerspiel* reflects the early modern condition in Reformation Europe and thus registers the profound disruptions of seventeenth-century European society. Key aspects of Reformation culture, which constitute *Trauer*'s backdrop, thus contribute to a vision of the world beset by fragmentation, calamity, and confusion. Central to Reformation culture, of course, is Martin Luther's momentous schism with the Catholic Church in the early sixteenth century. His ninety-five theses, posted on the cathedral door at Wittenberg in 1517, expressed his disdain toward the Church's selling of indulgences, a money-raising practice that claimed to shorten the deceased's time in purgatory. Yet this criticism of indulgences later flourished into a more comprehensive assault on Church doctrine and culture, including such institutional staples as papal authority and the seven sacraments. Ultimately, then, it was an entire worldview that was under attack, as Luther gradually became the apotheosis of the search for a more personalized religion unmediated by a wealthy, hierarchical institution with much temporal power.

Part of Luther's assault on the Church was his disagreement with Catholic teaching over the means to salvation. Luther stipulated that salvation comes through grace alone, that faith itself is enough to save us. This constitutes a radical rereading of Catholic teaching, which highlights the spiritual significance of social involvement and interaction. In rethinking the means of salvation, Reformation teaching severs the connection between human action and a spiritual mission, jettisoning the connection between what we do in this world and the possibility of redemption. Corporeal acts of mercy and other charitable gestures have no link to cairological time if faith alone points toward salvation. When faith alone saves us, then the many activities in which we busy ourselves claim no deeper correspondences. Luther had no argument against corporeal acts of mercy per se; still, at the extreme, his teachings sever our worldly existence and its expenditure of energy from the redemption we hope to enjoy. By contrast, withdrawal from community, at least in the form of quietism, was ultimately declared heresy by the Church. Good works must accompany simple faith, the Church teaches, and sin resides as much in *in*action as it does in action. Catechism thus stipulates that "the political community and public authority are based on human nature and therefore . . . belong to an order established by God," just as a Catholic prays, "I have sinned in what I have done *and in what I have failed to do.*"[20]

Certainly a distinguishing feature of modern political theory is its disaggregation of normative, theological assumptions from the sheer power play that temporal strength in fact assumes. The break between ancient and modern political thought carries with it an eschewal of normative considerations as principal organizers, which offers calculation, know-how, and general savvy a far greater role to play in ruling. In modern thought, politics becomes severed from religion, as Hobbes argued it should be, and the vast array of activities that contribute to human culture indeed become, as he predicted, little more than an ongoing power struggle: "In the first place, I put for a generall inclination of all mankind, a perpetuall and restlesse desire of Power after power, that ceaseth only in Death."[21] Indeed, the early modern recognition that power, not spiritual values or intellectual assumptions, is what drives human affairs contributes to a worldview in which *Trauerspiel* is implicated, a vision that registers in each painful moment the haphazardness of bonds and beings.

With the organic cohesion of the medieval world now overthrown, the resultant proliferation of religious interpretations, practices, and cultures produces an allegorical lament over the immanent world's severance from a lost unity. *Trauerspiel*, the baroque mourning play, employs a language that registers this lost connection thanks to the world's overnamed, overabundant status. The language of *Trauerspiel* eschews cohesion in favor of reinvention and reinterpretation: rather than acting as "pure bearer" of a single meaning, its words gravitate toward other possibilities—they seek out something *new*. In "The Role of Language in *Trauerspiel* and Tragedy," Benjamin writes: "The word as the pure bearer of its meaning is the true word. But alongside this, we find a word of another sort that is subject to change, as it moves from its source toward a different point, its estuary. Language in the process of change is the linguistic principle of the mourning play."[22] The language of *Trauerspiel* thus encapsulates modernity's principle as defined here, for it gravitates toward new and different meanings as it leaves behind a former cohesion. There is sadness contained in the genre's very use of words, then, as these register not a singularity of purpose, but a manifold of options.

Within this manifold there is the tragedy of purposelessness and of a deep sense of life's absurdity. *Trauerspiel* thus acknowledges the quality of taedium vitae, for if the immanent realm's fullness claims no spiritual correspondence, then it can only point toward death and ruin. This is why a baroque sensibility is characterized by extravagance and ostentation, an overabundance of humanity's material presence and intellectual expression. The opulence of baroque culture insists on the world's fullness against the backdrop of a lost antecedent. A world heavy with its own creatureliness is haunted by its own chaotic purposelessness; it is overwhelmed with interpretive possibilities. This "nonsense," witnessed in "the onset of an arbitrary rule over things, is the origin of all allegorical contemplation."[23] Too many signs and symbols, too much meaning can only reveal life's absurdity.

As a dramatic genre, *Trauerspiel* thus marks an important shift from classical drama. Whereas classical tragedy is characterized by a unity of time and place—an outcome is predicted from the start, some denouement must be delivered within twenty-four hours, the moral dilemma is clear—in *Trauerspiel* there is no such conception of things. We are onlookers in a life of meaningless activity, the exhausted observers of ornate exaggeration. In "*Trauerspiel* and Tragedy," Benjamin thus explains how the mourning play of this category lacks all resolution but is filled with ambiguity, delays, and catastrophes that are repeated in an allegorical manner. As a dramatic event, it is above all unfulfilled and unredeemed: its chaos leads nowhere. "Its events are allegorical schemata, symbolic mirror-images of a different game. . . . The time of the mourning play is not fulfilled, but nevertheless it is finite. . . . [It] is inherently nonunified drama, and the idea of its resolution no longer dwells within the realm of drama itself."[24]

Indeed, the allegorical nature of this genre means that immanent reality's robust presence claims no antecedent as its sensual, corporeal nature points violently toward decay and ruin. The baroque acknowledges that human life shares in the evanescence of nature, the overripeness of fruit, and fleeting beauty whose profound lamentation speaks of a lost connection to transcendent meaning. It witnesses an overabundant, ostentatious quality whose essential link to God has now been severed. Its vision is thus focused on the transient quality of living things, on nature's fleeting duration and inevitable decay. "Thus, one might say, nature remained the great teacher for the writers of this period," writes Benjamin in *The Origin of German Tragic Drama*. "However, nature was not seen by them in bud and bloom, but in the over-ripeness and decay of her creations."[25]

Although nature itself may have been the best instructor of the period, those playwrights most capable of dramatizing this sensibility were, for Benjamin, Shakespeare and Calderón de la Barca. Both playwrights dramatize the notion of time as chaotic and unfulfilled, busy with activity yet pointless and absurd. Indeed, the belief that life's energies ultimately serve an illusory end, claiming no deeper spiritual basis, explains Shakespeare's famous assertion that all the world is a stage, and that life's creaturely, performative aspect ensures our enmeshment within drama without endowing that drama with deeper meaning. Surely one perceives the admixture of overabundance and despair in the famous soliloquy from *Macbeth,* wherein the materiality of language assists in conveying the weight of unredeemed time. "To Morrow, to Morrow, and to Morrow . . . Life's but a Walking Shadow, a poor Player Thus Struts and Frets his hour upon the Stage, and then is heard no more. It is a Tale Told by an Ideot, full of Sound and Fury, Signifying Nothing."[26]

The transience of life encoded in nature's ruin, the absurdity of relationship revealed in language's materiality, the impossibility of meaning registered in the emblem—these are the themes that *Trauerspiel* recounts as it points, allegorically, to modernity's pathology. Indeed, Benjamin's deeper interest in *Trauerspiel* stems from the allegorical insight that it provides into the early modern condition. A seventeenth-century reading of the world's fallen state operates as the precursor, the earlier guise of a depleted existence that typifies the modern experience. What the baroque expression of melancholia succeeds in conveying through overripe fruit and fallen trees also foreshadows the modern experience of life overwhelmed by change-as-progress and the simulacrum of performativity: there is no antecedent. Before us is a hollowed-out reality of melancholic repetitions, a depleted existence caught up in the exile of vanished connections. Hence the melancholy of baroque allegory offers the prototype of modernity's experience as it itself replays the themes of Babel.

Yet, for Benjamin, the expression of *Trauer* to be found in the early modern period was later channeled into the restlessness and anxiety of high capitalism. If the early modern period saw a fundamental rupture from God's intended purpose encoded "not in bud and bloom, but in . . . overripeness and decay," later centuries witnessed this same creatureliness in capitalism's ability to produce. Now, it was not so much an earthly transience that revealed the modern world's rupture from an older order as it was the output of machinery. Capitalism's logic revealed the chaos of arbitrary meaning, an abundant materiality that lacks an antecedent. And if later modernity's focus on output, innovation, and performance was simply another way to strut and fret amid a tale told by an idiot, it brought with it its own signature contribution to the prevailing melancholia: a constant search for *something new.*

Baudelairean Correspondances *and the Critique of the New*

Benjamin especially credits Charles Baudelaire, the French lyrical poet of the nineteenth century, as an important yet misunderstood allegorist who understands modernity's obsession with the new. Benjamin maintains that many critics typically saw in Baudelaire's lurid, shocking poetry merely the desire to offend his readership and to scandalize their understanding of the purpose that poetry serves. Surely this is the manner in which *Les Fleurs du Mal,* which appeared in 1857, was initially received. Yet according to Benjamin's reading, this collection of poems aims at much more than simply unnerving the reader and disturbing the conventional wisdom that poetry should be pleasant and beautiful. More than this, Baudelaire's poems use allegory to unveil the melancholy in modernity and the encoded manner in which this melancholy reveals itself. "Baudelaire's genius, which feeds on melancholy, is an allegorical genius," wrote Benjamin in the 1939 exposé intended to adumbrate the arcades project.[27]

For Baudelaire, modernity's obsession with the new helps reveal its melancholy nature. This is because its concern with newness, *la nouveauté,* is so indicative of the fragmented, ruptured, even shock-filled nature of modern experience that it incessantly points to the very loss of an antecedent that I have described. Baudelaire's many descriptions of the Parisian cityscape and its defining features—the depravity and human misery, the prostitution and drug abuse, the life of the boulevards, and especially the crowds—allegorically reveal the degree to which his modern urban experience is the experience of melancholia. In Baudelaire's work, Paris is an opulent, bustling, ever-changing world capital whose constant display of the new in fact recounts a longing for a unifying substrate, for its "long echoes," he writes in "Correspondances," are long precisely because they intermingle in a "deep and mysterious union." They resonate and trace back to something withheld within the new. The modern world's obsession with the new thus has its dialectical counterpart in Baudelaire's concept of *correspondances,* which register the trace of a collective past unfamiliar with modernity's performance- and profit-oriented ethos.

Baudelaire's theory of *correspondances* registers the manner in which modernity's time is the time of rupture and fragmentation, a time lacking the sense of connection that so pervaded an older sensibility. Many things in the modern experience contribute to its ruptures and the sense of shock that this induces: newspapers, department stores, the panoramic gaze that is opened up on the boulevards, the phantasmagoric-like experience of strolling through a crowd or visiting the elegant nineteenth-century version of a shopping mall, known as the arcades. Each of these presents the world in the manner of montage, wherein many unrelated fragments appear alongside one another, often overwhelming the viewer with an abundant disharmony. Newspaper articles are brief, fact filled, and often sensationalist; they are arranged amid other articles that typically have no bearing on one another. They recount events to which the reader often cannot relate directly. The shops, the boulevards, the arcades and their enormous crowds—these similarly present a disjointed, cacophonous world that is filled to the brim yet appears to have no other guiding logic than that of economic incentive and the demanding performance principle of the marketplace.

Thus, in "Some Motifs in Baudelaire," Benjamin explains that "ritual elements" are now missing in contemporary society that formerly joined people, not to "the crowd" (*la foule*) with its connection to capitalism, but to "the collective." The collective distinguishes itself from the crowd in that it implies a narrative extending much further back in time, a story line that connects the individual to a larger group with rituals, festivals, and stories. "The collective" thus relates to an older worldview unbeset by the absurdity that prevails when meaning is lost. It invokes a spirituality wherein creatureliness corresponds to transcendent purpose. Conversely, the atomized nature of modernity, seen plainly in the impersonal, disjointed, hustling and bustling "crowd," displays secular humanism's commitment to rationalism and the performance principle, for it characterizes a world intent on delivering results. Hallmark of modernity's furibund ambition, it contravenes—but does not eclipse—what Baudelaire terms *correspondances*: a recognition of a lost antecedent that restores transcendent meaning to life's ephemeral contingencies. The trappings of modernity—the disjointed newspaper articles, the traffic in the street, the impersonal crowd, the constant supply of new items on sale in department stores—seem only to recall the surface reality that confronts us.

Yet poetry can help salvage the "breakdown" wrought by society at large, for it can invoke the deeper correspondences that lie hidden within the experience of modernity. The poet's sensibility discerns in the obsession with newness a longing for something old; the ability of Paris to reflect a manifestly modern sensibility thus contains an occulted wish for a deeper correspondence. As in Benjamin's study of Adamic language and baroque tragic drama, the poet sees in overabundance and overnaming the trace of a vanished collective unity. Benjamin writes: "The important thing is that the *correspondances* record a concept of experience which includes ritual elements. Only by appropriating these elements was Baudelaire able to fathom the full meaning of the breakdown which he, a modern man, was witnessing."[28]

Aware of the melancholy embedded in modernity's time, the poet therefore reads the obsession with the new against itself, not as a sign of modernity's "progress" but as an indication of its lost mooring and its subsequent, wandering imagination. Baudelaire recognizes this obsession with the new, a signature pathology of the modern world, as the by-product of a culture overripe with meaning and too full of possibilities. This insight, for many, has garnered him the status of *the* modernist poet par excellence. Indeed, many claim that a modern sensibility—with its anxieties and longing for opulence, its obsession with the new, which nevertheless fuels its desire—has its first articulation in Baudelaire's writings. This sensibility is reflected in the poet's allegorical approach to modernity's themes within the context of Paris.[29] World capital of the nineteenth century and paragon of modernization's progress, Paris thus becomes an urban center fraught with layered connotations in the context of the poet's writings. It is a site whose abundant life speaks simultaneously of lost origins and whose many outward signs of progress thus contain a compacted, melancholic underside. Paris's lurid cityscape, its changing architecture, infrastructure, and restless crowds thus provide ample occasion for the experience of *correspondances* as an urban, industrialized life overlays an older order.

That the poet's writings allow this urban, cosmopolitan center to present allegorically the absurdity of a world severed from its origins is seen immediately in Baudelaire's own definition of art, whose necessary registering of life's ephemeral quality resonates so clearly with modernity's devotion to progress and change. For Baudelaire, art examines the interplay between the transience of immanent reality and the often unrecognized traces of modernity's now-missing foundation similarly identified by Benjamin. "By modernity, I mean the ephemeral, the contingent, the half of art whose other half is eternal and immutable," Baudelaire wrote in "The Painter of Modern Life."[30] Presumably, then, the task of art in the modern setting is to capture the pregnant interplay between the changing world of contingencies, so emphasized in change-as-progress and a focus on the "new," and the deeper meanings to which material reality still corresponds. It is to emit "long echoes" and thereby register the interfusion of apparent and latent meanings whose headiness surrounds us yet whose reality often lies hidden.

Such interfusion allows for an allegorical approach, given that it sees the immediate, changing world partaking of a deeper narrative based on what Baudelaire termed "universal analogies."[31] These analogies were often perceived amid the most depraved elements of Parisian life. In this, Baudelaire's poetic insights parallel Benjamin's understanding of *Trauerspiel,* with its emphasis on decaying nature, unfulfilled time, and catastrophic ruin.

The raucous, at times celebratory description in Baudelaire's poetry of the dark underside of nineteenth-century Paris was surely shocking to a society enamored of such literary figures as Victor Hugo. The latter's moral tenor and aesthetic sensibility were far more conventional and reinforcing of the culture at large than the shocking statements of Baudelaire's verse. That drunkenness, drug addiction, prostitution, and the languor of ennui should serve as the subjects of verse was not consistent with mainstream public morals. Yet the depraved, shocking quality of nineteenth-century Parisian society was presented as a by-product of the city's modernizing. For Baudelaire, advancements in technology and industry were intimately connected to the physical and spiritual suffering that modernity breeds in its evisceration of a former substrate. Indeed, in demonstrating this evisceration, he revealed an unintended allegorical depth. These depraved features had existed in earlier societies, but Baudelaire concerned himself especially with their modern, *urban* incarnations, and with their ability to unveil modernity's often hidden thematics.

Paris was the city that, between the years 1853 and 1870, had been redesigned at the hand of Baron Haussmann under the directive of Napoleon III. Haussmann had altered the city's urban plan and revamped its boulevards, which were now widened and lined with trees, elegant department stores, and cafés. Greatly embellished, Paris hosted world exhibitions, scientific and cultural centers, and literary and artistic salons and boasted the Eiffel Tower. Because Paris embodied modernity itself, it forever promised something new. It was the city of inventions and innovation, of efficiency, opulence, and sensuality, filled with the display of the new. Yet the ephemeral quality of a buried transcendence is integral to Baudelaire's poems, for uncovering the moment of hushed transcendence that lies hidden in the modernizing world enamored of the new gives rise to poetic, allegorical insight.[32] The poet's task is to apprehend the interfusion of immanent and latent realities, and to intimate that experience through the sensuousness and nuance of language. "With Baudelaire, Paris for the first time became the subject of lyrical poetry," writes Benjamin in "Paris, the Capital of the Nineteeth Century." "The modern is a main stress in his poetry. . . . Just as in the seventeenth century allegory becomes the canon of dialectical images, so in the nineteenth century does *nouveauté*."[33]

For Baudelaire, the task of unveiling this dialectic contained in *nouveauté* and expressing it in language meant that the artist was no longer to be an aloof aesthetician, untouched by the more mundane, ugly dimensions of the contingent world. No longer was he or she to be concerned solely with what was conventionally beautiful, apart from the banal details and mediocre commonplaces of everyday life. The artist was now enmeshed in quotidian details, caught in the unbecoming machinations of urban life and commodity culture just like everyone else.[34] He or she was the person of the street who saw filth and depravity, tragedy and suffering, yet whose observance of such wretchedness was not without privileged interpretation. For Baudelaire, the artist is set apart only because he or she is capable of perceiving the embedded *correspondances* and universal analogies that lie hidden in every dimension of the changing reality of urban life. Thanks to the transformative power of this insight, the artist can apprehend the intimate and secret relationship of things, correspondences and analogies that make the world so full.[35]

Les Fleurs du Mal amply demonstrates the poet's concern with modernity's seeming elision of the meanings that, before the advent of industrialized relations, lent ballast to the culture at large. These poems explore the interconnection between a vast array of embedded meanings that invoke an originary site and the hollowed-out, evasive temporality of the lurid nineteenth-century Parisian cityscape. They examine the manner in which modernity always invokes premodernity, thereby recognizing the ironies contained in the former's infatuation with the new. The collection's title, for instance, invokes the premodern concern with sin and evil, and the manner in which sensuous pleasures are often interpreted to bring separation from God. Hence the title simultaneously suggests the Garden of Eden (union with God, an originary site) and expulsion from the Garden (separation from God, that moment when the immanent realm became burdened with strife and struggle). The plethora of religious, ancient, and mythical references that run throughout the poems allow Baudelaire to engage the theme of lost connections within the context of a changing, modernizing urban landscape caught up in the thralldom of the new. Modernity here becomes a replaying of an old condition, a repetition of the age-old problem of exile, now experienced using industrialized means and capitalist tools. Yet its reenactment of rupture, witnessed in each expression of *nouveauté*, does not truly advance the human condition, for an obsession with newness is in fact the hallmark of modernity's exile. "The *correspondances* are the data of remembrance," writes Benjamin of Baudelaire's poetry, ". . . of homesickness. . . . The murmur of the past may be heard in the correspondences, and the canonical experience of them has its place in a previous life."[36]

Baudelaire approaches the topic of modernity's severances in numerous ways, exposing the anguished underside of a revered *nouveauté* in which poetic privilege nevertheless finds traces of a larger narrative. One is through his frequent fragmenting of human bodily parts into inanimate objects that are incohesive and unfeeling, no longer parts of a body but tools of industrialized society. In certain poems, human flesh becomes hard and unyielding, as if made from cement; human eyes are steely and unemotional, as if made from metal. Baudelaire makes an obvious effort to reproduce the harshness of industrialized culture by dismissing bodily attributes and replacing them with the raw materials of industrialized relations. At the extreme, he presents the body as something that has no status prior to modernity; it does not cohere as an organic whole and, as a means to economic ends, has no spiritual dimension. Rather, as an absorbed and overtaken entity, it is colonized as an inorganic means to an end. Hence Baudelaire sometimes compares the body to a vessel of transport whose value is measured only in terms of its service to industrial needs. The body itself loses value, entering into the insatiable, demanding matrix of commodity culture and devolving into the forces of industry. The many registers of human exchange thus yield to the demands of progress in ways that deplete deeper meanings: the needs of high capitalism are such that instrumental rationality eclipses those aspects of culture incapable of turning a profit.

It is for this reason that many poems in *Les Fleurs du Mal* address prostitution, a socially marginalized yet integral part of the Parisian experience. Prostitutes floridly embody modernity's problematics, representing its lurid, fascinating pathologies in the flesh. This is because the prostitute is literally a human being and a commodity at the same time, a person whose body enters into economic exchange. In prostitution, human agency is acknowledged even as it is denied, for its success as an economic venture lies in the woman's ability to commodify herself. In a sense, prostitution is simply the most extreme, exaggerated, honest version of what modernity delivers to us all, a literal embodiment of what we experience figuratively. In "Le Serpent Qui Danse" (The dancing snake), for instance, the poet speaks to his dear indolent, *chère indolente,* and scrutinizes her various bodily parts in ways that clearly suggest fragmentation and a loss of humanity. The poem's first stanza likens her skin to a billowing fabric (*une étoffe vacillante*) that he finds attractive for its shimmering, silken quality. The allure of this feature is inseparable from the fact that her skin has taken on the qualities of fabric, and the moment of beauty is interfused with the comparison to inorganic life.

> Que j'aime voir, chère indolente,
> De ton corps si beau,
> Comme une étoffe vacillante,
> Miroiter la peau!

> Darling indolent, how I love to see
> Your skin shimmer
> Like a billowing cloth
> On your beautiful body![37]

Deliberately, the poem's amorous mood is undercut by the analogy forged between the woman's skin and a piece of fabric, such that even intimacy is not immune to the pervasive effects of industrial progress. The reference to a billowing fabric suggests a boat, which turns her body into a vessel. The fourth stanza continues with her body's fragmentation, suggesting the manner in which prostitution has ravaged the woman by fetishizing her within the logic of commodity culture. It describes her eyes as expressionless and cold, pieces of jewelry that combine gold and iron, yet reveal neither warmth nor hostility.

> Tes yeux, où rien ne se révèle
> De doux ni d'amer,

Sont deux bijoux froids où se mêle
L'or avec le fer.

Your eyes, which reveal nothing
Either sweet or bitter,
Are two cold jewels in which
Gold and iron commingle.

Most dramatic, however, is the manner in which the use of her body
reminds the poet of a ship on the water, *un fin vaissseau*, that is agile
and moves deftly, something skilled in its mission answering to the demands of industrial progress. The word *ship* suggests agency, purpose,
and usefulness, like a vessel used to deliver merchandise and to facilitate commercial exchange. Hence there is a skilled, professional maneuvering in the prostitute's actions that actually suggests a loss of self as
her body emulates an inorganic instrument designed to turn a profit.
Thus, although the following lines undoubtedly shocked Baudelaire's
public, his poetry in fact sought to deliver a deeper commentary on
modernity's impact.

Et ton corps s'allonge et se planche
Comme un fin vaisseau
Qui roule bord sur bord et plonge
Ses vergues dans l'eau.

And your body stretches out and lies down
Like a fine vessel
Swaying from side to side and plunging
Its spars into the water.

Seemingly, these allusions to fabric, metal, and ships make the woman
herself a force of production, something caught in the grid of capitalist relations with no intrinsic meaning apart from buying and selling.
Yet the deepest insight of Baudelaire's poem turns around the vestige
of some lost connection to be discovered in the immanent world's temporal expression: his ability to see in the prostitute something other
than her commodification. The most profound commentary of his poetic
expression lies in his art's ability to register some imprimatur of *cor-
respondance*, some trace of hushed transcendence that lies hidden in
the fleeting world hidden, for instance, in a visit to the brothel. Importantly, this poem's infusion of the female body with the demands of

industrialized culture still allows for the poetic intervention that sees in the loss of humanity the imprimatur of a former presence; in depletion, it sees a now hidden richness that allows for an allegorical reading of her profession.

In the second and third stanzas, the ability to reminisce becomes an important theme as the woman's presence awakens memories that undermine the present. The ability of sensual experience to recall the world's hidden depths succeeds in undercutting modernity's deadening effect, thanks to the transporting, enlivening memories that this encounter inspires. Ironically, something as transient as corporeal sensation holds the ability to countervail against the meanings of the modern world and to set in motion the suggestion of reconnection. This is because a reconnection to lost meanings indeed accompanies the prostitute's wretched existence, even in those places that seem to most indicate the erasure of her humanity. For instance, the poet delights in the experience of nostalgic transport in the woman's hair. Her colorful, perfumed tresses so engage his senses and carry him away that they cause his dreamy soul to cast off for a distant sky. In this way, what marks her as a commodity subverts the very system that categorizes her as such.

Sur ta chevelure profonde
Aux âcres parfums,
Mer odorante et vagabonde
Aux flots bleus et bruns

Comme un navire qui s'eveille
Au vent du matin,
Mon âme rêveuse appareille
Pour un ciel lointain

Upon your hair
Deep with acrid perfumes,
That is like a wandering and sweet-smelling sea
With blue and brown streams

My dreamy soul, like a ship awakened
With the morning wind,
Casts off
For a distant sky

Thus it is the woman herself, with her satiny skin, agile body, and perfumed hair that proves subversive to the system that sustains her. In a beautiful and nearly imperceptible irony, the transforming powers of memory and imagination that she stimulates contravene modernity's hold. At the extreme of her whoredom, she unravels the system that proves so dehumanizing by setting in motion the hidden correspondences, the secret analogies between fleeting sensation and latent meaning. Her ability to evoke a distant sky and to awaken a dreamy soul—to contravene modernity's performance principle despite her own commodified existence—fills the poet with a gratitude that he expresses toward his darling indolent (*chère indolente*), his beautiful one of abandoned pleasures (*belle d'abondon*). He is grateful for the transport she delivers, for it reveals not an abject depravity but some vestige of transcendent meanings. The immanent world is brought back to life, reconnected to another register, as her illicit work enlivens the senses. Although the prostitute is integral to Paris's lurid beauty, she simultaneously points to another world, another level of meaning as her appeal to the senses unknowingly restores innate value to contingent reality. It seems that her world of disavowed pleasure merely turns a profit and so confirms modernity's success. Yet, in fact, she uncovers the *correspondances* so often disguised within modernity's profit motive.

For indeed, when in her company, the poet's soul is itself a ship on the sea now brought to life by the morning wind. It is not a ship for industrial use, but, we might imagine, a vessel for discovering distant lands and distant meanings. The woman's status as a fine vessel, which at first blush announces her commodification, thus awakens him as if from a numbing, deadened reality, and he now "casts off" for another time and space. She brings to life the possibility of a distant sky that, with the help of memory's transport, holds out hope for the discovery of a lost antecedent. Thus what she offers far exceeds a moment's pleasure, for without knowing it she awakens the poet spiritually and joins him to a lost part of himself. The brazen descriptions of illicit matters therefore offer a glimpse of restored transcendent values, of latent meaning lost from the calculated demands of capitalism's instrumental rationality. For only when he sees the water rising again in her mouth can the poet drink a Bohemian wine as a liquid sky strews his heart with stars!

Quand l'eau de ta bouche remonte
Au bord de tes dents,

Je crois boire un vin de Bohême,
Amer et vainqueur,
Un ciel liquide qui parsème
D'étoiles mon cœur!

When the water of your mouth
Again reaches the edge of your teeth

I feel that I drink a Bohemian wine,
That is bitter and victorious,
A liquid sky that strews
My heart with stars!

The poet thus longs for the healing abandon of the prostitute's eroticism, which transports him to another register of time. His poetry
testifies to her ability to unlock the possibility of lost origins that the
Parisian cityscape so brutally elides. Another poem in the same collection similarly pays homage to the ironic, ennobled status of prostitution: "O magnificent filth! O sublime disgrace!"

Another example of the body's fragmentation into inorganic parts
that Baudelaire observes in modern culture occurs in "À Une Passante" (To a woman passing by). This poem beautifully captures the
ongoing fascination and estrangement of crowded city life, the harried
bustle that can be at once intriguing and painful. The urban crowd, *la
foule,* is indeed a central theme in Baudelaire, given that it takes us
immediately to the dense layering of modernity's meanings. For there
are many aspects of the crowded city streets that encapsulate the new
urban experience, setting it apart from former epochs aesthetically and
intellectually. The modern city streets are bustling and dynamic, throng-
ing and noisy. They stimulate the senses almost excessively, engaging
the pedestrian in an ongoing fascination with things to look at as the
crowd itself becomes a form of spectacle. Indeed, many have commented
on the increased, unique significance attributed to the gaze in the modern urban experience.[38] The cityscape opens up a vista that allows the
gaze to survey a wide array of disparate things; it brings together people and commodities in a way that puts them on display as never before.
This whirling, confused melange of disparate things, paraded in front
of each other inside the vortex of the raging crowd, plays a central role
in forging the modern consciousness, which is steeped in the rupture

and dislocation that are part and parcel of the progressive, industrialized world.

The modern consciousness thus adapts itself to a pervasive fragmentation, a shock value that exists due to the dynamics of urban life and
the phantasmagoric pleasure of the boulevards.[39] The energy of the
crowd highlights the loss of integration that becomes not only part of
the physical landscape but a central component of the culture's spiritual outlook. The crowd moves, surges, and bustles; it encourages a
phantasmagoric apprehension of other faces and of commodities on
display in store windows. Indeed, modernity breeds a fragmentation
that moves from the city streets inward, characterizing not only the
dynamics of the public life but the very structure of human consciousness. The streets are filled with people and noise, but, as in baroque
tragic drama, its vision of plenty leads nowhere. It is an overnamed
world that "Struts and Frets . . . full of Sound and Fury, Signifying
Nothing."[40]

In "A Une Passante," the poet happens upon a woman in mourning whose appearance captivates him yet whose moment of encounter
will always remain but a fleeting memory. Against the backdrop of the
city's uproarious din, as "the deafening street around me screamed"
(*la rue assourdissante autour de moi hurlait*), her charm and her evanescence remain forever conjoined as the poet observes her briefly,
in transit. Despite the inviting, even dangerous look in her eyes, the
sweetness that fascinates and the pleasure that kills (*la douceur qui
fascine et le plaisir qui tue*), she is eternally a fugitive beauty whom
the poet might have loved, but whom he will never see again. Yet her
striking appearance, which suddenly brought him to life again (*dont le
regard ma fait soudainement renaître*), succeeds in producing the same
transport, the same sensual evocation of intimate *correspondances*
against the backdrop of Paris's industrialized growth. The transport
incurred by this brief encounter thus holds the ability to reconnect with
a deeper register of transcendent meanings often occulted by modern
industrialized relations that are so busy delivering something new.

Appropriately, then, this chance meeting takes place against the
backdrop of a bustling Parisian thoroughfare, so that its healing power
might stand out in relief. The woman's ability to invoke *correspondances* stands in opposition to the street's harmful, deafening quality,
which is surely, at least in part, the by-product of its commercial use.
While the mysterious, fugitive woman in mourning brings his senses

to life, the modern milieu's deafening impact seemingly does the opposite. Hence there is a sharp contrast between modernity-as-progress, modernity-as-rupture, and what the senses can restore via the experience of *correspondances*.

> La rue assourdissante autour de moi hurlait.
> Longue, mince, en grand deuil, douleur majestueuse,
> Une femme passa, d'une main fastueuse
> Soulevant, balançant le feston et l'ourlet;
>
> Agile et noble, avec sa jambe de statue.
> Moi, je buvais, crispé comme un extravagant,
> Dans son œil, ciel livide où germe l'ouragan,
> La douceur qui fascine et le plaisir qui tue.
>
> The deafening street around me roared.
> Tall, thin, in full mourning and majestic pain,
> A woman passed by who, with an elegant hand
> Lifted and balanced her festoon and her hem;
>
> She was graceful and stately, with her statue's leg.
> And I, shaking like an eccentric,
> Drank in from her eye, pallid sky where the whirlwind brews,
> The sweetness that fascinates and the pleasure that kills.

The poet's attraction to this woman does not preclude his likening her bodily parts to inanimate objects, such that even a moment of romantic intrigue is mediated by industrialized culture. He notices her statue's leg (*jambe de statue*), on which he confers the qualities of stone or marble. Her leg seems hardened and insensitive to touch; like the prostitute, she is part human being and part inanimate object. And yet this bodily part has layered meanings, for surely *une jambe de statue* also implies arousal, which is echoed in the poet's tensing up and the whirlwind of the poem's following two lines. Indeed, as with the prostitute described earlier, modernity's dehumanized, fragmented influence simultaneously offers the moment of reconnection as it enlivens the poet, bringing him back as from a state of disconnection from himself. In similar fashion, the woman's eyes stir up so much in him, for they are a pallid sky where the whirlwind brews. Yet the reality of the crowd ensures that their meeting remains brief, as the woman's sudden disappearance recalls a different register of time.

Un éclair . . . puis la nuit!: Fugitive beauté!
Dont le regard m'a fait soudainement renaître,
Ne te verrai-je plus que dans l'étérnité?

Ailleurs, bien loin d'ici! trop tard! *jamais* peut-être!
Cars j'ignore où tu fuis, tu ne sais où je vais,
Ô toi que j'eusse aimée, ô toi qui le savais!

A lightening bolt . . . then night!: Fugitive beauty!
You whose glance suddenly brought me back to life,
Will I never see you except in eternity?

Elsewhere, far away! Too late! Perhaps *never!*
For I know not where you run to, you know not where I go,
Oh you whom I might have loved, oh you who knew it!

Baudelaire's closing stanzas thus foreground time's expansion and infinite distances, which contrast sharply with the hurried crowdedness of city streets and the congestion of urban development. In their mention of eternity, prolonged estrangement and what will never be in *chronological* time — *"never!"* — these lines highlight how modernity's essential restlessness delivers a loneliness and despair nevertheless mitigated by the possibility of something deeper, the possibility of a transcendent reality as invoked by a fleeting, beautiful vision. "Will I never see you except in eternity?" (*Ne te verrai-je plus que dans l'étérnité?*). Again, there is contrast between what modernity offers and a temporality unaligned with industrial culture. The intensity and liveliness of Paris produce a thralldom that engenders the fascination of looking, of viewing and of sampling everything that is new, in progress and in transit. Yet the beauty of a woman in mourning, a woman *agile et noble,* operates against this raging urban backdrop by setting in motion the *correspondances* that unveil a register outside of chronology, subverting the claim that modernity's inventions and commitment to the new constitute progress.

Baudelaire's loving response to a prostitute and fascination with a passerby both speak of restored connections made possible amid the very horrors of modernity that he laments. The connection to lost origins that they deliver invokes stars and a distant sky, a world not enmeshed in the grinding exhaustion of modernity so characterized by a cacophonous overabundance, a harried pace, the need to endlessly reinvent oneself. The world to which poetic insight returns him is one set apart from the deafening, whirling vortex of city streets caught up in the thralldom of the gaze. And although modernity's industrialized version of a deeper, seminal loss may be new, the loss of connection itself in the paradigm has been replayed again and again. This is why, for Baudelaire, the modern city streets so often refer back to ancient images and ancient themes, for to the discerning critic their correspondences contain the murmur of something past. Hence his poems frequently reference antiquity—Plato and Andromache, Styx and the Danaides—even as they focus on Paris in the nineteenth century. The progressive veneer of the industrialized world thus reveals itself as a lie, for such movement forward has only replayed a far more antiquated theme. This deliberate slippage between antiquity and modernity highlights the manner in which the nineteenth century merely presents an industrialized version of an older problem: the longing to uncover the "long echoes" that can restore transcendent meaning, thereby furnishing the modern imagination with its missing substrate.

"Harmonie du Soir" (The evening's harmony) testifies to those moments in which the missing substrate reveals itself in nature's evanescent sensations that have a brief, heady duration at dusk. The poem's four stanzas describe that fleeting moment at nightfall when flowers' perfume becomes especially intense, as they shed their scent amid a swirl of other commingled sounds and fragrances. The perfume they emit like a censer suggests a High Mass and counts among the beautiful, delicate qualities of the evening that reveal universal analogies between contingent reality and a deeper register. The evening's powerful scent, distant sounds, and sad, dramatic sky combine to arouse the poet's memory, which is heavily overlaid with religious themes. It is the poem's short-lived, temporal dimension that thus brings forth the topic of transcendence, for the appeal to the senses goes hand in hand with a religious solemnity whose purpose is commemorative. Indeed, the pleasures of the fading day are to be found in flowers that, getting ready to close up, invoke a hushed transcendence. In all their natural appeal, they suggest the sanctity of a church, as does the colorful sky at nightfall. The evanescence of the natural world corresponds, in other words, to another register's intervention into the immanent realm, for the sensations produced during this passing moment collude in suggesting religious ritual.

> Voici venir les temps où vibrant sur sa tige
> Chaque fleur s'évapore ainsi qu'un encensoir;

Les sons et les parfums tournent dans l'air du soir;
Valse mélancolique et langoureux vertige!

Chaque fleur s'évapore ainsi qu'un encensoir;
Le violon frémit comme un cœur qu'on afflige;
Valse mélancolique et langoureux vertige!
Le ciel est triste et beau comme un grand reposoir.

These are the moments when on quivering stems
Each flower emits its vapor like a censer.
Perfumes and sounds commingle in the evening air;
A melancholy waltz, vertiginous languor!

Each flower emits its vapor like a censer;
The violin shudders like a heart that grieves;
A melancholy waltz, vertiginous languor!
The sky is sad and beautiful like an altar.

The element of ritual invoking a premodern world can be grasped in nature's transitory sensations, or, rather, thanks to the sensations that mark nature's evanescence. Sensual immediacy thus contributes to the ability to grasp a deeper register. Yet the sadness felt in a "melancholy waltz" may be the sadness that comes with recognizing that this apprehension must remain but a passing moment, that recalling a hushed transcendence implicit in the immanent world cannot deliver us from the chronological register of time that creates an impossible desire.

Subsequently, the poem's closing stanzas clarify how the repetitions of nature's realm, like the repetitions of history wherein modernity recasts an ancient theme, culminate in a moment of remembrance. For the repeating phrases throughout the poem, repositioning words just as modernity repositions age-old concerns, find their conclusion in memory's power: "Your memory glows within me like a chalice." This mention of a chalice, like those of incense and an altar, reveals transcendence amid so many earthly sensations, an antecedent discovered thanks to the poet's privileged insight.

Le violon frémit comme un cœur quon afflige,
Un cœur tendre, qui hait le néant vaste et noir!
Le ciel est triste et beau comme un grand reposoir;
Le soleil s'est noyé dans son sang qui se fige.

Un cœur tendre, qui hait le néant vaste et noir,
Du passé lumineux recueille tout vestige!
Le soleil s'est noyé dans son sang qui se fige . . .
Ton souvenir en moi luit comme un ostensoir!

The violin shudders like a heart that grieves,
A tender heart that hates the black abyss.
The sky is sad and beautiful like an altar;
The sun is drowned in its own congealing blood.

A tender heart that hates the black abyss
Gathers all vestige of the luminous past.
The sun is drowned in its own congealing blood
The memory of you glows within me like a chalice!

The evening's heady floral scents, its eddying sounds and colorful skies are powerful but fleeting, and the languor that they inspire works to evoke memory. These sights and sensations call up *le souvenir,* causing a tender heart to gather all remnants of the luminous past and, amid their evanescence, to arrive at the transcendence of a chalice. The exquisite sorrow surrounding the memory in question may well result from the realization that the ritualistic elements perceived at this moment are usually missing from modern life. Certainly the third stanza implies a nostalgic longing, for the "luminous past" contrasts sharply with the current "black abyss." This brief insight grasps the potential for a life infused with cairological meanings and the ritualistic dimension missing from modernity's logic. Indeed, the poem's concluding line—"The memory of you glows within me like a chalice!"—is given only once, unlike many others that repeat. This draws attention to the word *chalice,* as does the fact that the word ends the poem. A chalice, of course, is a vessel for communion, which in the most literal sense causes immanent, material reality to be transformed into something that exceeds the bounds of chronological time. Thus the ritualistic themes invoked in the mention of a chalice contravene the repetitive nature of modernity's obsession with the new, as memory, *correspondances,* and ritual imply that something *truly different* has exceeded the time's register.

Moreover, the manner in which several verses repeat randomly throughout the poem disallows any clear temporality, for *le souvenir* involves drawing on the past and confusing time's measurement. Thanks to this haphazard repetition, the poem holds little linearity; rather, it foregrounds the swirling sensations and awareness of correspondences between material contingency and its deeper meanings that allow for memory's reconnection. The religious motifs of incense, an altar, and a chalice ensure that the luminous past recollected is not subject to the dehumanizing matrix of commodity culture. We know nothing about this past, but its transcendent qualities are what matter to Baudelaire, for they contravene the ugliness of the nineteenth century's high capitalism. Dialectically, they represent the obverse of modernity's eviscerated side, for even as *Les Fleurs du Mal* exposes the inhumanity of its surrounding culture, it concurrently demonstrates a reconnection to deeper meanings. The poet is transported to a realm wherein the fragment or fleeting moment has profundity, and the meanings of immanent reality are restored in an act that is healing and subversive. For Baudelaire, the sublime realization of originary meanings that nineteenth-century capitalism so threatens to expunge is thus found in a visit to the brothel, a brief encounter on the street, or the smell of evening flowers.

The allegorical dimension contained in Baudelaire's poetry, witnessed in his ability to interpret modernity with privileged insight, provides the armature for his critique of the new. This allegorical approach to modernity's newness creates parallels between his work and that of Benjamin, who drew deeply from the poet's literary contribution. Both authors locate a melancholic dimension to the obsession with the new, for the latter is the hallmark of a wandering imagination in search of a meaningful substrate. Their claim is that this obsession can result either in taedium vitae, a world overripe with meanings that collectively point nowhere, or in the promise of *correspondances*, to be had in moments of spiritual transport. Together, they help define the impossible structure of desire that is at the heart of modernity's melancholic outlook. For although some measure of reconnection is possible, located in what Kristeva calls transposition, such moments are surely unusual against the backdrop of modernity's pronounced fragmentation.

America's fundamental commitment to Enlightenment ideals, emanating from the philosophies of the seventeenth and eighteenth centuries, in some ways makes it *the* modern nation par excellence. The intellectual ruptures and fragmentations described above are what drive its ideological orientation, for since its inception it has claimed no ancien régime, no feudal ties, no vestige of Old World hierarchies. The United States necessarily embraced the philosophical first principles of the Age

of Reason and revolution, and wove these concepts into its most prominent political documents.[41] Many have commented on the deep intellectual affinities between European thinkers such as John Locke and
Montesquieu and the Founding Fathers, specifically Thomas Jefferson
and James Madison. For without question, America grew out of the
modern ideology that was intent on burying an Old World mind-set;
it was to be disenchantment in the flesh, the triumph of a rationalist
outlook over the superstitions, attachments, and obligations of an earlier time. "America has been dominated by pure bourgeois, middle-class
individualistic values," writes Seymour Martin Lipset, who explains
that such values have no history of the class revolutions central to modern European identity, no noblesse oblige to eradicate in the face of egalitarian principles. "Born out of revolution, the United States is a country
organized around an ideology which includes a set of dogmas. . . . Other
countries' senses of themselves are derived from a common history. . . .
Being an American . . . is an ideological commitment."[42] And the
American ideology of which Lipset speaks is that of modernity: it is the
ideology of democratic ideals, egalitarianism, a secular state, rugged
individualism, capitalist competition, and above all, progress—a commitment to the new.

This ideology, the ideology of the Founding "born out of revolution," has been interpreted differently by the American right and left.
In the subsequent chapters, I hope to demonstrate how these differing
interpretations have produced vastly opposing political agendas thanks
to their understanding of this cultural and spiritual substrate. For while
American conservatism holds fast to a foundation worth preserving,
the cultural left in many ways argues the obverse: that to be American is precisely to have an identity without foundations. A melancholic
motif thus resides at the core of America's unique experience, for we
are the modern nation par excellence built on rupture and fragmentation, a nation that has instantiated the modern sensibility from its
inception. And while the right strives to fill the void with a Founding
particular to America (but now dismissed and discredited by many),
the cultural left insists that all foundations are suspect given the performative nature of all political life.

Chapter 3

Overripe America

America, a Phoenix Reborn

We have seen that a cogent theory of melancholia rests on the bewildering reality of a world overripe with meaning, a world wherein a welter of cultural references no longer claims one established, unifying lexicon. In the Western world, this melancholia typifies the (post)modern condition, given the centrality of rupture and fragmentation to the contemporary experience. The resultant taedium vitae characteristic of a melancholic outlook often channels its energies into a frantic search for something new, an obsession with "progress" and linear time that in fact reveals a desire for an antecedent. This obsession speaks allegorically of a lost origin that, as beautifully expressed in Baudelaire's poetry, permeates the modern imagination. Thus the restless search for newness is in fact a replaying of something old, the longing for a different register of time hidden within the weight of chronology. And in the contemporary world overripe with meaning, taedium vitae may not express itself as apathetic lethargy, but play out as a hyperexcited, hyperactive form of overdrive enamored of novelty's thralldom.

The two theorists I have drawn on are both European. Nevertheless, their understanding of melancholia is pertinent to an examination of the contemporary United States, where a commitment to newness is deeply woven into the fabric of our cultural ideology. Their theory of melancholia helps probe the question of why, in the contemporary United States, the mythology of a former, happy decade unbeset by postmodern angst has such allure for Americans who are disillusioned with the current malaise. For whether Americans consider the 1950s a blueprint for progress or pie in the sky—whether they are to the right of the spectrum, to the left, or somewhere in between—they frequently have much to say about a revered past whose kinder, gentler temperament contrasts sharply with the internal depletion we currently experience.

Among those disappointed in our cultural malaise, resentment runs deep. They cling to an established agenda regarding our nation's (perceived) original mission and theological purpose, and in their conservatism are thus oriented toward the past (even as they propose change for the future). And indeed, from its inception, America's self-understanding carried with it theological overtones, as the New World sought to bring to fulfillment a new form of human community nevertheless modeled on its European origins. Since the earliest European settlers visited this land, our self-definitions have been heavily overlaid with the concept of a clean break, a fresh start, a new lease on life allowing for the older outlook to be abandoned in favor of newer, redeemed practices. Among the earliest arrivals, Americans understood themselves as the offspring of European forefathers who had ventured far in an effort to give an ancient culture a new beginning. They were pioneers who had left behind an old way of life so that a brand new tradition, a new take on older themes, might be established. Many saw America as an effort to revive an old covenant ruined by the vagaries of European history, a second chance at bringing theology into lived human history.[1] Thus our nation's self-definition necessarily carries with it overtones of a rupture, a radical break that would allow a fresh start to the Old World's antiquarian mind-set and revered traditions.

Importantly, the European settlers did not see America as simply a newer version of the Old World, a cognate of the European culture reassembled and replayed for a different generation. Rather than existing as the uprooted derivative of an established tradition, it was conceived as something genuinely new: a new space and a new time that would preserve the finer elements of the Old World in a novel and different incarnation. America was a new locale whose mission was to fulfill an older promise and, indeed, take the embattled European heritage into a new register of time. Because the earliest settlers over-looked Native American claims to the expansive territory they now inhabited, they could envisage this terrain as the site of a new begin-ning in human history.

Hence, as early as the seventeenth century, those embarking on the New World referred to America as the New Jerusalem, a New Israel, terms saturated with biblical inflections that unveil the profound reli-gious associations that accompanied the American experiment.[2] Sacvan Bercovitch explains that "America . . . was the new promised land, re-served by God for His chosen new people as the site for a new heaven and a new earth."[3] This amply demonstrates how the New World expe-rience was to parallel the Edenic splendor described in the Book of Genesis and in Revelation; it was to be a new city where the New Adam would finally see his mission fulfilled. On American soil, the Garden of Eden need not be thought of in strictly metaphoric language. Rather, America was to turn metaphor into the concrete reality of everyday life, a blessed place where lived reality matched the story of biblical promise. Indeed, in this new territorial expanse, the gap between idea and reality contained in figurative language was suspended. America was not a trope that alluded to God's promise, nor was it a temporal power that functioned as an analogy for God's kingdom. Instead, it was *to be* God's promise in a new place and a new time, a dream become real within the parameters of history. As Bercovitch writes, the Puritans perceived that "the Old Testament promises belonged to all true Chris-tians spiritually, but to God's New Israel historically and geographically as well. . . . It was a community at once purer and more political than its Old World counterparts."[4]

The promise contained in the New World was that of cairological fulfillment, the ability of a messianic dimension to imbue the heavy, painful chronological time of everyday life with God's presence such that immanent reality might take on a larger, more beautiful purpose. If Europe had lost its way in civil wars, religious battles, a profound philosophical debate over monarchy, secularism, and science, and the violence of class antagonisms, America was to be the peaceful land that saw God's true intentions written plainly in its very makeup. It was the place wherein human chronological time would finally be infused with cairology, the time of messianic fulfillment extending beyond chronological history in order to make God's covenant plain.

Importantly, simplicity was the keynote of America's blessed status as it threw off the corruption and degeneration that many held responsible

for Europe's decline. The New Adam was a man of simple manners
and of simple faith, a puritan who could experience redemption amid
human activity as he communed with nature. Simplicity ensured purity
of heart and a single-mindedness of purpose, staving off corruption and
contamination. The degenerative sophistication of Europe and richness of its culture was therefore countered by America's puritanism,
and the continent's many enclosed salons, with their hotbed of philosophical debate, had their nemesis, their cultural and intellectual foil,
in the untouched grandeur of America's pristine, wide-open spaces.
Alexis de Tocqueville thus wrote in the early nineteenth century of "the
emigrants who fixed themselves on the shores of America in the beginning of the seventeenth century, severed the democratic principle from
all principles that repressed it in the old communities of Europe, and
transplanted it unalloyed to the New World."[5] Thus "unalloyed" and
devoted to simplicity, the early settlers felt that the counterproductive
sophistication and unnecessary cultural breadth of European civilization had in fact backfired on the old country, wherein a prodigious
cerebral talent had helped alienate if not occult the spiritual dimension of life. Humanity's covenant with God had seemingly gone out of
the fabric of everyday life, and chronological time bore the heavy, repetitious weight of this separation.

The malaise of early modern culture discussed in the preceding chapter attests to the strife of European melancholy, as a repetitious, unredeemed chronology that has lost its deeper purpose recalls the unending
cycles of Dante's inferno. To the earliest non-Native Americans, Europe
thus represented catastrophic time and doomed space, the elements of
Trauerspiel lived out in everyday life. It represented immanent reality
deprived of a meaningful substrate, a world of spiritual potential now
marked by the absurdity of bonds and beings. Yet America represented
both a new time and a new space, a renewed chance at experiencing
God's covenant in the here and now. In the untouched expanse of
America's wide-open spaces, both nature and culture reflected God's
promise to redeem His people. The grandeur of the American terrain
thus responded to biblical purpose, as the "unalloyed" quality of American life demonstrated a renewed faith.

Rupture is thus integral to our nation's self-understanding, given
that the early colonists embarked on both a literal and spiritual departure from their origins. For the earliest Puritans, America was a rupture ordained to redeem God's people, a break with the past that would
rekindle and reinvigorate an old covenant. "America . . . was the new

promised land, reserved by God for His new chosen people as the site for a *new* heaven and a *new* earth."[6] These biblical themes allowed the new Americans to reinterpret human toil using the language of redemption. Indeed, the magnificent promise contained in the shift from Old World to New permitted the settlers to see redemption even in failure, hardship, struggle, and tragedy. Even the Puritans' errant gestures were interpreted as acts of God, a venue for purification that expedited their return to Him as they endured the flames of the refiner's fire. Even in their waywardness, an optimism animated the early Americans' belief that they were a unique people, a chosen population who even in hardship could discern God's redeeming hand.

> From the start [the Puritans] sounded a different note. Theirs was a peculiar mission, they explained, for they were a "peculiar people," a company of Christians not only called but chosen, and chosen not only for heaven but as instruments of a sacred historical design. Their church-state was to be at once a model to the world of Reformed Christianity and a prefiguration of New Jerusalem to come. To this end, they revised the message of jeremiad. . . . In their case, they believed, God's punishments were *corrective*, not destructive.[7]

Everything about the experience of early America, good and bad, thus pointed to the redeeming grace of God as it helped the misery of chronological time be radically changed thanks to the cairological purpose of the New World. America thus offered a version of time that combined mundane and theological registers, allowing the earthly experience of time's passing to be infused with biblical meaning. The early American experience comprised "a fusion of secular and sacred history,"[8] a union of earthly and Edenic purposes that redeemed even the hardest struggles.

This belief that America was truly unique among nations fueled an optimism that would, over time, become a hallmark of the American experience. So much of our self-definition rests on a conviction that America consistently demonstrates the power of a can-do, against-all-odds attitude capable of delivering a wealth of splendid results. The American dream relies on the premise of a rugged individualism that, braving the elements and taking great risks, dares to strike out on its own in a venture that ultimately proves successful. For instance, we love rags-to-riches stories, and the dream that an individual can become a millionaire thanks to hard work and determination continues to be a staple of American life. The stories of Horatio Alger indeed created a time-honored cultural hero who, struggling on a street corner and persevering despite misfortune, exercises his savvy to eventually become wealthy. Such stories are repeated again and again in a number of American icons—some real, some imagined—who go from similar lowly street corners to become pillars of society, wealthy operators who surpass their humble origins and, with resolve and an enterprising spirit, make millions.

Examples of real-life American rags-to-riches stories of course encourage this optimism. Many persons have literally struck it rich here, and there are reasons some still say the streets of America are paved with gold. People have discovered Texan oil, made millions overnight playing the stock market, become wealthy in Hollywood, or succeeded in industry by outsmarting competitors. Thus J. P. Morgan, the Rockefellers, the Vanderbilts, William Randolph Hearst, the Kennedys, Bill Gates, and Donald Trump not only count among our success stories but appear emblematic of the American dream: we refer to them as evidence of how our determination and savvy always pay off. Our reward in being true to our status as New Jerusalem, the argument goes, is that America can offer material success as nowhere else: upward mobility here is a commonplace. Subsequently, our fictitious cultural icons often play out this component of American exceptionalism, which stipulates that, as our nation is blessed like no other, we can easily enjoy a garden of earthly delights. J. R. Ewing of *Dallas,* Jed Clampett of *The Beverly Hillbillies,* and the televised wish fulfillment of *Who Wants to Marry a Multi-Millionaire?* all demonstrate how fervently Americans cling to the belief that fortunes are waiting to be had.[9]

The American attitude that the sky is the limit, that boundless opportunities are waiting to be developed, also derives from the wide-open spaces that have factored so prominently in our experience and in our imagination. Without question, the can-do spirit that has driven many to seek new opportunities for wealth owes much to the various frontiers that have factored into our nation's past. Laurence Shames argues that the frontier serves as a crucial American metaphor that organizes our thoughts, our desires, and our imagination: "The frontier, as reality and as symbol, is what has shaped the American way of doing things and the American sense of what's worth doing."[10] It compacts the thematics of geographic space and the enterprising spirit, the fact that there is so much to be invented, discovered, and explored in new, uncharted territory. The wide-open frontiers of the West, Alaska, the Great Plains, and the Grand Canyon, of outer space, and even, figuratively speaking, of a promising new industry, all contribute to the novelty and optimism that factor into the American mind-set. Indeed, as demonstrated in the doctrine of Manifest Destiny, in Kennedy's New Frontier, and in Johnson's Great Society, we think big in America. We have big plans when it comes to conquering, discovering, and colonizing what is new. We drive gas-guzzlers called Explorer, Cherokee, Yukon, and Odyssey, names that correlate with the frontier mentality that conquers wide-open spaces with constant forward motion.[11] The forward drive and rugged individualism that we so cherish are also illustrated in the bravado of such personas as the cowboy who sleeps under the stars, the astronaut in orbit, and the explorer embarking on new terrain. Going it alone, these individuals from the New World embody a brave spirit that longs to discover still more out there that is new. They wish to enlarge on the newness of things by expanding America's boundaries and extending its influence.

Because Americans are socialized according to these mythologies, we also act big. When I visited London in 1997 with a group of students from California, an English sociologist lectured to us about the body language that defines Americans and how different this is from the body language of the British. His training in sociology, together with steady input from his American wife, made him a keen observer of such Anglo-American distinctions. Americans use ample space, he said, and take up much room in the way we sit, stand, and walk. We spread out and use gestures that imply an upbeat attitude, confidence, and savvy. We're taught to smile broadly, to put a happy spin on things, and to use words like *great, wow,* and *awesome.* There is a largesse in our gestures that is supposed to correlate with a largesse in our mentality and with the hope of success. Moreover, the sociologist provided data illustrating how frequently Americans exaggerate their income, which goes hand in hand with how many Americans consent to ongoing debt. We consume voraciously and, because there is always more to be had, waste shamelessly.[12] To be restrained or discreet implies failure in America, he explained, unlike in Britain, where such mannerisms are read simply as politeness. The dynamism that Americans often express in their gestures can thus be read as a microcosm of our larger cultural mythology and the desire to hold onto the frontier mentality. We are the New Jerusalem, many believe, a favored nation to which has been given a new space and a new time.

Newness has thus always been deeply engrained in America's self-definitions. And although this newness was to be genuinely different from Europe, its purpose was to reestablish an old connection and pursue an ancient mission. America broke radically with Europe, yet the covenant it sought to revive had been integral to European civilization. Our purpose was to authenticate the cairological promise that European culture had allowed to atrophy, bringing biblical meaning into the reality of everyday life. And for many neoconservatives, this still is our purpose today.

Not everyone believed America could live up to this calling, or that the claim of American exceptionalism was anything other than a mythical illusion.[13] Yet this illusion was surely in place in our nation's earliest days, for in *Thoughts on Government* (1776), John Adams articulates with confidence the exceptional features of American government and of the American people. He states that Americans are characterized by "conscious dignity" and "good humor, sociability, good manners, and good morals." They are "sober, industrious, and frugal," exhibiting "some elegance, but more solidity," while eschewing "vanities, levities, and fopperies."[14] So unique is the blend of these qualities in Americans, and so outstanding the government that they formed, that our nation distinguishes itself throughout all human history. "How few of the human race have ever enjoyed an opportunity of making an election of government, more than of air, soil, or climate, for themselves or their children! When, before the present epoch, had three millions of people full power and a fair opportunity to form and establish the wisest and happiest government that human wisdom can contrive?"[15]

James Barry's allegorical aquatint, *The Phoenix or the Resurrection of Freedom* (1776) clearly illustrates the great expectations that numerous eighteenth-century thinkers conferred on America as a blessed community intended to live out a new lease on life. Completed at the time of the American Revolution, the aquatint is an illustration of very high hopes, for in America, a phoenix is reborn on top of a temple while European civilization draws to a somber, definitive close. In the foreground, European luminaries mourn the death of an outstretched Britannia, while mementos of Europe's past are strewn across the ground. We behold Algernon Sidney, John Milton, Andrew Marvell, John Locke, and Barry himself, all mourning this momentous passing under a darkened sky. In Europe, the heavy emotions being felt in front of an outstretched cadaver are echoed in the ruins that lie scattered about. Indeed, the darkened space of Europe stands littered with remnants of the past, and its soil seems the site of many battles. The fragments strewn on the ground suggest an exhausted culture that can yield no further results; they speak of a weary civilization capable only of displaying mementos of its illustrious but faded past. The land tells of the culture's demise, echoed in the leaves and flowers that fall from a fragment of garland.

Thus references to Athens and Rome, to numerous achievements and battles as well as an entourage of intellectuals can offer no hope, for the latters' bent heads and sad expressions tell us that all inspiration is gone. The outstretched body of Britannia evinces no sign of resurrection. Even the greatest minds of European civilization cannot breathe life into this corpse, whose very success may have killed it. This space, where so much took place, is thoroughly exhausted.

Yet across a body of water, a peaceful and prosperous civilization is newly under way. In contrast to the somber mood and ravaged terrain of Europe, America appears blessed with fertile pastures and growing industries, which its inhabitants enjoy peacefully under brightened skies. The space across the water experiences nothing of Europe's emotional desolation, as the various activities portrayed—dancing, farming, chatting—are carried out in an easy, lighthearted manner. A sunny land where sheep and cattle graze, America appears filled with hope and promise as the beautiful, bountiful terrain dominates the small figures. This is in contrast to the brooding European foreground, where the large, overwrought figures, some of whom point or wave at America, dominate the ravaged landscape. But across the water, the propitious mythological references assure us that this space is blessed and that it carries out an age-old mission in a new and different setting. America is indeed a land filled with mythico-poetic purpose, a place where the allegorical meaning of time-honored fables comes true, just as Gingrich asserts when he describes the United States as "a series of romantic folktales that just happen to be true."[16]

Hence, in the foreground, the three Graces hold hands and dance along the shore. They are Aglaia (Brilliance), Euphrosyne (Joy), and Thalia (Bloom). And on top of a Grecian temple, a phoenix—mythological symbol of rebirth and even immortality—perches confidently as it observes the surrounding scene. The inscription below the image tells us that freedom is being reborn, the freedom that Europe lost somewhere amid its numerous pursuits. It reads: "O Liberty, thou parent of whatever is truly amiable and illustrious associated with virtue, thou hatest the luxurious and intemperate, and hast successfully abandoned thy loved residence[s] of Greece, Italy, and thy more favoured England, when they grew corrupt and worthless; thou hast given them over to chains and despondency, and taken thy flight to a new people of manners simple and untainted."

Barry's deep allegorical interpretation of political life allows us to behold the dayspring of a happy, fulfilled, abundant civilization committed to simplicity. America, it seems, is the land wherein philosophical ideals and lived reality stand in alignment, where a beautiful unity between mind and matter offers a firm foundation to the social reality under way. Indeed, America's vitality, strength, and promise seem capable of correcting the misalignment between mind and matter that had so ravaged European civilization.

Contained in this aquatint are indications of how, for "the new people of manners simple and untainted," both space and time partake in their newfound cairological purpose, thereby fusing immanent reality with a larger theological purpose. With regard to *space*, this change manifests itself in the sharp contrast between a verdant, yielding American soil and an overused, belabored European terrain incapable of bringing forth anything new. The space in question is therefore a space that produces, a space that delivers a bountiful harvest thanks to humanity's ability to live in harmony with nature. Yet given the historical,

James Barry, *The Phoenix or the Resurrection of Freedom* (1776). Courtesy of the Yale Center for British Art, Paul Mellon Collection.

mythological, literary, and philosophical references contained in the aquatint, we know that it is not only crops that are being invoked. Figuratively, America will produce a great yield as a political project, for the simplicity of American manners and uncomplicated approach toward civilization's purpose indeed makes this land a New Jerusalem that will fulfill the messianic hopes and dreams of the now dying Europe. America is the space wherein cairology and chronology experience fusion: it relocates the origin that Europe had lost even as it breaks with the latter's colonial influence.

Given this auspicious beginning, America's historical trajectory was to be different from Europe's. It was destined, many felt, to avoid the melancholy state described by Baudelaire, Benjamin, and others wherein an abundance of arbitrary meaning had bred despair. To be sure, life would never reveal itself as ultimately absurd, it was hoped, because the abundance that America experienced would forever be imbued with God's purpose. Decaying nature was overshadowed by nature's freshness, the promise that immanent reality displayed the work of His hand. American exceptionalism thus lay in America's ability to uncover something truly new, to exist not as a mere derivative of an established European experience that had encountered melancholy. America both discovered and was the new origin; it connected to the past with a promise of projecting an old desire onto the future.

Yet America's acclaimed ability to fuse cairology and chronology indicates that it differs from Europe not only in *space*. It differs also in *time*, the understanding of history's movement and purpose that operates according to a new and different axis. On American soil, time unfolds an inner logic as it reveals God's purpose. It never allows outer reality to be severed from deeper meaning. Barry alludes to this in the aquatint through the freshness of the season and generosity of nature that contrasts with Europe's dark, chilly atmosphere. Whereas the latter's prominent cadaver, fragmented statuary, and falling flowers suggest the time of decay, in America a fresh start is under way with every indication of a confident and successful beginning. The seasons of the year in Barry's *The Phoenix* therefore run parallel to the larger registers of time and reveal the manner in which the American experience represents a new lease on life for European civilization. The time of America is thus the time of dayspring, the redemptive time that heals rather than repeats the mistakes of the past. Indeed, in 1776, when Barry's aquatint was completed, America was to be the antidote to melancholia's tenebrous hold, the time and place that furnished a missing substrate to the modern imagination. It would never become "a tale told by an idiot," but would allow history to start again.

America's Time as Jeztzeit

In its ability to fuse two distinct registers of time, America was to bring about what Benjamin calls *Jeztzeit*, "now-time" or waking time, the time that offers the present the possibility of change. *Jeztzeit* is the register that follows a radical break, a revolutionary dimension that inquires deeply into the impossible structure of modernity's desire and recognizes that this structure is less immutable, less heavy with permanence, than at first seems the case. It announces the fact that what seemed impossible to change can in fact be accomplished through political commitment. In his 1935 exposé on the Parisian arcades project, Benjamin alluded to a new experience of time, a "utopia that has left its trace,"[17] which, the later unfinished project would demonstrate, lies hidden as a latent potential within the current experience of modernity. *Jeztzeit* is a time that disallows the pain of overabundant, arbitrary meaning in favor of empirical, political fulfillment: it jettisons the melancholia of the present and ensures that history need not repeat itself endlessly in a search for something new. Because it affirms the potential of the present, insisting that the present need not simply repeat the past, it introduces a genuinely new register into human history, offering a true origin in the place of endless reincarnations of the same.[18]

Benjamin's concept of *Jetztzeit* indeed brings together empirical and redemptive understandings of time as it seeks to awaken us from the complacent lull that modernity offers, a lull due especially to capitalism's tantalizing, irrational logic. The taedium vitae explained in his *Trauerspiel* study can be appeased through the power of this awakening wherein the trajectory of human history finally stops repeating the same mistakes. The hopeful dimension of *Jeztzeit* correlates with the theological aspect of Benjamin's work, and with his long-standing interest in Jewish mysticism. His belief that time as we know it contains a latent, different register displays an indebtedness to a theological tradition rooted in the Kabbalah. Benjamin's work, taken as a whole, demonstrates that the theological axis of his thought interpenetrates with his political ideas and that his earlier grounding in Jewish mysticism later became the armature of his Marxian reading of capitalism.

Several scholars have carefully analyzed this relationship between the two poles of Benjamin's thought and have explained the manner in which seemingly irreconcilable positions can in fact interrelate.[19] Susan Buck-Morss, for instance, emphasizes the manner in which a Jewish mystical reading of time "saturates" Benjamin's writings, just as he himself stated in his copious notes preparing for the arcades project: "My thinking is related to theology as blotting pad is related to ink. It is saturated with it."[20] Yet both Buck-Morss and David Kaufmann insist that Benjamin's understanding of theology remains deeply rooted in the temporal world, such that theological intention offers direction to a Marxian analysis of class relations and the possibility of changing socioeconomic reality. As against the Christian understanding that redemption relates to an eternal life not of this earth, the Jewish mystical tradition focuses more on the here and now, and on the way in which theological purpose animates immanent reality. "Jewish theology differs from its Christian counterpart," writes Kaufmann, for "Judaism tends to speculate not on God's being, but concentrates on His relation to the world and on the world itself."[21] Because this focus on worldly matters necessarily forces theology to interpenetrate with the pain of chronology as we know it, Benjamin can easily use theology as a lens, a theoretical framework meant to guide his reading of modernity's impossible desire. "For Benjamin and Adorno," Kaufmann argues, "redemption is a question of *logic* . . . a necessary postulate for a form of reason that seeks to calculate the level of distortion of the fallen world."[22]

Theology is therefore a political venue for Benjamin, a lens meant to illuminate his reading of modernity's melancholia. It partakes of a logic that leads from theology to political praxis, allowing the latter to overshadow the former. Indeed, the segue to his statement regarding the blotting pad clarifies that theology is truly an armature in the service of politics: his writings do not serve theological ends per se. "My thinking relates to theology as blotting pad is to ink. It is saturated with it. *Were one to go by the blotter, however, nothing of what is written would remain.*"[23] Benjamin's theological framework thus informs his critique of contemporary "progress." This critique maintains that modernity's injustices, irrationality, and constant repetition of the same contain an occulted dimension as the movement forward corresponds, on a hidden level, to an older desire ensconced within the logic of human history—namely, the desire for a classless society. His understanding of *Jeztzeit* affirms that the theory of melancholy offered here gives an allegorical dimension to modernity's painful, frenetic search for the new. Just as the baroque emblematics in his *Trauerspiel* study spoke allegorically of a decayed nature still open to redemption, so too does the logic of capitalist desire in its enthrallment with commodity culture speak, allegorically, of modernity's potential to rectify its pronounced injustice.

Indeed, Benjamin's reading of the seventeenth-century world's fallen state operates as the precursor, the earlier guise of a depleted existence that typifies the modern experience. Fallen nature dialectically invokes its opposite, then, just as the modern world's irrationality carries within it the longing for a more just social order. What the baroque experience of melancholia perceives in an arbitrary overabundance thus foreshadows the modern, urban experience of life overpowered by commodity fetishism: a hollowed-out reality of melancholic repetitions, an eviscerated existence caught up in the exile of vanished connections.

Hence the melancholy of baroque allegory examined in *Ursprung des Deutsches Trauerspiel,* which laments the world's disjointed character, offers a seminal, prototypical expression of modernity's shock-filled yet repetitive experience. Its allegory provides the index for understanding how the world's arbitrary meaning delivers melancholia despite the appearance of fullness. It is in this way that the seventeenth-century baroque offers a commentary on the experience of modernity and that a study of a dramatic genre has bearing on commodity fetishism. For Benjamin's analysis of *Trauerspiel* provides crucial insight into his later, ambitious study of the Parisian arcades whose resplendent display of items for sale partakes of the same allegory contained in baroque emblematics. Like the prattle of language after the Fall, these items on display seem to be a jumble: a multitude of things thrown together whose values have no stability. Yet to the knowing critic they are dialectical images bearing the trace of a connection. Although their ensemble might have the appearance of a disorganized bazaar, for those who perceive their dialectical meaning they impart statements about *Jeztzeit*'s potential.

The theoretical connection between the allegory of baroque and the experience of modernity constitutes the linchpin of Benjamin's unfinished project on the Parisian arcades, the now famous, posthumously compiled *Passagen-Werk.* Many excellent pieces of scholarship already exist on this incomplete, extensive undertaking that studies the nineteenth-century prototype of contemporary shopping malls.[24] The arcades were indoor passages in Paris, "inner boulevards" that featured an array of shops, eateries, and open spaces for public spectacles that, like malls today, brought people together in a public ritual of shopping, strolling, gazing, and idling. Lit from above, the arcades were originally elegant, marble-paneled thoroughfares. Their names alone suggest their color and character, as an entry from Benjamin's collected notes for the project illustrates:

> Names of arcades: Passages des Panoramas [Arcade of the Panoramas], Passage Véro-Dodat, Passage du Désir [Arcade of Desire] [leading in earlier days to a house of ill repute], Passage Colbert, Passage Vivienne, Passage du Pont-Neuf, Passage du Caire, Passage de la Réunion, Passage de l'Opéra, Passage de la Trinité, Passage du Cheval-Blanc [Arcade of the White Horse], Passage Pressière [Bessières?], Passage du Bois de Boulogne [Arcade of the Bois de Boulogne, a park in Paris], Passage Grosse-Tête [Arcade of the Big Head or the Intelligent One]. [The Passage des Panoramas was known at first as the Passage Mirès.][25]

Originally constructed to market luxury items in the early nineteenth century, these inner boulevards offered gaiety and entertainment to Parisian society as they helped bolster its consumerist culture, for, as Buck-Morss observes, the city "was at the bursting point of unprecedented material abundance."[26] They gave rise to such public spectacles and diversions as the panoramas, which were large structures into which the public would peer and gain the impression of visiting other parts of the world at record speed. They allowed for *flânerie* and other forms of idling, and of course were sites of prolific advertising. Above all, the arcades promoted the deification of fetishized commodities, featured behind large panels of glass to be displayed if not revered. Hence behind the bustle of consumerism, one might perceive the semiology of a secularized religion with its own deities. To be sure, commodities on display in shopwindows are not all that different from the host on display during benediction: we come to pause and reflect on the communion that it offers.

Yet amid the melee of shopping, these arcades simultaneously offered an allegory of the modern experience, enabling visitors to witness a panoply of items on display in what was a multitudinous, cacophonous, overabundant presentation, bombarding the senses in the act of viewing. For Benjamin, the cacophony of consumerist goods and general phantasmagoria of public spectacle paralleled the baroque contemplation of the world's absurdity, the profusion of emblematics, just as it did the prattle of language after the Fall. The abundance of items for sale, and the striking incongruity in their presentation, echoed the logic of both the *Trauerspiel* and the loss of Adamic unity. Full of noise and commotion, yet utterly incongruous, their world was overwhelmed by a loss of former cohesion and now knew a depleted status whose hollowed nature spoke, dialectically, of a former union. It was the image of these items, their presentation *as montage,* that Benjamin believed offered insight into the modern condition. His original aim was to rely heavily on montage, and therefore to *show,* rather than explain, his theory of modern melancholia.

> In the crowded arcades of the boulevards, umbrellas and canes are displayed in serried ranks; a phalanx of colorful crooks. Many are the institutes of hygiene, where gladiators are wearing orthopedic belts and bandages wind round the white bellies of mannequins. . . . "Souvenirs" and bibelots take on a hideous aspect; the odalisque lies in wait next to the inkwell; priestesses in knitted jackets raise aloft ashtrays like vessels in holy water. A bookshop makes a place for manuals of lovemaking beside devotional prints in color; next to the memoirs of a chambermaid, it has Napoleon riding through Marengo and, between cookbook and dreambook, old-English burghers treading the broad and the narrow way of the Gospel.[27]

The abundance of the arcades, when looked at as montage, was the abundance of melancholy prattle, only now arranged to charm, intrigue, lull, and even shock the viewer. The disarrangement of their presentation encapsulated the disarrangement of modernity, whose severance from lost origins could be read in the allegory of fetishized commodities. Items for sale were like words after the Fall: a babbling confusion whose seeming disarray contained the trace of a former connection. Read from this angle, the arcades were "the hollow mold from which the image of modernity was cast. . . . A world of secret affinities: palm tree and feather duster, hair dryer and Venus de Milo, prosthesis and letter-writing manual."[28]

This welter of images presented in the arcades—the commodities for sale and items for amusement whose pell-mell profusion recalls the chatter after the Fall—thus succeeds in imparting the allegorical tale of modernity's disinheritance. The fragmentation that is part of their display recapitulates the fragmentation of the modern experience from which an originary site has now vanished. Montage, of course, encourages this insight, visually demonstrating the dislocation at the center of Benjamin's analysis. Moreover, it is fitting that during Benjamin's time, the arcades themselves were in disrepair, showing signs of wear and tear rather than the lustrous appeal one imagines them having in nineteenth-century Paris. Indeed, Benjamin deliberately chose to focus on the arcades as a central metaphor for urban capitalism because of the disrepair they were experiencing, a disrepair that parallels the baroque interest in nature's decay. For such disrepair "not . . . in bud and bloom, but . . . over-ripeness and decay" tangibly plays out the thematics of lost connection now witnessed in buildings that house the very material abundance that drives modernity's "progress."

Yet the commodities themselves also participate in this commentary, for they too register the passage of time even as they appear in such resplendent variety and abundance. The items for sale themselves re-count an allegory of exile as their enmeshment within the flux of market relations raises questions about the possibility of connection, of meaning, within the continuum of modern history. This mention of market relations of course brings us to the other pole of Benjamin's thought, his Marxist axis, whose theory of the commodity's relation to its price, its severance from human labor and subsequent fetishizing, further substantiates the preponderance of hollowed-out, eviscerated reality in the modern experience.

Interwoven into the spiritual framework of Benjamin's thinking, his intellectual commitment to Marxist theory prevents the future from simply reaching back into the past in an eternally repeating gesture. That theory's emphasis on revolutionary change precludes an eternal recurrence of the same that deadens even as it promises innovation and fulfillment. *Jetztzeit,* Benjamin hoped, would truly awaken the present to a new consciousness that might produce meaningful socioeconomic change, "rescuing" us from the dreamworld into which modernity's "progress" has lulled us. It is thus revolutionary time whose ability to fulfill a utopian dream relies on its deliverance of a classless society.

Within Marxist theory, commodities under capitalism are like language after the Fall: they are possessed of a hollowed-out status, a meaninglessness that emanates from their subjection to market forces. For under capitalism, commodities lack the stable, intrinsic value that would be determined by the labor time that produced them or the use value that they offer to consumers. Indeed, on entering the flux of market relations, they are severed from the human labor that alone brought them into being, or from the use value that they bring. Instead, they are assigned a "value" in their price. This price, of course, can fluctuate dramatically thanks to a host of factors utterly divorced from the commodity itself. Nor does a commodity's simple use value determine its value, for many useful things cost little, whereas many fashionable items serving no purpose are costly.

Under capitalism and the moods of the market, value is conferred according to price. And because market forces alone determine the price of things, the values assigned to things are utterly arbitrary; things are valued or diminished, costly or on sale, depending on the unpredictable, often whimsical and haphazard flux of supply and demand. "Fashion prescribes the ritual according to which the commodity fetish demands to be worshipped," wrote Benjamin in a 1935 exposé on the arcades project.[29] Indeed, the "worshipping," the "pilgrimages," the reverencing of items contribute to the price they can command when they are in vogue. For given the religious connotations that commodities assume under capitalism, their display in the arcades is not unlike the display of relics on side altars within a cathedral. Hence Benjamin wrote of the nineteenth-century world exhibitions as events to which people made a "pilgrimage to the commodity fetish."[30]

Because capitalism robs commodities of any intrinsic, abiding value, they appear bereft of stable meaning even as they abound in the marketplace. Their abundant existence is marked by an arbitrary relationship to value, as the reverencing of consumers beholden to fashion helps determine their price. Under capitalism, then, it is not the use value or labor value of something that straightforwardly determines its cost. Rather, commodities are "social things," fetishized objects that take on mystical, unpredictable meaning and value once they enter the marketplace. In Marx's words, "A commodity appears, at first sight, a very trivial thing, and easily understood. Its analysis shows that it is, in reality, a very queer thing, abounding in metaphysical subtleties and theological niceties."[31]

On this reading, the logic of capitalist relations thus parallels the logic of melancholia, as items on sale in the inner boulevards of Paris show the world, thanks to their changing price tags, the arbitrariness of their value. To the knowing critic, a stroll through the arcades is a montage of images that unveils how the vicissitudes of the marketplace recapitulate a life in abeyance. It points to an allegory of how the experience of modernity is, at its core, about the loss of connections. As with language after the Fall, items on sale partake of a prattle whose abundant proliferation only reveals the contingency of their value and the flaccidity of their worth. If the nineteenth century was noted for its "bursting point" of material abundance, then it follows that this period delivered an especially robust supply of "hollowed-out" items. It was a time that initiated the reenactment of baroque allegory in an especially dramatic way, wherein fetishized commodities took the place of emblems whose meanings vacillated.[32] Indeed, commodities themselves are now a register for allegory, a repository for the melancholy contained in *Trauerspiel*. In its own fluctuating state, the commodity under capitalism is thus similarly eloquent.

How the price of goods is arrived at in each case can never quite be foreseen, either in the course of their production or later, when they enter the market. It is exactly the same with the object in its allegorical existence. At no point is it written in the stars that the allegorist's profundity will lead to one meaning rather than another. And although it once may have acquired such a meaning, this can always be withdrawn in favor of a different meaning. The modes of meaning fluctuate almost as rapidly as the price of commodities.[33]

And yet the fetishized, hollowed-out items for sale succeed in acquiring a mystique. As mentioned, they are reverenced, indeed worshipped, within the ethos of modernity whose capitalist relations provide a secular religion. Therefore, to claim in Marxian fashion that commodities display "metaphysical subtleties" and "theological niceties" is, on the one hand, to acknowledge the arbitrariness of their price, the mystery of how they are assigned value. Importantly, however, such language also suggests the manner in which items for sale relate as much to the dream-filled realm of wish fulfillment, "a time in the present that can respond to the desires of the collective unconscious," as to the immediate realm of purchasing power.

It is vitally important that the revered commodity plays on what Benjamin believed to be an unconscious collective desire for utopia, a longing to invoke images of an archaic past that will answer to the need for a classless society. In all their "newness," commodities actually present an intermingling of the old and the new, a desire to work out an old utopian dream stored in the collective unconscious through new and different items. The new images of modernity are thus, simultaneously, "wish images," the images of a new possibility to actualize a stored collective desire that has left its trace on each and every novelty. It was therefore Benjamin's hope that a montage of such images would unleash the revolutionary energies needed to realize this wish.

Indeed, in the 1935 exposé, Benjamin made it clear how central this theoretical tenet was to his argument, explaining that newness becomes esteemed under the new forces of production for reasons that have nothing to do with commodities' use value. The unconscious desire for a classless society thus constitutes the redemption he spoke of in *The Origin of German Tragic Drama;* the mythic longing for a healed relation between humanity and nature is in fact a longing for socioeconomic justice—a classless society. In keeping with the logic of baroque, then, newness was revered because the wish image contained in its appearance allowed a novelty to appear "wedded to elements of primal history,"[34] thus offering hope for utopian realization. If commodities contain the allegory of modernity's lost connections, if their fluctuating price registers the melancholy of arbitrary meaning, their newness holds out the hope of fulfilling an old wish, for "utopia . . . has left its trace upon a thousand configurations of life, from enduring edifices to passing fashions."[35]

The combined theological and Marxian poles of Benjamin's thought, which at first blush appear so irreconcilable, are thus joined in this notion of a new register of time, a register wherein chronology and cairology unite, awakening the present to an unfulfilled wish of the past. *Jetztzeit* truly breaks from mere chronological time by privileging a redemptive element that radically alters how we read history, bringing us deeper into the present moment. For with now-time, we are no longer searching for novelty and expansion, the "progress" similarly disdained by Baudelaire in his reading of modernity's horrors. Rather, now-time marks the answering of a collective wish, a way of experiencing the present that dispels a life in abeyance by engaging both past and future in the meanings that directly confront us. In a 1935 essay titled "Paris, the Capital of the Nineteenth Century," Benjamin writes of how the search for the new in fact reveals an older wish for social justice:

> Corresponding to the form of the new means of production, which in the beginning is still ruled by the form by the old . . . are images in the collective consciousness in which the old and new interpenetrate. . . .
> In the dream in which each epoch entertains images of its successor, the latter appears wedded to elements of its primal history (*Urgeschichte*)—that is, to elements of a classless society. And the experience of such a society—as stored in the unconscious of the collective—engender, through interpenetration with what is new, the utopia that has left its trace in a thousand configurations of life.[36]

The images presented in the Parisian arcades—dialectical images—thus bring together the messianic and Marxist poles of Benjamin's thought, allowing for a reading of modernity that both recognizes its melancholia and unveils a repository of withheld, utopian potential. The ability to wake up in the present, to stop reliving a spiritual dislocation, is thus contained in the dialectical image of an origin whose redemptive potential, "an eddy in the stream of becoming,"[37] the discerning critic can unearth. It comes as little surprise that Benjamin drew deeply from Baudelaire's allegorical insights into the lurid nineteenth-century Parisian cityscape and saw in that poetry a reading of time and of connection similar to his own. In addition to writing several essays on the poet, Benjamin devoted an entire section, or "convolute," of his arcades project research to the study of Baudelaire.[38] Benjamin especially saw parallels between the poet's ability to perceive correspondences in the ugliness of urban capitalism and his own analysis of dialectical images, between the former's purview of the city's horrors and his own theory of redemption. For just as Benjamin apprehends allegory in the commodity's hollowed-out status, so Baudelaire discerns the moment of correspondence amid the many shifting terrains of Paris. Both search for the "new" amid modernity's incessant, infernal repetitions.

Baudelaire closes *Les Fleurs du Mal* with an invocation to death, a force that, along with poetic insight, can alone countenance the weight of modernity. In "Le Voyage," death ensures the break with repetition that will alter modernity's grasp on our imagination and thus deliver something genuinely new. Indeed, so eager is the poet to escape the death delivered by endless repetition that it scarcely matters whether heaven or hell awaits him: "the new" resides in experiencing something other than the constant return of the same, the constant efforts at "progress" delivered in everyday modern life.

O Mort, vieux capitaine, il est temps! Levons l'ancre!
Ce pays nous ennuie, ô Mort! Appareillons!

Nous voulons, tant ce feu nous brûle le cerveau,
Plonger au fond du gouffre, Enfer ou Ciel, qu'importe?
Au fond de l'Inconnu pour trouver du nouveau!

Oh Death, old captain, it is time! Let us pull up the anchor!
We tire of this land, oh Death! Let us cast off!

So much does this fire consume our minds
That we desire to dive into the beyond

Hell or Heaven—it matters not!—
To the depths of the unknown to discover—something new!

We have seen that, at its inception, America was to be something new, a political and cultural experience that truly offered the world a different register of time like that alluded to by Baudelaire. Barry's aquatint plainly illustrates the extent to which so many eighteenth century intellects felt certain that America embodied a crucial, world-historic awakening that parallels Benjamin's now-time. Yet today, there exists an obvious difference of opinion among Americans as to whether this origin is true. Is America an expression of the new, or does it bear the weight of chronology as does every other country? On the one hand, neoconservatism often speaks of restoring this foundation that God ordained. "The fact that God, not the state, has empowered us puts an enormous burden on our shoulders," writes Gingrich.[39] George W. Bush agrees when he argues that we are living in "historic times." Yet the cultural left counters by stating that the mythology surrounding such an origin is utterly pernicious: there is no true foundation for us to hark back to. Unlike most other countries, it insists, America lacks a common narrative and a common history, and by its very nature illustrates the signifier's performative inauthenticity. America is postmodernism writ large, a (meaningful) fiction that gives the lie to "true" identities.

The film *Pleasantville* contains a brief interlude that demonstrates this ideological division between the American right and left, who differ so strongly on the question of our nation's foundation. It dramatizes how, within the logic of contemporary neoconservatism, the 1950s stand imbued with the same messianic attributes given play at the Founding. This interlude engages the biblical theme of Eden's innocence, simplicity, and abundance versus the enraged overripeness of contemporary culture. In the safe, predictable world that the sitcom brings to life, 1950s American society truly operates as the New Jerusalem, so unlike the unsettled, even tormented, world of the late 1990s from which David and Jennifer have been temporarily removed. Because this interlude establishes a clear parallel between 1950s culture and the Garden of Eden, it brings out the thematic of our (for some dishonored, for others fictitious) theological purpose.

Contained within the TV-land city of Pleasantville there exists a lovely clearing called Lovers' Lane. Situated beside a pond, it is a serene, secluded spot where fruit trees grow. Initially, couples go there simply to sit and stare at the water, for in their innocence they can't imagine what else they might do. Yet once Jennifer qua Mary Sue seduces Skip Martin, thereby introducing sex into the community, this quiet place is charged with romantic, erotic energy. Couples go there for intimacy and guiltlessly have sex in their ample, shiny 1950s vehicles. As in the tale of Genesis, they experience pleasure in a beautiful garden without shame or remorse. A 1950s-style rendition of the song "At Last" plays in the background.

Importantly, sex brings color into the black-and white world of 1950s simplicity, and the screen comes to life in vivid hues that imply that this innocent world has found happiness. Indeed, no sooner does Skip Martin take Mary Sue home that fateful evening than, to his amazement, he spots a brilliant red rose on a bush of otherwise colorless blooms. Subsequently, throughout the town, flowers turn beautiful shades of red and pink, automobiles take on all colors of the rainbow, and people's clothing comes to life. David qua Bud is seen visiting Lovers' Lane in a bright yellow convertible. Women's lipstick turns scarlet, as does their nail polish, and their dresses and hats are radiant with color. The association between color and sex, color and subversion, causes some to worry what others will think.

Pleasantville, the dramatization of Rockwellian charm, now starts to change. Mr. Johnson, the malt shop manager, explores his artistic side and succeeds in producing vivid, erotic tableaux that eventually embellish the city streets. Ignoring his chores at the shop, he paints imaginative murals whose bold, colorful expressions shock the more conservative elements of the town. Where he used to be obsessed with cleanliness and routine, with sparkling countertops and well-stocked supply rooms, he is now engrossed in art and is fascinated with his palette's potential. He even paints Betty in the nude, transforming the former paragon of domestic duty always dressed like June Cleaver into an erotic beauty. For a brief period during the film, then, Pleasantville is truly a garden of earthly delights. That Pleasantville equates with the Garden of Eden is made manifestly clear when a woman, Margaret, picks an apple at Lovers' Lane and offers it to Bud.

And yet the introduction of sex and color into this innocent town also sows the seeds of discord. Pleasure foretells exile and infighting as the vast array of colors corresponds to meaning's ambiguity. Literally and figuratively, things are not black-and-white anymore, as shades of color imply shades of meaning. Pleasantville begins to factionalize as those wedded to tradition are outraged at the disruption of routine.

They are incensed at the murals and shocked when a double bed appears for sale ("You mean one of those *big* beds?"). They remain distraught when their basketball team loses for the first time ever. They don't know how to respond to inclement weather, and they never knew the fire department did more than rescue cats. As life becomes unpredictable amid showers, fires, and failure on the basketball court, the town separates dramatically into two groups: those committed to the status quo (those who prefer things in black and white) and those favoring reform (those favoring color, those favoring meaning's ambiguity). Life is quarrelous and unstable, with no script to guide it. For the first time, no one knows what will happen next in Pleasantville. Something of the 1990s has thus been brought into the 1950s. The fractious climate and ensuing debates guarantee that the town's status as Eden cannot be sustained.

This gradual exile from a blissful state is clearly demonstrated when Mr. Johnson peruses an art book given to him by Bud. After a series of black-and-white reproductions, the first color plate that he comes upon is Masaccio's *Expulsion from Eden* (1425–27). The overwrought, wailing figures of Adam and Eve depart the garden of earthly delights in shame, their arms covering their naked bodies. Aggrieved, they are expelled, just as Pleasantville itself must depart its state of perfect routine, harmony, and union. Pleasantville gradually becomes more like America in the 1990s as social cohesion breaks down: the referents no longer refer back to what they always meant. Mary Sue has already learned in geography class that all roads lead back to Pleasantville; incredulous, she realized that the inhabitants of this TV-land town have no point of reference outside themselves. When she challenged the teacher on this count, asking, "What's outside of Pleasantville?" the other students stared at her in disbelief. Half bemused, half caught off guard, the teacher responded, "I don't understand." Yet now, with the introduction of sex and color, Pleasantville residents begin to suspect that what Bud has told them is true: out there, where life is "louder, scarier, and a lot more dangerous," the roads just keep on going, extending to parts unknown.

Pleasantville's ability to dramatize the contemporary struggle between American neoconservatism and the cultural left's tolerance of shifting signifiers is made clear when the city's mayor laments the unwillingness of Pleasantville housewives to perform wifely duties. Both George and his friend Roy have registered complaints that the city is changing too quickly and for the worse: Betty has failed to prepare

George's dinner, and Roy's wife, careless in ironing his shirt, has scorched it. The mayor's language is unequivocally that of the right as he speaks of American values that are eroding. His mission is to restore a cultural traditional while shoring up the city's cohesion:

> My friends, this is not about George's dinner. It's not about Roy's shirt. It's a question of values. It's a question of whether we want to hold on to those values that made this place great. So the time has come to make a decision. Are we in this thing alone, or are we in it together?

The cohesion touted by the mayor in the name of conservative values thus parallels the mission of many on the right. And if their politics maintains that the postwar era resumed America's cairological mission begun at the Founding, it follows that for neoconservatives—perhaps for many Americans—the late 1990s and early twenty-first century have lost a unifying substrate and have lowered us to the reaches of hell. Indeed, there can be little doubt that the late 1990s from which

Today, American neoconservatives seek to rehabilitate the 1950s-style family values made explicit in television shows such as *Make Room for Daddy*. Yet *Pleasantville* makes clear that this rehabilitation is now impossible, given that our country is "louder, scarier, and a lot more dangerous" than these sitcoms suggest.

David and Jennifer have vanished know a hellish sense of meaning-lessness. Melancholia keynotes the world from which these teenagers come for all the reasons theorized by Benjamin: the postmodern nine-ties display a dizzying swirl of unstable signifiers whose wide range of potential meanings disallows cultural cohesion. Theirs is an overnamed culture, a culture too saturated with signifying potential, heavy with sorrowful potential.

Although there is pleasure, playfulness, and creativity in this free fall, the film does not fail to dramatize the fact that an absence of cul-tural cohesion can produce despair. This is made visible in the repeated efforts to find meaning within the parameters of an infernal, unre-deemed time: David constantly watching his sitcoms in an effort to escape the present, Jennifer and her mother constantly searching for the right man. The former withdraws into himself, whereas the latter seem to argue with everyone. Their shared, unspoken sense that life in postmodern America might in fact be full of sound and fury, a tale told by an idiot signifying nothing, is hinted at in the vicious arguments, the constant disappointments, the restlessness and desperation that drive each one's efforts to find fulfillment. "What the hell am I doing?" sobs their mother at the kitchen table after reneging on a weekend get-away with her current boyfriend. "It wasn't supposed to be like this!"

The mother's statement begs the question that is bound to arise in a discussion of our foundations: What was it supposed to be like? How was life, the family, the way we spend our weekends supposed to turn out in America? How can we tell if things have gone awry? American neoconservatism offers answers to these questions by supporting a polit-ical and cultural agenda that seeks realignment with (what it believes to be) America's true intended purpose. If we can understand its full vision of our national realignment, then we can understand why it considers contemporary America, infected by the cultural left with its radically different sensibility, to be so lost. The following chapter thus analyzes the neoconservative understanding of America's intended mean-ings. By unpacking this movement's mission, we will better grasp the deeper connotations of its disappointment with unprepared dinners and scorched shirts.

CHAPTER 4

Making Love with Absence:
Neoconservatism and the Fifties

A firm foundation ostensibly undergirds American neoconservatism, a solid basis that offers its followers a reliable, unchanging matrix through which to read our culture. This foundation operates as a sanctuary that strives to protect its inhabitants from the anxieties of cultural indeterminacy, shielding them from the interpretive free fall that now surrounds America's meanings. This is why the right invokes the 1950s sincerely and with nostalgia, urging America to regain the pleasing leitmotif and homey aura that it feels constitutes that decade's signature. This leitmotif will eradicate the pernicious influence of more recent epochs, the right argues, and cover over the scars, the tragedies, and the failures of the intervening years. Yet perhaps most important, it will expunge the insincerity of postmodern pastiche and the confusion of multicultural welter, for the absurdity of an over-named world may be the hardest thing to endure.

This chapter offers a critical reading of this longing for cohesion and explores the anxious self-referencing that such longing reveals. I argue here that the gesture of turning in on oneself, of forever referring back to an imagined wholeness, emanates from an inability to accept America's overnamed quality. It reveals a worried outlook un-rooted in the present that fears its own unraveling. Caught in the free fall of multicultural, postmodern indeterminacies—what defines a fam-ily, *do* we trust in God?—such a loss of origins experiences the pres-ent in abeyance and, in an effort to reconnect with anterior referents, projects the past onto the future. Part of the right's agenda, therefore, lies in re-creating the *Pleasantville* ethos of picket fences, malt shops, and "Honey, I'm home!" For to locate this past would be, according to its logic, to find something "new." It would be to exit the current welter of confusion and rediscover the potential for chronological time to be imbued with deeper meaning. The right's mission thus recaptures America's inaugural pupose: to exit the Old World and rediscover the new in chronological time.

We have seen that, for neoconservatives today, midcentury America was undoubtedly a golden age in our history, a lost Eden that we now must recapture by stringently adhering to a stated agenda. The 1950s (and to a lesser degree the 1940s) were an innocent, simple, straight-forward time, a time of obvious truths and well-honed rights and wrongs, a decade characterized by American wholeness and spiritual integration. Gingrich again makes plain the right's connection between America's true identity and the 1950s: "I believe we can revitalize American society, restore the greatness of American civilization, and reinvigorate the American economy while we remake the structure of American government. . . . Older Americans who grew up with the cer-tainty and convictions of World War II and the Cold War are eager for a rebirth of American values."[1]

This is why much of the right's mission resides in recovering a sense of national integration. In many forms of the right's parlance—in the language of Ronald Reagan, Pat Buchanan, Ralph Reed, and Gin-grich—the 1950s loom large, revered as the era that must serve as the current American ideal. Restitution, realignment, recommitment, re-birth—these themes inform a good deal of neoconservatism's political stance, whose unmistakable nostalgia projects a reading of America's former identity onto its future.

Indeed, the general tenor of the right's current discourse succeeds in upholding a fifties paradigm often without mentioning the decade directly. Thanks to the power of political rhetoric as it taps into our nation's collective imagination, it takes little to imply a lot. Even oblique comments can set in motion images of Dad at the office in a double-breasted suit with cuffed pants, Mom at home wearing a ruffled apron and a string of pearls, kids in striped T-shirts bicycling through well-kept neighborhoods. Because the 1950s operates as a saturated metaphor, it issues garrulous commentary with few words. Thus in 1992, when Pat Buchanan announced that the far right planned to "take back our country," what he meant was implicitly understood: he wanted to take back America's meanings from the newfangled sensibilities of left-liberals and return them to an ethos commensurate with Norman Rockwell paintings.[2] The ideological substrate of the 1950s lay embedded in Buchanan's comments, for he referred to a "cultural war as critical to the kind of nation we shall be as the cold war itself."[3] Hence, in constructing parallels between the cultural wars of the early 1990s and the Cold War of the 1950s, Buchanan clearly aligned the right's agenda with the associations surrounding Ozzie and Harriet. "The terms of these early nineties battles were transparently set in the early fifties," writes Alice Jardine, for whom the cultural wars "directly echoed fifties McCarthyism."[4]

Similarly, the emphasis on "family values" so pronounced during the 1992 presidential campaign made abundantly clear how the 1950s now function as a highly charged trope surrounded by a host of associations that Americans educe even in the absence of full elaboration. Dan Quayle undoubtedly created more of a stir than intended when he condemned the "cultural elite" of our nation for its assault on fatherhood, its deviation from traditional family values, its condoning of newfangled practices and alternative lifestyles. Aided by Marilyn Quayle's fifties-style flip hairdo, with its turned-up shoulder-length curl, the vice president provided an anachronistic, backward-looking semiology as he chided elements of Hollywood for portraying values incommensurate with an old-fashioned American narrative. Together, these husband-and-wife statements pointed to the dayspring of a renewed America, the awakening to a "new time" and a "now-time" that will reach back into the past to confer rich meaning on the future.

This sidestepping of the present while focusing on an idealized past and romanticized future of course takes the focus off the imperfect present, the overnamed America with loud, scary, hellish attributes. Insisting that we *can* connect with a more perfect version of ourselves in a register of time where chronology and cairology cross parallels Rockwell's insistence that if it's not a perfect world, it should be, such that—at least in his earlier days—he claimed, "I will not disturb my audience."[5] At the extreme, then, a form of Rockwellian denial informs this collective episteme, for flashing back to kinder, gentler times—

using either the remote control or, for instance, the Contract with America—keeps the present in abeyance.

Karal Ann Marling has observed that, in an attempt to deliver a clear political message, Ross Perot often posed for photographs in front of his Rockwell paintings, "as if to connect his biography and political values to their content."[6] Family values, reduced government spending, freedom in the private sector—these ideological tenets mesh well with cheerful scenes produced from Rockwell's palette. The artist's vision of an undisturbed America to which neoconservatives cling thus serves as a firm foundation on which they propose to build our national identity. Yet we have seen that the gesture of positing an origin always stands freighted with mythical and emotional connotations, enmeshed in a complicated, convoluted dynamic of anachronism wherein past and future are deliberately, usefully entangled and the impossible nature of desire is reaffirmed. Melancholia displays an interest in the past and future coupled with the inability to take root in the present, a mind-set laboring beneath the weight of an impossible desire nevertheless capable of imagining that a beautiful, seamless unity will someday reinspire our lived reality. Thus Max Pensky writes, "Origin is an image in which the linearity of mythic time is doubled back upon itself, in which the category of anticipatory hope is cast upon the past, in which the category of recollection is imposed upon the future."[7]

This doubled-back gesture of casting and imposing, of reaching backward and projecting forward, thus sidesteps the present, importing ideas and emotions from other eras in order to reconfigure—if not deny and avoid—the current constellation. Such logic posits the present as an aporia, a strange ellipsis that allowed a former, cheerful unison to become bewilderingly overnamed. This logic travels through other decades hoping to take the present with it, hoping that an imagined former bliss will take the place of the pain and confusion that often characterize the present.

The American Right, Remnant of "the Great Tradition"

The concept of exile that pervades neoconservative discourse is in part borrowed from the movement's forerunning predecessors. As with the old right, much of neoconservatism's self-definition still draws on its long-standing exile from mainstream American politics, its ostracization from the liberal hub that positions it on the outside looking in. Even after Reagan's rise to power and the movement's subsequent electoral victories, this motif has persisted. Neoconservatives have typically understood themselves as the surviving remnant of a former epoch, the remains of a wiser time that they seek to reestablish within the contemporary setting now so dominated by the left. They define themselves in opposition to the various forms of prevalent liberal sensibility and liberal institutions that, they feel, have left their imprimatur on American culture.

Admittedly, certain features of today's neoconservatism are genuinely new: specifically, its unique combination of fast-paced corporate culture and down-home American values, its ability to promote groundbreaking technology side by side with Grant Wood's *American Gothic.*[8] This admixture of high tech with down-home, of being folksy while getting rich, has been enormously appealing, given that, for many, it combines the best of both worlds. It allows American populism to retain its outward commitment to such old-fashioned values as hard work and frugality while also endorsing the good life. It sends the message that opulence is entirely commensurate with American traditionalism and that it is possible—in fact desirable—to be at home on the ranch and techno-savvy, plain talking and plugged into globalization, all at the same time.

Still, this movement understands itself as related to an older conservatism, for it, too, is the remnant of a former, sensible world now ensnared in a frazzled confusion wrought by liberal folly and postmodern pastiche. Even in the face of electoral victories, it still claims a disinherited status given the extensive revamping of American meanings that began in the 1960s and that still continues today. Consequently, the obvious disagreement over America's foundations that today separates neoconservatism from the cultural left only confirms the former's sense of disaffection. The right's purpose is to reclaim what was tampered with, to realign what has derailed.

Itself a variegated group marked by profound philosophical distinctions, the old right in America can nevertheless be characterized by its comprehensive dismay over the erosion of our nation's moral and economic framework. It maintains that organized religion, laissez-faire economics, and an unambiguous social ordering long upheld such a framework, which ensured American social cohesion.[9] Far from constantly rewriting the rules and rethinking the agenda, such stability allowed our country to focus on what it does well, to stick with one identity and adhere to that. Scholars such as Friedrich von Hayek, Frank Meyer, Russell Kirk, Irving Kristol, Walter Berns, Allan Bloom, and William F. Buckley Jr. now represent an older guard of conservative thinkers relentlessly perturbed by what they feel is America's ever-worsening disarray: a harmful, sloppy, expensive disarray sanctioned by the wasteful, permissive liberal mainstream. With our nation gradually disintegrating into a flotsam-and-jetsam state of anarchy lacking any clear vision, conservatives have long seen themselves as anguished voices crying in the wilderness, a solitary collective of clear thinkers aghast at America's fall from grace.

For this reason, conservatives are armed with an agenda to revive America's fine tradition, an agenda that always recommends *going back*. Von Hayek and Kirk, for instance, have both deplored the cultural disarrangement of contemporary life wherein traditional tenets no longer hold and have expressed longing for the organic cohesion that characterized earlier centuries. Along with other conservatives, they lament the social disintegration that has occurred since the 1960s and therefore resent the influence of multiculturalists, feminists, psychoanalysts, deconstructionists, cultural theorists—anyone falling under the rubric "postmodern" and intent on eroding the Western canon. "We see so far only because we are elevated upon the accomplishment of our ancestors," writes Kirk, "and if we break with ancestral wisdom, we at once are plunged into the ditch of ignorance."[10] Kristol holds similar views, which he expounds in a treatise aptly titled *Reflections of a Neoconservative: Looking Back, Looking Ahead*. This piece, whose title alludes to the doubled gesture of reaching backward and projecting forward, laments the unraveling moral fabric of Western culture brought on by lax morals, permissive attitudes, and a misguided interest in "difference." According to Kristol, such indulgences are like pornography in that they are "inherently and purposefully subversive of civilization and its institutions."[11]

Bloom, perhaps the most widely read among the old guard, similarly condemns almost everything about the 1960s, whose legacy, he argues, continues to wreak havoc on the country. In his disdain for such disruptions, Bloom applauds the stable 1950s as a time of enviable intellectual freedom and praiseworthy scholarly rigor, a time when meaningful public exchange was unhindered by the fruitless hypersensitivities of later decades. For in their constant deference to gender, class, and race, the latter shift the focus of cultural discourse and hone a sensibility whose relaxed relativism Bloom finds disturbing. During the 1950s, Bloom reminds us, the boundaries were clear and the parameters respected: writing and interpreting texts offered far less room for maneuver. Interestingly, this produced greater intellectual freedom.

One of the myths is that the fifties were a period of intellectual conformism and superficiality, whereas there was real excitement and questioning in the sixties. . . . The fact is that the fifties were one of the great periods of the American university. . . . Academic freedom had for that last moment more than an abstract meaning, a content with respect to research and publication about which there was general agreement. The rhetoric about the protection of unpopular ideas meant something.[12]

Eager to revisit an earlier America in which "much of the great tradition was here,"[13] Bloom dismisses the intervening decades as damaging to American life, for a blinding disorientation and regrettable loss of focus are what stand as their legacy. Intent on countering the "liberal establishment" and its (supposed) collusion in this process, the conservative school thus promulgates a discourse defensive of the "great books" tradition, Judeo-Christian tenets, traditional gender roles, and, for the most part, free market ideology. It clings to a cultural matrix now under siege by critics who query "the great tradition" so promoted by Bloom.

Sidney Blumenthal insists that it was the New Deal of the 1930s that truly galvanized American conservatism, allowing it to organize against a high-profile, high-powered enemy that served to sharpen its raison d'être.[14] The success of the New Deal's liberal agenda gave conservatives something to focus on; it lent them an archenemy to react against, a nemesis to condemn and to contradict. In the decades to come, then, American conservatism gained focus and honed its identity as the indignantly disinherited. The dynamic between liberal establishment and conservative counterestablishment was laid, and it is one that has greatly informed American politics since the early 1980s.

This dynamic substantially widened the purview of conservative expression. The forties saw the founding of the American Enterprise Association and the American Liberty League and the publication of *American Mercury*. William F. Buckley Jr.'s *National Review* appeared in 1955, as did Daniel Bell's *New American Right*. The John Birch Society was founded in 1958, and Young Americans for Freedom organized in 1960.[15] Yet the proliferation of such reactionary efforts could not stanch the liberal establishment's success or curtail the degree to which an ever-expanding federal presence became a mainstay in Americans' lives. Rather, a succession of administrations, from FDR to Jimmy Carter, saw to it that the federal government grew significantly, expanding federal programs, raising taxes, increasing the power of the federal branches in ways previously unforseen. This gave the right even more grounds for disaffection, heightening its growing sense of for-lorn disinheritance due to the resounding success of liberal expansion. By the 1970s, the federal government was bigger and richer than ever before, with an increasingly developed bureaucracy and a long list of programs on which many Americans had come to rely.

This served to augment the conservative sense of exclusion from the hub. "*Il n'y a que la vérité qui blesse. It is only the truth that hurts,*" wrote Pat Buchanan in 1975, conceding that in the United States, conservative ideology never translated into actual policy by gaining meaningful entry into the corridors of power.[16] At that time, a stalwart conservatism had no significant impact on the inner circles of Washington, D.C., Buchanan admitted, for somehow that environment always managed to transform a reactionary agenda into something more liberal. A conservative ally in Washington thus "ceases to be one of our friends."[17] Yet the marginalized, cantankerous existence of the older, pre-Reagan right had the salutary effect of giving the conservative movement purpose and cohesion. It sharpened conservatives' self-understanding by bringing their consummate disinheritance into focus.

This sense of ostracization also complements the populist strain mentioned earlier that has typified much conservatism. A conservative populism gives added play to the struggle over American definitions by offering a specific concatenation of political values and spiritual themes. It pits urban decay against pastoral simplicity, differentiating newfangled, overly tolerant liberals ready to try anything from filiopietists true to the Founding. To some degree, populism thus emphasizes the differences between our nation's coasts, especially the East Coast, and its heartland, between heady European cultural imports and its homegrown, healthy American elements. It keynotes that conservative strain in American culture that deliberately turns its back on foreign influence and relies only on a self-referencing, self-contained national identity. "They lived in God's country," writes David Halberstam of midwestern Republicans circa 1950, "a land far from oceans and far from foreigners, and they were all-powerful in their own small towns."[18]

Of course, the erudite cosmopolitanism of reactionary intellectuals such as Allan Bloom, William F. Buckley Jr., and Dinesh D'Souza cannot be denied, for their writings reflect a cultivated acumen different in tenor from the down-home variety of neoconservatism. Yet their worldly sensibilities and urbane manner do not prevent them from similarly opposing the liberal outlook, which they perceive as having wrongly thwarted American culture. For them, a conservative intellectual necessarily looks askance at such policies as affirmative action, the intellectual efforts of the cultural left to rethink academic canons, and the subsequent endorsement of poststructural, postmodern and postcolonial discourses that subvert a Eurocentric, patriarchal episteme. "Diversity, tolerance, multiculturalism, pluralism—these phrases are perennially on the lips of university administrators," D'Souza laments. "They are the principles and slogans of the victims' revolution. . . . the current academic revolution on behalf of minority victims moves at a swift pace. Nothing interrupts it or gives it pause."[19]

Hence the worldly, literate stance of these authors does not make for a political interpretation all that different from that of their more populist colleagues.[20] Indeed, the many varieties of American conservatism, erudite or down-home, all impart a sense of disinheritance, a disaffected removal from the political mainstream that garners them a platform suited to political outcasts. Gingrich has thus argued that Rush Limbaugh's seething attack on the mainstream liberal establishment expresses the true opinions of the average American. In his willingness to name the blundering errors, moral waywardness, and embarrassing peccadillos of his nemeses, Limbaugh is to be commended for giving voice to deeply felt yet typically unexpressed American sentiments that have been unjustly cowed by leftists. Little wonder, then, that the latter's radio show and books have received a warm welcome among Americans, because in them "the news was being interpreted by someone whose values were much closer to the average American than were those of the elite media. The average American began to enjoy listening to someone puncture the liberals' balloon."[21] Indeed, the most extreme expression of populist outrage goes so far as to dismiss the American press, media, bureaucracy, school system, and courts as tools of an orchestrated liberal conspiracy.

The Reagan Revolution and the Importance of Home

When the movement I refer to as neoconservatism gained momentum in the late 1970s, it inherited this sense of ostracization and spoke in terms of finally moving in on the liberal establishment by turning the ideological tide in this country. The collective feeling of failure and dwindling confidence that many Americans felt under the Carter administration, especially during the hostage crisis in Iran, abetted the neoconservative effort to assume a high political profile and to win public esteem. Many argued that Jimmy Carter made Americans feel indecisive and weak, and that he came to represent our nation's decline and fall. The political and economic troubles that beset his administration, along with his gentle southern nature and thoughtful manner, made some feel that we were regressing domestically, losing our edge in the world arena, and failing in our collective mission. In his quiet, compassionate way, Carter represented the softhearted liberal par excellence, whose good intentions and kind manner offered a vision of the presidency that differed from that of his predecessors. He was a reflective, principled Christian man not given to displays of machismo; his administration has thus come to be associated not with flexing our collective muscles but with controlling them, not with whetting our imperialist appetite but with curbing it. In Roger Rosenblatt's words, Carter's presidency was "characterized by small people, small talk and small matters. He made Americans feel two things they are not used to feeling, and will not abide. He made them feel puny and he made them feel insecure."[22] Although I personally disagree with this reading of Jimmy Carter, there is no disputing the fact that, by the late 1970s, America was experiencing a crisis in confidence.

Carter was cut from different cloth than many other American presidents. He gave us a different vision of the powers of the office and deliberately distanced himself from the philosophy and style of his predecessor Richard Nixon. Carter's Christian principles led him to prefer diplomacy over military intervention and cooperation in the world arena over unilateral action. His administration sought to get away from America's image as a bully, the biggest country with the most, the one who always wins and always gets its way. He thus asked Americans to cut back, to reevaluate our actions, and to be mindful of our wastefulness. To reduce our dependence on foreign oil, he asked that we conserve energy and perhaps give up some things. His focus was on the shortage of supplies as he asked Americans to take responsibility for our part in the depletion of world resources.

Americans aren't used to presidents who ask us to look inward and to reevaluate ourselves; rather, we celebrate those who tell other countries what to do. We applaud presidents who reaffirm our notion that we are the world's central point of reference, reassuring us that, consequently, other countries want to be like us. Americans don't want someone in the Oval Office telling us that we can learn from other countries and that part of our problem is us. Yet Carter's kindhearted

manner and principled approach offered a version of American manhood not at all in keeping with our standard mythologies and time-
honored folklore. Although Carter was formerly a peanut farmer who
spent many days working the land, his image doesn't mesh with that
of the rough-and-tumble cowboy that we love, the rugged individualist who refuses assistance and can go into attack mode at any moment.
Carter's trust in diplomacy didn't fit with the John Wayne, strong-and-
silent type that we love, who says little but acts aggressively, decisively,
and without hesitation. Once in the White House, then, Carter sought
to take much of the pomp and regality out of its character, getting rid
of guards' Prussian-style uniforms and ending the practice of playing
"Hail to the Chief" on his arrival.[23] The day of his inauguration, amid
the energy crunch, he walked to the White House.

By the late 1970s, many Americans were plagued by self-doubts,
troubled by a sense that we would never again live up to our manifest
destiny. Our glory days were vanishing before our eyes, it seemed, as
the leading role we had assumed in the world arena following World
War II seemed to slip away. Economically and militarily, America was
losing ground. Andrew Ross has argued convincingly that the late 1970s
was a time of renewed anxiety concerning America's ethnic makeup,
national boundaries, and national security, for that decade had seen
enormous amounts of foreign capital poured into the United States as
the globalizing economy encouraged new immigration into the service
sector economy.[24] New York, Ross writes, "had become home to the
cultures of the globe" in new and different ways than at the turn of
the century, for multicultural communities that "had no common Western traditions."[25] Such anxieties were in many ways a replaying of the
worries experienced during the Rosenberg case, when many feared
that America's military and technological strength were threatened from
within by agents cooperating with sinister foreign elements. This new
influx of non-Western populations, together with the economic and
cultural changes taking place in seventies America,[26] created a crisis in
confidence and the collective sense that our nation had truly lost its
way. For many, the drawn-out, painful ordeal involving American hos-
tages in Iran dramatized the bitter reality of our atrophied strength
and waning self-confidence.

This ideological setting, of course, amply laid the stage for the theme
of lost origins that would soon be given play on a national level with
the rise of neoconservatism. It set in motion the thematics of lost origins that would feature so prominently in that movement's discourse,

accompanied by the promise that we could, happily, find our way home if only we changed course politically. Although the seeds of this social movement had earlier been sown in ways that would abet its organization at the national level,[27] the late 1970s were primed for a national figure who would assuage Americans' growing doubts and uncertainties, making them feel that the slippage from a place of international prominence was only an aberration. We were ready for someone to make us feel comfortable in our old role, allowing us to replay the theme songs of our old cultural mythologies so that we could feel good again about those quintessentially American qualities—our individualism, our vitality and optimism, our sky-is-the-limit ethos—that, we believed, had made us powerful. Americans wanted to feel big again after the privations and humiliations of the Carter years, to broaden our shoulders and ride tall in the saddle. We wanted to believe in the American dream, to know that the weight of chronology still bore traces of a redeemed register of time.

Rediscovering this dream, for many, was tantamount to being taken home, back to a place where law and order prevailed. It was comparable to being transported back to a time when as in *Pleasantville*, Mom stayed home and made Rice Krispies squares, when Father knew best and, on returning from a day's work, shouted, "Honey, I'm home!" and hung up his hat. Allowing the old American mythologies to prevail once again, we no longer had to consider a new course that, like the harsh realities Carter had made us confront, jettisoned the belief in America-as-New Jerusalem and simply forced us to deal with the present.

As a man, Ronald Reagan projected an image that was both fatherly and tough, both benevolent and strong, all of which played beautifully into Americans' need to be reassured that we weren't floundering. Certainly much of Reagan's popularity was due to his friendly, down-to-earth personality, which nevertheless went hand in hand with his tough-mindedness and tough body. His persona was always tainted with frontiersman attributes thanks to his having acted in westerns, along with his penchant for being photographed in jeans and cowboy hat. This image of him, by now so familiar, augmented his popularity by reminding us of his acting career and of the extent to which all Americans want to be able to write their own script, trailblaze their own success, and determine their own role in society. Our deep-seated commitment to individualism implies that we can take any situation and, as in a Hollywood movie with a good cast and special effects, turn a disaster into a happy ending. By invoking the frontier ideology so ingrained in the American mind-set, Reagan thus drew on our shared mythology from the past and projected that mythology onto the future. He made us feel that America is an adventure based on wide-open spaces and endless opportunity, a nation where more, not less, is what we can expect.

Because Carter had taken a different path and drew on different spiritual sources, next to Reagan he seemed like the aberration, the unusual president who had forgotten America's meanings. But Reagan, to many, spelled home. The charm that emanated from him has been described as a "magical" quality that could easily, convincingly blur the boundaries between fact and fiction and make real life seem like a script. This suggested that Washington and Hollywood were part of a larger American continuum, and that the culture of the former was interchangeable with the story writing and satisfying endings particular to the latter.[28] As many have noted, Reagan was keenly adept at projecting an image, at playing a role that was as rough and tough as it was family oriented, as committed to combating communism as it was devoted to down-home, traditional American values. His reassurance that it is okay to escape to TV-land and flash back to a better world, to dream a cohesion rather than confront the reality of America's overnamed status, had a greatly rejuvenating effect on many. "As a performer, Reagan is far from panicky," wrote Garry Wills in 1987. "He is equitable in temperament and regular in his habits. His confidence and optimism impress everyone who knows him."[29] This confidence, this resolve that promoted a political and cultural backlash, appealed to many Americans, for whom Reagan became a long-awaited hero. Although he was the oldest president, it has been said, he made us feel young again, for he gave us the confidence to believe in our dreams.

Michael Paul Rogin and Susan Jeffords are among several authors to recognize the importance of fantasy, Hollywood scripts, and embellished success stories to Reagan's presidency.[30] For fantasy was more important than fact to those who felt belittled by the former president and by former administrations: we needed to believe that America is a series of folktales that just happen to be true. Reagan's romanticized quality and Hollywood appeal thus directly inspired a kinder, gentler America located either in TV-land or in an imagined Rockwellian past. It allowed the veneer of an imaginary wholeness, a totalized image, to appear real. "The screen . . . takes the place of a mirror," writes Rogin.

"It obliterates the referent: a self who sees from all angles fragments *and disappears into his image*. Self-sufficient, the screen dispenses both with external history and with the historically formed human interior. . . . Reagan has, to be sure, deliberately quoted movie lines to make himself the hero of American cultural myths."[31]

Jeffords concurs that Reagan quickly surmised the importance of allowing a Hollywood larger-than-life romance—a story that always turns out well in the end, that has episodic adventure and romantic intrigue but always winds up where it should—to be part of Washington's grimmer, harsher reality. Thanks to his background in acting, "Reagan learned a vital political lesson: that the success of the story, especially a story in which he could figure as a hero, was more important than any facts involving the events themselves. . . . Reagan cast himself as hero, but many in the country seemed to be reading from the same script."[32] This script, which put Reagan in the lead, featured America's high corporate culture, its religious, traditionalist sensibilities, and the small-town good old days so linked to the 1950s. Reagan supplied the cheerful outlook and indomitable demeanor that allowed these discrete components to combine into a single formation intent on circumventing the present and projecting the past onto the future. His affable persona lent a cohesive finish to these formerly distinct elements, bringing together Wall Street, computer technology, organized religion, and white picket fences in a movement that claimed a cohesive vitality. He was both reminiscent and forward looking, attuned to foundationalist meanings yet acting on behalf of future investment, future growth, and future aggrandizement. "The ultimate reassurance was that the society could have it both ways . . . early modern fundamentalism and postmodern agnosticism," writes Sheldon Wolin.[33] Given the bond this formed between capital and ideology, between a high-tech, corporate culture and Smalltown, USA, the Reagan Revolution was primed to cash in on the embittered but above all melancholic mood of Americans who longed to reestablish the nation's waning sovereignty.[34]

On taking office, Reagan keynoted the theme of national regeneration, seeking to assure Americans that the re-creation of a revered former era is eminently possible. In his inaugural address of January 1981, he exhorted Americans to "begin an era of national renewal," to *go back* to our former identity, search the past for forgotten meanings, and re-create a former, more innocent version of ourselves. Taking over from his beleaguered predecessor, Reagan embarked on the laborious process of dismantling the liberal legacy: "It is my intention to curb the size and influence of the federal establishment and to demand recognition of the distinction between the powers granted to the federal government and those reserved to the states or to the people."[35] Coupled with this domestic agenda, of course, was his desire to rehabilitate the American military and to revive our prominent military status in the world. All of this would facilitate *going back* to an earlier definition of American foreign policy. This revival would deny the reality of détente, ostentatiously reassert American military strength, and, importantly, resuscitate the rhetoric of the Cold War—the rhetoric of the 1950s.

It is no accident, then, that one associates Rambo, the Terminator, RoboCop, and other pectorally resplendent icons with the Reagan era. All these eighties Hollywood creations reflected a nation intent on doing battle with the Soviet Union through a revived manhood, hard bodies, a new commitment to individual responsibility, and, of course, increased military spending. In movie theaters across the country, Rambo's rippling chest and bulging biceps announced a hard-boiled resolve to do battle anew with the evil empire. His formidable girth and unsmiling face amply filled up the big screen, affirming in no uncertain terms that our nation's stint as kindhearted mediator in the world arena was over. Resuscitated Cold War energy would supplant the milksop performance that had made stooges of us in years past; American was strong again. The impressive musculature and aggressive demeanor of this cultural icon thus instantiated an entire social commentary, as the very body of Sylvester Stallone imparted a range of ideas that fueled Reagan's vision. Hence Jeffords writes that after the "feminine" Carter years, "Reagan America was to be a strong one, capable of confronting enemies . . . of using its hardened body . . . to impose its will on others."[36]

Echoes of the 1950s can thus be traced in the bulky physiques of eighties cultural icons. Stallone, Schwarzenegger, RoboCop, and others revived Cold War ideology, conveying through their bodies the need to reconnect with an anterior location whose embedded, abiding meanings were well worth fighting for. And in 1983, after much economic downsizing, military maneuvering, and confrontation with Congress, Reagan claimed that he could in fact see "a great spiritual awakening in America" that was allowing the country to heal.[37]

Reagan's efforts to heal the country, to re-create Rockwellian tableaux, successfully spawned a cultural revolution in America keynoted by melancholia.[38] For even when Reagan's political rhetoric was not informed by a metaphoric "fifties," his frequent referencing of Hollywood movies and talent and making reality seem like a film was enough to encourage the mythical illusions so important to the neoconservative position in which America is "a series of romantic folktales" that are nevertheless true. Today, as George W. Bush carries forward the torch, this position still adheres to much the same vision, striving collectively to rejuvenate America and to prevent Reagan's project from petering out.

Among certain spokespersons for the right, there still can be heard a lament suggesting that, although we may be on our way given recent electoral victories, serious obstacles still prevent the neoconservative agenda from reconnecting us with an anterior wholeness. This is true, for instance, in terms of globalization; certain neoconservatives feel that America's overinvolvement in the world economy has the undesirable effect of depleting our integrity. Although the right certainly desires an expanded American economy, some conservatives view globalization as an impediment to our nation's larger cultural mission. Globalization causes us to forget our uniqueness, they claim, by causing us to be excessively enmeshed in other cultures and other economies. It blurs the distinction between what is American and what is not, and thus threatens to contaminate and to confuse our unique, inspired mission. Pat Buchanan has warned against involvement in globalizing markets given that these detract from our true "destiny," the destiny made plain by the Founding Fathers in their plea that America not overinvolve itself in foreign affairs. "America today is as overextended as any empire in history," Buchanan wrote in 1999, concurrent with a request that our nation above all "reclaim" its destiny and "recapture" the ability to make decisions based solely on national interest. "We need to rediscover the lost chapters of our history . . . to know the ideas and ideals of the Founding Fathers and America's great men, who would not believe where our leaders are taking us now."[39]

Buchanan's exhortation that we relearn "lost chapters of our history" is of course commensurate with the charge that America now suffers a damaged life and that to return to an earlier mind-set would be to discover something "new," away from the weight of contemporary chronology. His is a backward-looking impulse rife with the implication that America is now not where it belongs and that a better, truer destination awaits us once we overcome the countervailing influences that keep us from our goal. Buchanan thus laments the present disarray, now through the lens of globalization, and urges a return to a truer foundation. "Now, back to the beginning," he concludes.[40]

Buchanan's exhortation that we go "back to the beginning" fuels the belief that America's original, cairologically charged mission has given way to the hellish culture we now endure. This rhetoric is both the cause and the effect of melancholia's grasp, both the impetus giving rise to the melancholic imagination and the lament that claims to be the cause of it. Importantly, neoconservatism *constructs* America's current hellish attributes thanks to its own discursive tools, even as it claims *to suffer from* a state of exile. It introduces the language of a living hell even as it strives to combat that hell politically. By clinging to the substrate of our eclipsed foundation, it fully articulates in distinctly American terms the melancholic tendencies that the (post)modern condition ensures are latent in us all. It is, in short, this movement's own rhetoric that puts into play the impossible nature of desire, acting as both cause and effect of the melancholia it seeks to overcome.

"Where's the Rest of Me?": Creating the Veneer of Cohesion

We have seen that Reagan's talents as an actor helped revive key elements of American mythology, catapulting many Americans into a mind-set that sought to engage a mythic origin in the hopes of imposing that past on the future. This temporal relationship of casting backward and projecting forward typifies melancholia, whose premise is that the present, overnamed world lacks an anterior wholeness and so renders our existence absurd. As opposed to the claim that all cultures, ideologies, and indeed individuals are essentially fragmented, the right holds fast to a desired totality (which, the cultural left argues, can be only the veneer of totality, given desire's impossible structure). With the aid of Hollywood's visual culture—perhaps *visual ideology* would be the more correct term—neoconservatism allows Washington to be on a continuum with the world of the big screen that writes its own scripts and has the ending turn out the way it wants. And that image is anachronistic, a 1950s-style world meant to counter the indeterminacies of globalizing, postmodern America.

But is it possible that the era of the 1950s *itself* utilized visual culture in order to project the image of wholeness? Was the era so contented, so happily self-contained to those living through it, or do we tend to misread what is simply the look of completion? It may be that 1950s America simply celebrated wholeness in the same way that

multicultural America celebrates diversity; yet neither of those cele-
brations makes the image real. If *Far from Heaven* is anything to go
by, there was a great deal of attention paid to the *image* of complete-
ness during the decade, which in fact covered over (or tried to) the
era's inconsistencies, hypocrisies, and internal confusions. The beautiful
interiors, the color-coordinated sets, the scenes portraying successfully
catered parties and well-organized functions—all give the impression
of a society that *looks* so good on the outside because it was so under
control on the inside. Indeed, Cathy Whitaker travels in social circles
that place a high premium on looking good. And she does look good,
just as she also organizes parties down to the last detail in hopes that
they will run smoothly. Yet her husband's soon-to-be-revealed homo-
sexual tendencies, along with her own attraction to a black man, assure
us that 1950s visual culture—carefully schematized, organized, under
control—was in fact a veneer for a more ambiguous reality. For if the
elements of mainstream 1950s culture could in fact open themselves
up to dispute, then America might degenerate into an overnamed society bearing no resemblance to Eden's serene state of bliss. It would
be, as the title suggests, far from heaven, where not everyone is white,
middle-class, Christian, or heterosexual, and where much rougher language makes "ah geez" sound like an innocent lament.

The television shows, commercials, films, and advertising that
abounded during the 1950s surely contributed to a configuration of
visualized totality, to an image of wholeness that was genuinely new
in the American experience. Thanks to the media's expansion and to
its economic prosperity in general, a seamless image, a *look* of completion, did become part of everyday life during the 1950s and helped
promote the veneer of cohesion. Television especially allowed for the
culture to understand itself as an integrated whole, a self-referential
entity that Americans eagerly viewed on their rabbit-eared sets, and
then imitated in real life. The sitcoms, the variety shows, the increasingly lively and sometimes bizarre commercials—all helped create the
impression of a full, ample, rich culture not lacking in anything.

Indeed, the decade's economic expansion meant that it produced a
culture abounding in things to do, to buy, to *see:* it was a visual culture of show-and-tell. New cars were on display in the showrooms,
and new power tools were being demonstrated in the department stores.
New food items appeared on grocery store shelves, and frozen foods
made marketing more convenient. The fashion industry was expanding to include Dior's New Look, with its full skirts and fitted jackets,

as well as the sack dress, the Halston pillbox hat, the wide-brimmed chapeau, and a revived emphasis on color and texture, satin and silk. For those in more comfortable attire also eager to look and see, to be persuaded that American culture was a culture of completion, a Walt Disney theme park waited to be explored. This was an expanding theme park now replete with Adventureland, Frontierland, Tomorrowland, Fantasyland, and Main Street. Disney's various motifs worked to convince people that the safeness, the innocence, the carefree visits and happy endings found within its expanding parameters paralleled American society at large.[41] To see Disney's family appeal, with its rides, its storybook characters, its gift shops and souvenirs, was to be presented with the veneer of a social totality, a society in which there is no missing substrate because no antecedent was ever lost. In this way, it has been argued, Disneyland allowed for "psychic redemption" because its art and architecture "fused postwar enthusiasms for imagination, horror, hallucination, and magic with deep-felt desires for safety, security, restraint, and direction."[42]

The visual culture of the 1950s—its big screens,[43] televisions, billboards, floor shows, showrooms, and theme parks—thus abetted the latter's reading of itself as a home, an abundantly rich image committed to maintaining a self-referencing, self-sufficient veneer. Despite the marauding collective angst concerning impending doom and infiltrating enemies, there was much in the decade that saw itself as an enclosed totality, an organic whole whose needs and desires were satiated. Its look of integration, its patina of wholeness, created a dazzling effect as compelling as the beautiful tableaux that make up *Far from Heaven*. It was a visual culture whose visual magnificence projected an image of Edenic wholeness. Yet we know that this veneer conceals a less glossy truth, given that the decade had no dearth of strife, conflict, anguish, and violence.

Today, this veneer of wholeness operates as a metaphor in American culture capable of drawing on our most deep-seated, long-standing mythologies. Because the right of the political spectrum longs to affirm and sustain the latter—keeping alive such concepts as rugged individualism, rags to riches, the wide-open spaces of the frontier, the premise of mind over matter—it uses the metaphor of the 1950s in its approach to the present. Although George W. Bush is clearly the ideological heir of Reagan and thus has been characterized as "Eisenhower with hair," Reagan's initial efforts to turn the country back to an earlier ethos and undo the damage of the intervening years more poignantly underscores the connection between neoconservatism and a missing substrate.

Reagan's autobiography *Where's the Rest of Me?* explains how a return to the political right offered him a form of psychic redemption by providing him with the substrate missing from his spiritual center. Reagan's life prior to this internal metamorphosis was filled with the highs and lows of a Hollywood career. As it does for most actors, the Hollywood experience offered him the full complement of exhilarating creativity interspersed with periods of intense loneliness and emotional disconnection. Yet he was successful, and the confidence he gained in making more than fifty movies easily translated into his political career. His ability to project an image and remain at ease in front of the camera surely heightened his awareness of the disconnection between image and reality, illustrating how powerfully a carefully crafted image can play on the mind, making us believe in a reality that is, at bottom, a fiction. Reagan's livelihood depended on his ability to blur the distinction between image and reality, to deftly make the performance seem real as the image fascinates, seduces, and anesthetizes. According to many cultural critics, acting, with its task of creating the image of wholeness and the veneer of totality, never left Reagan's professional repertoire.[44]

Where's the Rest of Me? engages this same disconnection, given that its apparent narrative about Reagan's career and external life changes is not its real story. For the book simultaneously recounts the deeper, internal tale of his ideological reorientation, his movement away from the liberal pluralism he had long embraced toward a conservative worldview utterly at odds with his former ideological position. Published in 1965, *Where's the Rest of Me?* explains the emergence of that nostalgic weltanschauung and conservative commitments that would have such great impact on American culture fifteen years later. The book's title, taken from a line Reagan delivers in the 1942 film *Kings Row,* suggests lost bodily parts and a missing spiritual connection. It alludes to castration, with its attendant feelings of emasculation, disempowerment, and the chaos that accompanies the phallus's loss of signifying status. Yet the title also implies a loss of relationship, for "the rest of me" could just as easily be a person. It could be a spouse, but, given our insights into the longing for reconnection that characterizes neoconservative melancholia, it is a pre-oedipal mother whose all-powerful, abject presence has been lost to the realm of culture. The autobiography thus establishes the desire to reinstate a missing bond, a bond that lends the individual cohesion, as a central theme merely with its title.

The reader soon gathers that the vagaries of Reagan's life as an actor were also fed by his liberal politics, which added to the sense of confusion and disorientation that governed his existence for so long. He was floundering, uncertain, and in search of a center. This spiritual disorientation caused by his liberal outlook proved to be not utterly fruitless, however, for it came into play when, in making *Kings Row,* Reagan uttered the line, "Where's the rest of me?" These words are the agonizing first utterance of an accident victim just regaining consciousness after losing both legs. Having no experience of amputation or dismemberment of his own to draw on, Reagan did extensive research in preparation for this scene. He consulted doctors, psychologists, and disabled persons in an effort to understand what a life without legs must be like. He toiled over the line's delivery, rehearsing it incessantly, "in corners of studios, while driving home, in the men's room of restaurants," at all hours and in odd places, "trying to brew in myself the caldron of emotions a man must feel who wakes up one sunny morning to find half of himself gone."[45]

Yet the book's ultimate interest in this line has nothing to do with Reagan's acting career. Instead, it makes use of this dramatic moment to explain his later conviction that it is American conservatism that can help us find the rest of ourselves, supplying our missing part and reconnecting us to the antecedent we lack. For indeed, Reagan underwent a true internal conversion later in his life that led him away from liberal politics and the Democratic Party. What marks this text as neoconservative, then, is Reagan's assertion that the frailty and bewilderment of a floundering human identity can indeed be overcome through ideological forcefulness, that the painful irresolution and uncertainty of our subjective narratives can be healed by political discourse. *Where's the Rest of Me?* clearly maintains that we need not retain the lack essential to our inauguration into culture, but can actually reconnect with a lost origin after a lifetime of fragmented dislocation.

Reagan's text is therefore optimistic where the healing of our fundamental fissure is concerned; it is upbeat in its belief that the imprimatur of loss can be forever erased, supplanted by a sense of wholeness and completion. Importantly, the means of attaining such reconnection are not spiritual or intellectual, not artistic or erotic. For Reagan as for others, they are political in nature, revolving around interpretations of truth and power, generating rhetorical strategies and articulated platforms. It is his implicit argument that within the contemporary American context, neoconservatism alone provides the venue for overcoming the sorrows of a fragmented existence wrought by liberal folly. His journey home to the right, which helped him recover a lost part of himself, can thus be a journey on which we all embark, out of exile and back to the lost Eden, where we can all utter the jubilant cry, "Honey, I'm home!" And as he closes his autobiography, the fluid continuum linking Hollywood to Washington that was so crucial to his personal odyssey remains intact, for he invokes America's future while making reference to Clark Gable. Leaving behind the city for the ranch—two metaphors of ideological space—he is serene knowing that the ranch is now home. Nancy, and a long-lost missing substrate, stand ready to embrace him.

> The days stretch out ahead with promise. The city closes in on the ranch—we prowl the countryside scouting a new location. I should turn to the sages for some profound utterance to close out these words. Still, it is more fitting that a remark by the King of actors, Clark Gable, sticks in my mind. Clark said, "The most important thing a man can know is that, as he approaches his own door, someone on the other side is listening for the sound of his footsteps." I have found the rest of me.[46]

Yet in the setting of a cacophonous American pluralism, in the context of a globalizing, multicultural world radically unsettled with regard to its meanings, this confident optimism is not shared by everyone. Whereas Reagan ponders the future while insisting on the reality of an anterior wholeness partaking of Hollywood glamour, others would insist that the pretense of having found our missing antecedent must always remain something fictional. Because there is no true foundation to locate in America's past, all we have is the performative effort to make such a foundation seem real. Read in this light, neoconservatism thus appears to cling to the phantom of a vanished space, the simulacrum of a renewed wholeness that in fact claims no authentic origin. The movement's efforts to identify now-time in a replaying of the 1950s in fact only increase the melancholic thematics that saturate it, for its invocation of our past glory creates the very exile from which it claims to suffer. Kristeva describes how the one suffering from melancholia is in fact in love with the absence he or she laments. In this state of spiritual exile, the melancholic experiences an unmistakable pleasure undoubtedly akin to watching *Pleasantville* reruns or old Hollywood movies with our favorite stars. The melancholic is the "lover of a vanished space . . . that he will never be able to recover . . . a dreamer making love with absence, one exquisitely depressed."[47]

An exquisite depression that clings to "the fifties" is not a depression one would attempt to get over. This is especially true when, in our case, letting go forces us to renounce imagistic wholeness and the American mythologies that inform it. Renouncing these would leave us only with America today, which is by any standard a louder, scarier, more dangerous place, hardly reminiscent of a Clark Gable movie. How to approach this place without succumbing to the feeling that it is absurd? How to read America's contemporary cultural landscape and not perceive it as a tale told by an idiot? Immersing ourselves in our contemporary struggles without becoming overwhelmed, or melancholic, or even just "exquisitely depressed," surely demands a different reading of America's embattled terrain.

CHAPTER 5

X-Ray Vision and the Powers of Performance: Letting Go of the Fifties

Look, Up in the Sky!

I have argued that the exquisite depression of melancholia arises from an absence whose erotic thrill derives precisely from the fact that it is beyond our grasp. For it is only in remaining ineffable that an imaginary wholeness can so illuminate the present, causing some to look backward in the hopes of regaining something that will then be projected onto the future. In contemporary American culture, such a melancholic outlook is evident on the right of the political spectrum if we look deeply into its claim that America has lost its way, that its formerly "continuous civilization" is now an inconsistent amalgam of too many things. This backward-looking gesture clearly indicates a strong erotic attachment to an absence, even if its tone is upbeat and cheerful. For within the current setting, it is beyond our grasp to bring into focus "a clear sense of what it means to be an American" as painted by Norman Rockwell. America is too conflicted, too problematic, too enmeshed in foreign economies, and too internally fragmented for any "clear sense" to emerge. Besides, Rockwell himself admitted that his vision was often euphemistic: "It's not an ideal world."[1]

In order for the current, overnamed reality of our culture not to prove so emotionally debilitating, a different approach to our nation's bewildering fragmentation is needed. What is called for is a theoretical framework that endorses multiplicity and that looks askance at unification, a cultural critique that embraces the ambiguities of American identity and that accepts an unsystematic reading of our political foundation. From within the melancholic matrix, this would mean being able to embrace overnaming while still finding an erotic connection that fuels our desire to act. It would mean being able to accept America's quintessential lack of unity while still finding meaning in the overcrowded, incongruous cultural landscape. This acceptance would not read the present as in abeyance and would breed a "new" commitment to political action undisturbed by thoughts of a missing antecedent. The new would instead leave behind the phantom of an antecedent and find a way to treat the current melee as home.

If the imperfections of the present are not absurd and need not jettison our ability to enter now-time, our understanding of "the new" necessarily changes. Above all, it would entail embracing rather than sidestepping the present, letting go of an imaginary wholeness that the pilgrims, the Founding Fathers, the Constitution, and the flag never conferred. Indeed, "the new" would no longer imply reconnecting with the past, for neither our nation's earliest days nor the 1950s correspond to a true foundation. Letting go of the magical, mythical qualities of history—the narratives that many cultures tell themselves in order to enjoy cohesion[2]—would root us solely in the history now being made as it disregards the entire concept of America's larger-than-life origins embodied in a phoenix reborn on a temple. To begin in chronology and stay here, then, would no longer endorse an anesthetized state of foundational myth. This version of "the new" shuns the damaging implications of that ideology in all its Eurocentrism and instead refers to an America that has no essential cultural identity. Its premise is that, Native Americans aside, no ethnic group can claim a true American identity or a continuous experience of American civilization, for the simple reason that this does not exist. The nation is a political experiment made up of cultural imports, no more cairologically ordained than any other group of people. It is an amalgam of different things whose lack of cultural unity constitutes its most distinguishing feature. Although there is a history to recount and a story to tell, neither narrative succeeds in conferring an essential identity on the American people.

These statements about our nation's cultural incoherence are entirely consistent with Lipset's assertion that to be an American is to commit to an ideology, to endorse the political ideals that constitute American liberalism. This portion concedes that there is an abiding *theoretical* core, an intellectual basis to our constitutional framework that has not changed since the eighteenth century. The Constitution, of course, is a text like any other, a document open to interpretation and responsive to historical change. As is true of any other example of political writing, its meanings interrelate and interpenetrate with other texts, historical settings, actors, and situations. Nevertheless, the basic intellectual tenets that define American liberalism claim a stability that allows one to state along with Lipset that "being" an American in fact describes an *ideological* commitment grounded in constitutional principles and American political thought. Although one may deny that the Founding Fathers pursued a "sacred" mission imbued with cairological purpose, then, there is no denying that the political theory they advanced remains, in many ways, intact today.

Yet American *culture,* which interprets and lives out that theory at the everyday level, can claim no such consistency. The fact that our nation does not cohere around any single ethnicity, and that only Native Americans can be called true Americans, contributes enormously to the fragmented, disjointed quality of American culture, which borrows so heavily from here and there. America has never been linked to one religion, one set of cultural practices, one royal family, one common ancestry. Like many nations, it has never been one color, but today it is perhaps more colorful than most countries. In fact, it is anticipated that, before long, white America will be overshadowed by African Americans, Hispanics, Asian Americans, and other persons of color. The ongoing debate about bilingual education in California already encapsulates the question of whether our English heritage truly claims a privileged status in our makeup and whether the Anglo-American elements of our culture weigh more heavily than others.[3] For if the ties that bind us as a country are primarily theoretical, grounded in ideas rather than in a cultural past or a genetic makeup, one has to question the assertion that our "roots" are English, or Judeo-Christian, or even European.

To be sure, the diversity that distinguishes us and the waves of immigration that have affected us easily preclude any one shared historical experience. Instead, ideas unite us—ideology, concepts, stories, narratives, heroes who bring ideas to life. We love our heroes, especially when they recap something vital about the mythologies we live by. It has been argued, for instance, that Superman exists as an American cultural icon precisely because he embodies so many of the qualities that our collective imagination understands. Gary Engel writes that Superman, the man of steel who doubles as a shy, self-conscious reporter, may seem exotic, but in fact he plays out many of the attributes that are central to Americans' self-understanding. Primary among these is Superman's immigrant status, the fact that not only is he not from America, but he is from another planet. Superman is above all an immigrant and an orphan, someone literally flown in from elsewhere whose origins are not of this soil and whose constitutional makeup differs radically from our own. A cultural import, he reminds us of us and of who we would like to be: someone whose roots are elsewhere, yet whose valuable personal resources make him respected and needed in American society. "It is impossible to imagine Superman being as popular as he is and speaking as deeply to the American character were he not an immigrant and an orphan," writes Engel.[4]

Hence both the comic book series and the 1950s television show tell of this man's ability to fit into a society that is not originally his own. He is a hero whose physical prowess designates that he cannot be from this soil, for the superhuman powers he brings from Krypton—his strength and agility, his ability to fly, his X-ray vision—are not American made. That Superman is from elsewhere is thus demonstrated in each episode's dramatic high point as he stops an oncoming train, holds up a falling building, catches people as they fall from a collapsing bridge. I clearly recall how the distinct sound of a strong wind told the viewer that Superman was now flying through the air, arms and legs extended, ready to come to the rescue. I was glued to the TV and in love with his heroics. Then, mission accomplished and eager to share in others' joy, he would quickly reinvent himself back into Clark Kent so as to remain self-effacing even as he heard the praises of Superman being sung around him.

Yet what also explains this icon's success as a cultural hero is the fact that, although foreign-born, he has grown to love America and wants to be part of her cultural fabric. A big part of him wants nothing more than to be one of us, an average working citizen who blends in amid the daily routine. Superman thus never remains in costume after his heroics have finished: the S, the cape, and the tights all humbly mutate into a workingman's suit. This is why, Engel maintains, Superman's double is so bland and undistinguished, so mainstream and unassuming. Indeed, the "mild-mannered reporter" Clark Kent fits into the crowd perfectly, easily, and without effort. Quiet and obliging, a hard worker and team player, he is a man one easily overlooks given that he disappears into the background. Who would ever imagine that he isn't an American through and through, that *he* is the one flying through the air faster than a speeding bullet? His shyness and retiring manner, his restrained body language and unexcited responses, all denote a person who is just one of us, an average citizen doing a day's work.

By validating the fact that people from other parts of the world can make it in America, the two sides of Superman's persona succeed in relieving the anxieties of assimilation. Such anxieties were of course very pronounced in 1933, when the comic book version of these adventures first appeared. Yet, as mentioned earlier, such anxieties continue to plague both those who come to American soil today in search of a new beginning and those already here whose sense of a stable American identity is subsequently threatened.[5] If the man from Krypton can hide behind the person of Clark Kent, appearing quintessentially American when in fact he is an immigrant, mild mannered when he is really made of steel, then anyone can assimilate into American culture and leave behind the worries surrounding a foreign identity. Superman thus delivers assurance to the American mind-set that assimilation is eminently attainable, even to the most foreign-born, and that it is possible to appear American while retaining attributes from an entirely different culture.

Yet if Superman assuages our fears, he also serves to remind us dramatically that America is a mishmash of people from other places, very few of whom can claim to be authentically American. "Immigration, of course, is the overwhelming fact in American history," Engel writes. "Except for the Indians, all Americans have an immediate sense of their origins elsewhere."[6] This icon thus highlights a unique feature of our identity: the fact that we are an overarching text that claims no single, true antecedent, that admits imports from all over and that allows foreign elements to be alloyed to our diverse metanarrative. We have a plurality of antecedents and a wide vista of starting points, so much so that none of these starting points is the original. We come from everywhere and, in a sense, from nowhere.

Americans thus strongly identify with Superman's ability to transform himself from one identity to the other, to morph from the quiet Clark Kent who fumbles with his glasses and apologizes about his awkwardness into the dynamic, strapping hero who leaps out the window and flies through the air. In order to pursue the American way, he changes his identity from one persona to the other at the drop of a hat, as if to be American is to not cling to one identity for too long. All that is needed is a closet, a back alley, an empty office where Clark can undergo metamorphosis without being noticed, emerging the cultural savior with a huge S on his shirt. Growing up, I watched *The Adventures of Superman* regularly, and a question that my siblings and I always had revolved around the location of this metamorphosis: Where will Clark Kent change his clothes today? Will anyone ever see him changing, and thus discover his secret? Importantly, however, the series never showed Clark actually taking off his clothes and putting on his Superman outfit, all of which made his transformation appear seamless and natural, something that occurred without effort. Each episode depended on Clark's ability to transform one identity into another without trouble, just as the entire series depended on his ability to be both Clark Kent and Superman without anyone's finding out.

The combined inauthenticity and heroic powers of Superman are thus qualities that Americans relate to, for they reassure us that the reality of our immigrant status need not prevent us from being accepted by the culture at large and performing well within it. Yet we have seen that this inauthenticity is precisely what neoconservatism rejects, insisting instead on a unified founding that confers on us an undisputed, cohesive identity. The political right thus promotes the stable substrate that Engel, and a host of other readers of American culture, adamantly denies. Whereas neoconservatism interprets our nation as a series of folktales that just happen to be true, other cultural critics, and certainly the cultural left, take a stance more aligned with Engel's Superman: inauthentic, dissembling, *performing,* yet in love with the idea of America. It's as if Superman's X-ray vision allows him to see that, for anyone except Native Americans, this substrate is a phony, a pretense of the Thing that in fact isn't real.

To be sure, the fact that Superman is not authentically American does not keep us from needing his performance. His roles as both superhero and shy reporter are needed by the culture at large, whether we know of his foreign origins or not. Once we see his behaviors as a theatrical effort to appear American through assimilation, it changes nothing, for Superman's performative existence is the existence of nearly all Americans told in a dramatic way. Indeed, an alternative reading of America's essential inauthenticity, its mishmash culture made up of foreign derivatives, views our fragmentation as the cause for a different politics and a different cultural ideal. This position does not endorse a complicity of origins, thereby reading American culture as predominantly absurd. Rather, it finds in the critique of origins a commitment to the tolerance and pluralism that are so central to the American imagination. Indeed, an alternative reading to the claim that we currently disrespect our origins interprets America's absent foundation as the very reason our nation should spawn a progressive politics based on the democratic ideal of diversity. It would argue that relinquishing our Edenic past, the phantom of the Thing, is not only politically feasible, but ethically desirable. This position of the cultural left maintains that there exists a theoretical connection between the deconstruction of stated origins and an openness to alternative interpretations, one insisting that the inauthenticity of simulacra can only endorse a political tolerance open to change.

This position grounds itself in a performative politics committed to relinquishing foundations. Indeed, the renouncing of stated origins is the epistemological basis of poststructuralist and postmodernist theories, lending itself to the focus on difference—or, as will be explained, on *differance*—that so distinguishes the leftist embrace of this philosophy from a conservative position convinced of authentic origins. A commitment to performativity thus locates itself at a place diametrically opposed to the melancholy of the right. Although it may have its own sources of sorrow and regret (to be discussed in chapter 6),[7] the melancholy I have described that stands in search of a lost foundation will never motivate the left's politics. Instead, the cultural left argues that America's incohesive, inchoate qualities make it especially hospitable to—indeed, the paragon of—postmodernism's shifting signifiers. It is far more aligned with turbulent social movements and unsettled meanings than with reputed foundations resistant to change. Thus the years that Reagan lamented, the disquieting 1960s and 1970s, were in some ways more typically American than the 1950s. For, as Superman assures us, America needs to undergo metamorphosis in order to stay alive, reinventing itself in a seamless manner in order to keep the story going.

America and the Politics of Performance

The inauthenticity that characterizes performance politics is commensurate with the epistemological commitments of postmodernity. At all

costs, these commitments resist being complicitous in the originary sites
that allow one to claim having lost one's way. The premise is that
a belief in true origins, while illusory, breeds a dangerous political
outcome nevertheless familiar to the Western mind-set. In *Of Grammatology*, for instance, Jacques Derrida argues that to embrace a "complicity of origins" necessarily lends itself to the hierarchical structure
of binary oppositions on which Western philosophy traditionally rests.
To posit an origin is to construct a legacy, a trajectory infused with
claims to authenticity that facilitates dismissing others unalloyed to
that trajectory. It is to introduce the logic and dynamics of an episteme
that must, in ordaining the center as authentic, characterize all outly-
ing postions as marginal and inauthentic. The resultant worldview thus
vacillates between authentic origin and devalued, unfaithful margins,
between a true foundation and the simulacra imposed by distance.
This, at least, is the case in the Western tradition, wherein the authority of Greek philosophy further justifies its own belief in logocentrism:
the positing of one form of utterance, speech, as more genuine than
any of the subsequent forms that seek to re-present the philosopher's
own word. Hence writing, publishing, copying, and so forth are all
engagements with philosophy that suffer from the inauthenticity of distance. They are forms of discourse that suffer from an increasingly
decentered, damaged outlook given their intellectual distance from the
philosopher's own voice.

The logocentric episteme necessarily privileges the spoken word over
the written one, the written word over that which is transcribed, transcription over technology's various forms of reproduction, and so on,
in a signifying chain whose growth ensures that each utterance is increasingly disloyal to the source. The distance that ensues with each
subsequent iteration condemns it with a greater level of dissembling
and insincerity; the further we are from the philosopher's ostensibly
pure speech, the more troubled is our text by the confused, mediating
factors that have sullied the pristine foundation. The more deferred the
meaning, in other words, the more different its significance. The more
different its significance, the more intellectually inferior and morally
suspect it is. Hence the metaphysics of presence that characterizes so
much of Western philosophy supports the notion of true origins, true
foundations, and pristine beginnings, all of which is viewed with suspicion by the deconstructive process.

In his critique of the metaphysics of presence, Derrida argues that
this belief in a pure foundation is a dangerous illusion that breeds

harmful political consequences. This is because what posits itself as the foundation is merely another relational iteration whose meaning flows entirely from its relation to other iterations. Each moment in the stated trajectory is relative to others, having no primary identity outside of the trajectory. All meaning is contextual, relational, the outgrowth of other meanings. All is by-product, and the discipline of philosophy can be approached only as a world of texts, each of which takes its meaning in relation to other texts. Within the logic of deconstruction, this intertextual nature of meaning prevents the purported origins from claiming the authority that has traditionally been accorded them. For there exists no true origin, only the mind-set that longs for one given its need for a guiding discourse, a singular truth, an authoritative father. Derrida thus writes that this "complicity of origins" is, from the start, misconceived:

> A signifier is from the very beginning the possibility of its own repetition, of its own image or resemblance. It is the condition of its ideality, what identifies it as signifier, and makes it function as such, relating it to a signified which, for the same reasons, could never be "a unique and singular reality." From the moment that the sign appears, that is to say from the very beginning, there is no chance of encountering anywhere the purity of "reality," "unicity," "singularity."[8]

This passage makes plain two of the principal tenets of Derridean *differance*: that meaning is always different and deferred, always existing in relation to other meanings in an unending intertextual play, having no preexisting authority of its own. Hence the signifier ("America") is part of a text ("American history," "American culture," "the American people") that has no hermetically sealed meaning; rather, it takes on meaning only in relation to a variety of other texts. To posit one unchanging meaning to this ambiguous, overnamed signifier is to privilege that meaning in a hierarchy of cultural meanings, when in fact its meanings are always different and deferred, constituted only in relationship and in historical context.

The complicity of origins proves politically dangerous due to the cultural hierarchies that it tends to support. The fact that originary texts and originary authors have exerted such influence over the trajectory of Western philosophy ultimately stands culpable of the intolerance that is part and parcel of the Western mind. For the linear, hierarchical mindset that such an epistemological outlook produces cannot approach intellectual ambiguity and political pluralism in anything but a skeptical way. There must be a binary opposition, a serial ordering that assigns value to ideas in keeping with their closeness to the vaunted center. Yet the act of safeguarding a unique origin, an unspoiled beginning whose metaphysics of presence lays an undisputed foundation is, for Derrida, itself a morally suspect act in that it gives rise to a politics that, at the extreme, displays intolerance. The political intolerance of racism, sexism, and homophobia thus emanates from the epistemological premise of a true foundation whose authority and authenticity should never be challenged.

This critique of logocentrism and subsequent endorsement of *differance* throws open the entire question of philosophy's privileging of antiquity and the Eurocentric, phallocentric implications that accompany this. According to Derrida, the authority that Greek philosophy has exerted over the Western mind cannot be divorced from the oppressive politics that has ensued within the Western tradition and that continues to inform the canon of Western cultural literacy. Because logocentrism denies the intertextuality of stated meanings and decries the impurity of distanced, colonized meanings, it cannot admit the plurality of meanings that has come to terms with the world's admittedly overnamed quality. Ironically, in clinging to the metaphysics of presence, it cannot now live in the present without forever referencing a reputed foundation. This is evident in the cultural primacy of antiquity, whose authority in the Western experience causes us to deny that it, too, inhabits the overnamed landscape of meaning, the fact that it simply is one cultural experience among many rather than a seminal, founding moment. Derrida asks, "So by what right can it be supposed that speech could have had, 'in antiquity . . . ' . . . the sense and value that we know in the West?"[9]

This critique of logocentrism that impugns a worship of the past, as indeed of any origin, unearths the problematic political ideology among those who insist on America's true foundation. The filiopietism of American conservatism indeed exhibits the same intolerance that Derrida identifies amid the metaphysics of presence. Filiopietism's devotion to the past and to the Founding Fathers reads America as one stable text unreceptive of new and different interpretations, a text grounded in one set of cultural values refusing to be alloyed to others. It views America as forever tied to the vision made clear in Barry's aquatint, a vision revived within numerous Rockwell paintings positing "the fifties" as our true identity.

This static cultural interpretation that emanates from the complicity of origins stands diametrically opposed to the politics of performativity that helped explain what makes Superman "so darned American." In that it relinquishes foundations and denies a priori identities, the politics of performativity sees value only in the intertextual play of *differance* according to which meaning is always different (never stable or fixed) and always deferred (constantly changing as things change). Because this intertextuality perceives fixity as suspect, it readily lets go of America's connection to Europe, a literalist interpretation of the Constitution, and a mimetic attitude toward eighteenth-century culture in favor of the many cultural and demographic changes that our nation has undergone since its inception. It feels at ease with letting go of the belief that America represented something "new" in its guise as Europe's second chance and instead strives to see "the new" in an engagement of America today. Although the gesture of relinquishing foundations is potentially terrifying, it disallows the intolerance that clinging to the past tends to justify under the guise of filial devotion.

Because it lets go of anterior claims, performativity adheres to an ideology that admits only the reality of simulacrum. In a world that is essentially overnamed, the concept of an original must cede to an acceptance of variations, by-products, derivatives, and spin-offs: a copy of a copy, a new interpretation on the heels of so many others. The challenge of this position, of course, is not to allow this plethora of meanings deprived of an antecedent to result in absurdity, producing a melancholic orientation that views life as a tale told by an idiot. This is indeed a challenge, because to confront meaning's wake and the confusion this engenders can be a saddening experience that shatters not only our vision of cultural cohesion but even our sense of internal consistency.[10] This shattering, to say the least, is a disturbing experience, and at the extreme it gives rise to psychosis in the individual. The hard work would therefore be to embrace a performative politics in the name of pluralism and not give in to melancholy's grip. It would be to confront meaning's wake with the hope of new and different dreams that correspond more directly to the world before us, rather than to the dreams of an imagined world of fifty years ago. To adhere to this worldview is to take a leap of faith and allow that the "new" actually resides in America's *lack* of an antecedent. Only this version of the new can unlock the potential of the present and awaken us from an anesthetizing dream concerning the pilgrims, the Founding, and a battery of other mythologies and heroes. Performativity delivers this leap of faith — "Look, up in the sky!" — as it focuses on identity's tentative, unfinished quality.

The advocates of performativity, who dismiss the entire concept of a missing antecedent, insist that the focus be not on the bewilderment of an overnamed reality but on the liberating potential of simulacrum. The flip side of free fall's potential sadness is performativity's uncompromising focus on the present and our awakening to the fact that the present's meanings will escape us if we read them through a retroactive matrix. The unique beauty and energy of the present will be lost if we see it only in terms of a romanticized past whose authority is unfounded. Just as Benjamin insists that a society's liberating potential can be grasped by the critic who knows how to read capitalism's debris, so would the one awakened to America's potential discover the new amid our embattled cultural landscape. Remaining in the here and now, staying focused on the idiosyncrasies of a given performance, delivers a politics that avoids the appropriating gestures of traditional social engagement. It gets away from time-honored readings of political categories (e.g., the politics of national identity, of class, gender, race, and sexual orientation) and allows us to approach these topics not through the filter of a preordained matrix but in terms of the present's demands. Performativity thus radically deconstructs the engrained assumptions of traditional politics and advocates instead the multiplicity of meanings that keynotes a postmodern world.

In the act of deconstruction, what emerges is an awareness of the signifier's excesses and theatrical room for maneuver. Because it does not produce a closed reading whose meanings are already decided, it instead demonstrates an overflow of different meanings that take their bearings only in relation to other terms. This signifying excess is not consistent with tidy, pristine categories that keep "America" easy to read, but, because the term is saturated with conflict, chaos, and nuance, makes for a signifying abundance whose purpose is often hard to discern. Hence American political culture claims no missing antecedent now lost amid the melee, but experiences the overnaming that has always been our distinguishing feature. Its culture is the culture of simulacrum. America spells free fall, and its meanings are to be found in the beauty and enjoyment of that fall.

To admit our overnamed status and embrace, rather than condemn, the resultant confusion allows us to resist the reverie that longs for "the fifties." In denying the totality that this decade's look strove to imply, the focus would then turn to the many gaps and fissures that prevent the nation from living up to that model. It would look to the current performance of the many players involved, and, unmindful of a former mandate and earlier representations, locate venues for social change in the present. "Precisely because of representation's supplemental excess and its failure to be totalizing," writes Peggy Phelan, "close readings of the logic of representation can produce psychic resistance and, possibly, political change."[11]

Hence postmodern pastiche might cause us to mourn meaning's passing as we contemplate the overnamed landscape filled with relations that temporarily elude us. Yet if we fully embrace the logic of free fall, with all its political implications, there must follow an awakening very similar to Benjamin's *Jeztzeit* and to Kristeva's thrill of transposition. Recognizing that we can furnish the imagination with a missing substrate based not on a point of origin but on the reference point that confronts us now liberates us from having to definitively locate the Thing, the pre-oedipal mother, the cairological register unsullied by chronology. It opens us to the possibilities of this performance and the meanings that are surely contained in an immediate, ongoing engagement. Why go "back to the beginning," then, if that gesture only breeds rage at the present? Why go back if the promise of a pristine anterior moment will only disappoint and cause us to miss the beauty of the present? A more demanding politics is one that looks for meanings hidden in the present and that locates an attachment in the heart of imperfection.

A Missing Substrate: So What?

Pleasantville dramatizes that the act of letting go indeed opens up new vistas of personal and cultural growth. This turning point occurs during the course of the city's gradual falling away from its state of innocence toward something more closely resembling the fractious, raucous United States today. As mentioned earlier, the charming TV-land community undergoes significant changes once David and Jennifer infect its 1950s Rockwellian sensibility with a dose of the shocking 1990s. As soon as Jennifer introduces sex to her friends, everything changes. Commensurate with the film's cairological themes, the introduction of sensuality into the community inaugurates its fall from Edenic grace, bringing both the wonderment of color and the anguish of failure, calamity, and disgrace to its repertoire. Pleasantville's exile from a state of bliss is therefore an ambiguous affair, for the joy in discovering earthly delights — in color and sex, art, and a sense of adventure — is coupled with a sudden recognition of human fallibility witnessed in lost basketball

games, inclement weather, divisive political stances, and rebellious housewives. Pleasantville's transition from a 1950s weltanschauung to the
fractious 1990s thus brings with it a joy in sensuality coupled with a
recognition of the essential frailty of immanent reality. The loss of innocence made explicit in the film's heightened color thus holds a deeper
underside that brings maturity to the town's inhabitants, for they now
perceive that life is not so predictable.

The implications of this maturity for David qua Bud are beautifully
dramatized during what is perhaps the film's most crucial transition.
It occurs when Bud's mother, Betty, realizes that she, too, is slowly
beginning to turn color, morphing from an obedient 1950s housewife
into a woman more aware of her own autonomy and eroticism. Jennifer qua Mary Sue plays a significant role in this metamorphosis, just
as she does with the town in general. She has shared with her mother
some lessons in female desire, such that Betty has now begun to imagine a more voluptuous existence beyond the twin-beds relationship she
has long had with her husband. Yet as she experiences the efflores-
cence of desire, which eventually pushes her into a brief relationship
with Mr. Johnson, Betty is overwhelmed with guilt, for the color now
visible in her face announces to the world the magnitude of her longing. It tells the world that she no longer fits nicely into the confines of
Pleasantville's Rockwellian mentality, but has transgressed its moral
strictures by imagining herself something other than a dutiful wife and
homemaker who makes Rice Krispies squares.

Bud comes on Betty as she stands at the kitchen sink, overwhelmed
with shame. Her face has turned from the black-and-white signature
of Pleasantville conformity to a colorful visage denoting her alliance
with the city's subversive forces. Humiliated, she at first refuses to look
her son in the face, for she knows that he is aware of what her color
means. It means pleasure and nonconformity, a world wherein the roads
do not lead back to Main Street, but just keep on going. It means
unpredictability and the fact that time has switched registers in Pleasantville. Yet Betty's fear of Bud's disapproval is mingled with her need
for his help, for whatever feelings of disappointment he might have will
be no match, she knows, for her husband's opprobrium. For although
George has been unaware of Betty's transformations the entire time
they've been occurring, he has expressed dismay at what is happening
in Pleasantville. He is a law-and-order man who sides with the mayor.

Bud is at first nonplussed at the sight of his sad, terrified mother.
Can this keeper of an immaculate house, this meticulous woman who

always has meat loaf dinners and Rice Krispies squares on hand, now be longing for passion in her life? Can her frame of reference be anything larger than her home, the grocery store, and her occasional card games with the girls? Bud's bewilderment soon yields to the desire to help, however, and this change in attitude is crucial to the film's deeper commentary on why the TV-land world of Pleasantville eventually had to come unraveled. It may be that Bud feels identification with his mother when he perceives her shame, for just as she is now out of sync with "the fifties," so was he out of sync with 1990s America. Whatever the reason, he chooses not to stay focused on his own surprise and dismay, but to help her. He leaves behind the ideas in his head and moves to action. He thus sets about powdering his mother's face and blackening her lips in an effort to return her to the original 1950s visage she always had. This will help her with her immediate problem of confronting George. In unspoken terms, as he powders her face he offers assurance that her secret is safe with him: she is not the perfect wife and mother she appears to be, but that's okay with him. She is moving away from the Pleasantville he so loves, but he can accept that.

This act of powdering Betty's face and accepting her imperfections produces a great emotional turning point in Bud. Her transformation away from her former role, and subsequent need to feign that role's continuing existence, causes him to recognize that feigning has long been a part of *his* life. David has been living in a dreamworld under the spell of a television show, imagining, hoping that life could be just like the *Pleasantville* episodes he enjoys. His enjoyment of this show has allowed him to escape from his real life and to avoid taking risks in the loud, scary, dangerous environment he inhabits. For instance, in an early scene in the film, David is imagining a conversation with a young woman at school whom he doesn't dare approach. He chats with her and arranges a date in what we quickly realize is an encounter that is all in his head; in reality she is much farther away from him than he imagines, and she is busy chatting with other people. Thus David only dreams of connecting with someone; in reality he goes home to watch his favorite television show, *Pleasantville*.

But now, when he sees Betty's changing face color, he realizes that it's time to start living his life and to stop watching television. He understands that Pleasantville doesn't exist—that "the fifties" do not exist—and that it's time to wake up from his dream and reach out to the present. For just as Betty is not the perfect 1950s housewife who provides the perfect 1950s home—*that* woman does not exist—

neither is there a perfect wholeness or innocence to be discovered somewhere in America's past. There is only the present, and the manner in
which Bud touches Betty's cheek while putting on her makeup tells us
that the present is good enough for him.

Bud's great epiphany thus arrives when he understands that Betty's
feigned role playing is emblematic of the entire sitcom logic that rules
his imagination: Pleasantville itself is all about role playing and pretending, because in truth there never existed an Edenic community as
safe, happy, and integrated as the one he has been watching on television. The Rockwellian 1950s he has long dreamed of is a facade,
behind which there are people just like himself in 1990s America. Why
did he allow his imagination to be appropriated by this mesmerizing
logic of an Edenic past? Why did he fall into melancholia's grasp? As
he arrives at this realization, he touches his mother's cheek, and the
camera focuses exclusively on his wide eyes lost in amazement. Bud
conveys to his mother that her imperfect, conflicted state is all right
with him, just as his own recognition of Pleasantville's unreality is all
right with him, too.

This moment when Bud touches Betty's cheek corresponds to an
emergence from melancholia's grasp. He does not emerge because he
has filled his imagination with a missing antecedent once and for all,
for he has not changed the basic structure of desire. Rather, when Bud
touches his mother's cheek, he realizes that the ability to satiate desire's
essentially impossible structure can be fulfilled (however imperfectly
and temporarily) as much by a present lack as by a former wholeness.
The joys of Kristevan transposition are to be found, he feels, not in
the escapism that technology or art provide, but in a conversation with
his mother at the kitchen table, the moment when her imperfections
are made manifest. Coming to terms with the fact that a desired wholeness is in fact a facade, a misperceived state answering to our own
internal fragmentation, liberates David from the unending search for
a missing antecedent and causes him to act. Now he can give up his
search for a perfect past and a perfect mother, and—without changing the basic, impossible structure of desire—at last feel engaged. He
can confront the overnamed quality of multicultural, postmodern America, and not feel so melancholic, because what is overnamed need not
be absurd. Postmodernity may be cacophonous, but it is not a tale told
by an idiot. Thus he finds "the new" and touches his mother's cheek.

Bud soon travels back to 1990s America, having once again become David. This implies that this encounter in the kitchen has indeed

liberated him from melancholy's hold and allowed him to live in the present. (Jennifer, meanwhile, has decided to stay in Pleasantville, having given up her obsession with sex and become quite studious.) His exiting the TV-land sitcom signals a deep internal change in him, for his eagerness to furnish the imagination with a missing substrate has now translated into the desire to engage with life in the 1990s. David feels the full extent of his liberation when, no sooner home, he once again comes on his mother crying in the kitchen. Importantly, it is his real mother this time: divorced, angry, a woman who feels that her life isn't turning out the way she wanted, that it's all a meaningless pursuit. She has decided not to go away for the weekend with a younger man and instead sits sobbing at the kitchen table, her head in her hands. "What the hell am I doing?" she sobs as her makeup runs.

As she cries, insisting that her life has gone wrong, David sits down with her. He touches her face, just as he touched Betty's, and offers her reassurance. He explains that the imperfections of the present needn't be so devastating. In answer to her lament, "It wasn't supposed to be this way!" he responds "It isn't supposed to *be* anything." The camera again focuses exclusively on David's wide, searching eyes as he reaches out to his aggrieved mother. His ability to touch his mother with love and to feel compassion for her denotes that his own acceptance of life's overnamed, embattled quality no longer overwhelms him. It *is* an overnamed world, and the free fall we encounter amid America's globalizing, multicultural, postmodern indeterminacies *does* create the desire for a missing antecedent—even if that antecedent doesn't exist. Yet the transformation that has taken place in David dramatizes the fact that melancholy's hold need not be indefinite, for he can look meaning's tenuousness in the face and still live with it.

If David's experience is to be trusted, the melancholic mind-set can be overcome even if we no longer believe in a true missing antecedent. The mirage of maternal wholeness, of the Thing, the utopian trace, can be recognized for the facade that it is even as we dispel melancholia's grip. Indeed, even if it is not a facade, it will never enter this register of time and will thus always be something more likely to stymie meaningful engagement than to produce it. Thus, in David's case—in ours too—it is precisely because he has let go of his hopes for perfect happiness in a perfect world that he is able to enter the present at last. He connects with his real mother in the 1990s only after he lets go of believing in a perfect, pristine mother. David locates the missing substrate of his imagination—his mother in the 1990s—only after he stops believing in that substrate's perfect wholeness: Betty in the 1950s, clad in apron and pearls. In so doing, he lives in this present register of time and discovers "the new" in his decision to take action. *Jeztzeit* is thus his resolve to reach out to other people despite their obvious imperfections, to live in the time given us rather than a perfected time when America was its true self. America *is* its true self: loud, scary, and dangerous.

Because performativity assumes a world of simulacra devoid of true foundations, it endorses a politics conducive to letting go and to finding "the new" in the present. As I will explain in the next chapter, the cultural left adheres to this performative logic and thus denounces neoconservatism's participation in the complicity of origins. Its radically different view of American political identity disallows the kind of mythmaking and revering of mythology that exist on the right. Ideally, then, denouncing the complicity of origins should inspire a performative politics that never cedes to a new form of exquisite melancholy. Yet, as I will be explain, the left at times displays a melancholy of its own and is no less culpable of the same disengagement from the present as the right. It, too, is at times the melancholy lover of a vanished space, exquisitely depressed for its own reasons, caught up in its own mythologized identity. It has its own "Betty" to let go of, and only letting go will allow it to engage fully with the present moment.

CHAPTER 6

The Left Reviews "the Fifties"

One would naturally doubt that the decade of extended McCarthy hearings, censorious Smith Act persecutions, and the doctrine of containment has much in common with any form of politics indebted to socialist precepts. There is little to bind any leftist position—be it Old Left, New Left, or cultural left—to the decade that sought to erase that end of the political spectrum in this country. Yet, as we shall see, it is more the foundational meanings of the metaphoric fifties, the portrayal of this decade as an originary site and its implications for America, that most drive the critique of the decade examined in this chapter. Indeed, the cultural left necessarily looks askance at any foundational politics and views the claim of disinheritance to be fundamentally misbegotten. For origins, it argues, are always mythical, partaking of a fabulist's world that clings to the mirage of foundations often serving strategic ends.

The American left is in many ways a diffuse and variegated group of people whose politics frequently conflict. In part, this is due to the fact that the politics of the left by now stands imbricated with that of more mainstream liberals, taking its cues from the tradition of the New

139

Deal and Great Society, but more recently allowing market mechanisms to play a role in its economics. Today, a leftist presence is most strongly felt in sub- and countercultural contexts, such as in the ecology movement, alternative medicine and therapy, alternative bookstores and natural food markets, the arts, and academe. It is not a mainstream movement but, in taking issue with the predominant values and practices of American society, it challenges some of America's most basic self-definitions as a globalizing superpower. It of course still identifies with organized labor and typically opposes the amalgam of capitalist, technological, and military elements that combine to make what Ben Barber has called "McWorld," an expression that stands for corporate ideology as it seeks to normalize and sanction globalizing capital, often through political channels.[1] The cultural left surely includes itself in the critique of McWorld's "soft imperialism" given that the latter's economic success in the world arena carries with it a host of normative assumptions about Western democracy's meanings.[2] The extent to which McWorld has successfully appropriated those meanings, occluding alternative understandings of capitalism, America, and the West, causes this position to assume an oppositional stance vis-à-vis corporate culture and the anti-intellectualism it often promotes.[3]

As we have seen, it is especially the foundationalist commitments of conservative positions that the cultural left opposes. Its criticisms of secure foundations are many, but what interests us here is the manner in which such foundations elide the beauty and potential of the present by focusing exclusively on a static interpretation of America grounded in a mythological reading of our Edenic past. This oppositional status explains why the American cultural left does not identify with either the historical 1950s or the fifties-as-metaphor in anything but a distanced, at times ironic, way. This chapter examines the left's disaffection with both the 1950s and "the fifties" and thus with neoconservatism's promotion of (what it deems) a regressive politics. Yet, as will be made clear, this chapter holds that a sense of melancholia, of missed opportunities and life in abeyance, also exists at this end of the spectrum, which is not always true to its antifoundationalist claims.

The Left's Disassociation from the 1950s

The American left's critique of the historical 1950s begins with the obvious reason: namely, that the left tells a very different, much less glowing story of the decade than does the right and highlights the hypocrisy of its censorious politics. The left is far less convinced that the decade was as happy, as prosperous, or as unified as the Rockwellian vision suggests. Although it may be true that the *Father Knows Best* version of the era existed for some, it is incorrect to portray that experience of the decade as typical.[4] Relentlessly, the left insists on the decade's ongoing economic injustices, its familial strife, its sexism and racial tensions.[5] Michael Harrington's *The Other America,* which appeared in 1962, was enormously successful in that it brought to the attention of the American public the manner in which poverty had been successfully erased from view even though it was an integral part of the 1950s (and other decades). Harrington brought to light the "invisible Americans" who would become the focus of President Johnson's Great Society. Harrington's text, which chronicles the lives of Americans living through dire poverty, thus inspired and galvanized the American New Left by offering a model of self-criticism and self-awareness that played itself out in many forms of 1960s radicalism.

In its criticism of 1950s complacency and self-congratulation, then, the left today similarly highlights the many ways in which the decade was a painful struggle. For many Americans not featured on television sitcoms, the postwar decade was a time of hardship, discrimination, and censorship. For them, the American dream never came true despite the culture's outward appearance of opulence and expansion, of robust status and endless opportunity. Stephanie Coontz argues that one-quarter of the American population, forty to fifty million people, lived in poverty in the mid-1950s.[6] And although American society became less and less white during the decade due to immigration and the migration of blacks, the latter did not enjoy the society's wealth.[7] African Americans were perceived to be in a society that was moving forward while most of them were being left behind.[8] Even among two-parent black families, the poverty rate was more than 50 percent.[9] By 1960, only 6 percent of public schools in America were integrated. And as is well-known, episodes of racial violence, such as lynchings, rapes, beatings, and other forms of abuse, were rampant.[10]

Many other dimensions of 1950s America help undermine the truthfulness of the Rockwellian image, thereby casting aspersions on Gingrich's claim that a continuous, cohesive, "clear sense" of what it means to be American prevailed during the decade. The racial unrest, the beats, the Klan, the misfits portrayed even in as mainstream a film as *West Side Story* all present a very different image of America than that suggested by the covers of the *Saturday Evening Post*. And Cathy Whitaker's heightened awareness of her society's racism and homophobia in *Far from Heaven* reminds us that even for the well-to-do, the decade's oppressive conformity squelched the joie de vivre that people were so urged to convey. Thus her husband's "sickness" causes him to be utterly clandestine about his desire for other men, whereas the African American man to whom Cathy is attracted is shouted at threateningly on the street for touching her arm.

Moreover, the abundance of science fiction films mentioned earlier undermines any claim that the 1950s radiated great mutual trust. On the contrary, this was an anxious decade beset by fear and paranoia, a nervous time in which many Americans were convinced that various enemies resided not only outside of the nation's boundaries but within American parameters, marauding our neighborhoods, silently invading our homes, corrupting our children. Not even the respected doctor of *Invasion of the Body Snatchers*, Miles, can keep the malevolent foreign forces from overtaking those he loves, for their strategy is too cunning for him. Nora Sayre thus recounts that, during the decade, the media amply portrayed haggard communists as disturbingly ubiquitous, too wily for the average American to outsmart. "The vigilant eye registered how they tended to lurk on street corners [in] trench coats, and walk on a forward slant revealing their dedication to the cause."[11]

Elaine Tyler May contributes to this picture of the decade's malaise in her study of the American family in the postwar period titled *Homeward Bound*. May chronicles the extent to which the larger doctrine of containment, stemming from fear of cunning communist invaders, played an important role in determining the 1950s ideology of the family.[12] To a good degree, May argues, family life was keynoted by the underpinning that containment of international communism begins at home. Hence the decade's focus on rigid gender roles, respect for authority, patriotism, and hygiene was part of a larger fear that our nation might unravel from within. Much of the decade's emphasis on strong family life was a response to the anxious sense that malevolent internal forces, such as those caricatured in *Invasion of the Body Snatchers*, might destroy America's integrity and sense of purpose. This connection between the doctrine of containment and the nation's domestic scene meant that home life in midcentury America was in fact *not* so insular. Rather, the home was on a continuum with political life in the country at large, and the doctrine of containment informed numerous practices at the everyday level. Thus May urges us to remember that

McCarthyism, whose high level of publicity undoubtedly caused it to exert a great deal of influence on the collective imagination, sought to root out *internal* dangers, not *external* threats.

Many excellent studies disabuse us of the idea that family life was excellent during the 1950s, the work of Coontz, May, and Betty Friedan among them.[13] May and Friedan both highlight the fact that married life was often not nearly as blissful as we tend to imagine in retrospect. For instance, May recounts that husbands and wives interviewed during the 1950s or early 1960s often gave conflicting accounts of the state of their marriage. Typically, husbands seemed more content with things than their wives and were often oblivious to problems their wives perceived as significant. "Women were twice as likely as men to report that they were dissatisfied or regretted their marriage. Nearly half the women, but only a third of the men, said they had considered divorce."[14] Friedan adds to this picture, in her acclaimed *The Feminine Mystique*, a portrayal of unhappy housewives at midcentury who, like Cathy Whitaker, spent their time attending to hearth and home, scurrying from the grocery store to the PTA meeting, to family barbecues and cocktail parties, all the while feeling deeply dissatisfied yet afraid to express their unhappiness. They had a "problem with no name," for although their lives appeared utterly complete to the outside observer, they were in fact quite unhappy. In one woman's words: "You wake up in the morning, and you feel as if there's no point in going on another day like this. So you take a tranquilizer because it makes you not care so much that it's pointless."[15]

These elements of authoritarianism, patriarchal control, rigid social stereotyping, and attention to outer appearances all help explain why the left disdains the historical 1950s, whose ideological priorities were surely different from the left's own. Yet perhaps the most obvious reason the various strains of the contemporary American left distance themselves from the decade revolves around the fact that the 1950s sought to erase the left. It sought to expunge any version of leftist politics, however benignly democratic and removed from orthodox Marxism. This is witnessed in the fact that the Cold War characterized socialism only in terms of highly contentious totalitarian experiments whose disregard for human rights and emphasis on commitment to the cause tended to resemble the political right. The fact that Big Brother defined socialism in 1950s America, existing as the only version of the left that the mainstream would allow, illustrates the narrow vision of socialist politics promulgated by those in power during the decade. There was no room for revisionist thought in the mainstream, only the worst depiction of the worst elements that the left had to offer.

Thus the writings of Frankfurt Institute scholars, so influential in intellectual circles given their thoughtful reexamination of the meaning of Marxian tenets in twentieth-century Western societies, went unacknowledged in the culture at large. True, Irving Howe could publish "The Age of Conformity" in a 1954 issue of *Partisan Review,* bemoaning the American left's absorption into the university and its silencing, co-opting impact on the forces of political dissent. Yet the appearance of Howe's piece hardly altered the nation's staunch anticommunism and ignorance of revisionist thought. Indeed, by this time Frankfurt Institute scholars themselves had close connections to American universities and research centers; still, our perception of socialism could not divest itself of violent images emerging from the Soviet and Chinese settings. If socialism and totalitarianism went hand in hand, why muddy the waters by reading Herbert Marcuse on repressive desublimation, or Theodor Adorno on negative dialectics?

This meant that, for many, the left was read only in terms of a crude economic determinism and that the many other cultural, psychological, and artistic elements now included in its repertoire were largely ignored. It is true that economic issues in American society were targeted, even by Frankfurt school scholars, as important contributors to a host of social and economic problems. Among these were the excessive power of corporate America, our growing materialism and consumerist ideology, a never-ending search for new markets, and excessive military spending. Yet revisionism insisted that a vast array of other disciplines inform its use of Marxian categories, which it delivered in a far more synthesized version than simple economic determinism. This is demonstrated, for instance, in the critique of prescribed attitudes central to several of the Frankfurt scholars' research, which nevertheless went unacknowledged by those who refused to see the left in anything other than the most simplistic, black-and-white terms. Marcuse takes aim at these attitudes when he observes that the appealing, rewarding opulence of a consumerist culture often succeeds in blinding the average person to the reality of that culture's intellectual decay:

> The means of mass transportation and communication, the
> commodities of lodging, food and clothing, the irresistible output
> of the entertainment and information industry carry with them
> prescribed attitudes and habits, certain intellectual and emotional

reactions which bind the consumers more or less pleasantly to the producers and, through the latter, to the whole. The products indoctrinate and manipulate; they promote a false consciousness which is immune against its falsehood.[16]

Thus, following the lead of such persons as Marcuse, Adorno, Frantz Fanon, Tom Hayden, Michael Harrington, and Paul Goodman, leftists of this generation wanted to change not just the economic and political structure of American society but the very fabric of our value system as well. They were convinced that a shallow consumerism and a mindless greed were becoming the norm, as Americans were being sucked into the vortex of an expanding market ideology. And it was this ideology and its surrounding value system, as much as any structural issue, that was the problem. Instead of relying strictly on Marxian economic categories, then, what eventually became known as the New Left incorporated a broad array of social, psychoanalytic, and philosophical issues into a more traditional leftist outlook, thus widening its analytic purview.[17]

For the left, recent allusions to the blissful 1950s are thus wishful creations that only display the melancholic vision of neoconservatism. So distorted are current allusions to the 1950s as glory days that they can now be invoked only with irony, presented as something that turns back on itself and that undercuts its very articulation. This position argues that the sole function this trope now performs is to suggest how unattainable the fifties dream is, or perhaps ever was. On this reading, to invoke the 1950s through political stance, rhetoric, dress, or mannerism is to introduce critical, skeptical distance between that matrix's former status and its contemporary revival. It is to offer it as ruse, introduced hand in hand with a corrosive irony that at first blush seems to divest its replaying of all seriousness.

Little wonder, then, that a leftist panel critique of the 1950s historical tenure, delivered in 1996 and sponsored by *The Nation* magazine, was titled "All Shook Up: Lessons and Legacies from the 1950s." Little wonder that the panel might use an Elvis Presley song title to undermine the decade's legacy. Participants were Allen Ginsberg, Nora Sayre, Barbara Ehrenreich, Fred Hellerman, Ring Lardner Jr., Morty Sobell, Paul Robeson Jr., Susan Reed, and Bud Trilling, and Victor Navasky served as moderator. For these panelists, the decade stands as a dark, ominous chapter in American history filled with unfortunate episodes concerning political intolerance and excessive cultural conformity.

It tells the unsavory tale of just how regressively authoritarian, police-like, and anti-intellectual our society can be once its critical edge has been bought off by a shallow commercialism. Indeed, the most progressive features of any society are domesticated if not silenced once commodity culture succeeds in controlling them. Hence we are left with "the rational character of . . . irrationality,"[18] as the affluence that would presumably accompany openness and tolerance in fact delivers its opposite.

This is why Fred Hellerman, a charter member of the folk music group the Weavers and participant in the panel, described the decade as "mostly a time of defeats." He recalled the time span as a sad interval in American history wherein a deplorable, stultifying oppression was overshadowed by the diversion of economic expansion, an upswing in the standard of living that encouraged people to conform. Along with the other members of the Weavers, Hellerman was blacklisted for three years and suffered personally, professionally, and economically because of this. "The big victims of that time were the American people," he stated, "who had . . . to suffer all the movies that were never made, all the books that were never written, all the songs that were never sung, all the thoughts that were never thought."[19] According to Hellerman, this explains why the early days of rock 'n' roll—the days of Elvis Presley, Buddy Holly, the Spinners, and the Platters—coincided with the practice of blacklisting, for these artists produced music that was, in his view, utterly vacuous.

Two other panelists, Ring Lardner and Morty Sobell, went further in their denunciation of the decade's censorious tactics, arguing that such measures were fascistic in everything but name. Given that these panelists were punished so severely for their transgressions during the 1950s, it comes as little surprise that their memories of that time are so embittered. A successful Hollywood scriptwriter and member of the leftist Hollywood Ten, Lardner remembered how the 1950s thoroughly disappointed the elated 1945 impression that fascism was defeated and that compulsory devotion to nation, organized religion, and patriarchal structures was a thing of the past.[20] In reality, he insisted, the decade did not mark the true defeat of fascism, but merely rehabilitated this ideology along more insidious, familiar, all-American lines. In its facile demonizing of anything remotely to the left of the spectrum, midcentury America repackaged the very fascist enemy we had just defeated in ways that masked its ominous dimensions, turning more sinister aspects of a totalitarian ideology into practices and ideas that were so palatable to Americans as to appear harmless. This was the danger in it all: that the 1950s were in fact so authoritarian while pretending to promote democratic ideals. Lardner spent ten months in jail in the early 1950s. Once released and in search of work, he had to resort to professional subterfuge, for his prospects of finding work in Hollywood were very bleak. He thus wrote under a pseudonym and sold scripts abroad knowing that they would then be sold back to American filmmakers.

Sobell expounded on Lardner's claims that America was protofascist during the 1950s, offering a more explicit rationale for why such a seemingly exaggerated, hyperbolic statement is in fact true. He confirmed that Washington was indeed ready to implement several defining attributes of fascist rule during the 1950s, for the FBI had been directed to devise an emergency detention program whose various authoritarian components would flagrantly violate Americans' civil liberties. One component was a security index to be compiled by the FBI, an index that listed some twenty-six thousand people deemed suspiciously un-American and worthy of surveillance. This measure, Sobell explained, would have sufficed for placing people under arrest in the absence of individual warrants—all that would have been necessary was that one's name be on the list and that a master warrant be issued. Added to the security index were such distasteful things as the government's readiness to suspend habeas corpus and its willingness to resurrect the use of concentration camps (as, of course, it had done with Japanese Americans). Indeed, according to Sobell, the federal government was willing to take the first steps to a fascist state in order to weaken the left's influence on American culture. It is Sobell's conviction, however, that such egregiously authoritarian measures as those mentioned above were never necessary given the level of paranoia that developed on its own within American society. Fear of communism, he argued, was the major product peddled by Washington.[21]

It was an era that prevented many Americans from being too outspoken, subversive, or out of the ordinary, because, in Sayre's words, "life was safer if you had no politics."[22] Indeed, Americans were exhorted to be "mature," to fit in, to blend in with the surroundings and conform to the mold. Even the training in literature that Sayre received while at college often encouraged the eschewal of social and historical considerations. She was taught that these would only sully a work's literary and artistic values by widening its purview onto the larger cultural framework, thereby detracting from the elements that were strictly literary. Literature thus partook of the aesthetic sanctuary, a realm unscathed by the realities of everyday life, unsullied by the dissonances of the social setting. And at the time, Sayre admits, such self-referential introspection seemed natural to the literary field. In the classroom as in the world at large, she and her classmates consented to staying close to hearth and home, to repeating what was already known and familiar by allowing literature to pursue a self-conscious inwardness. The important thing was to fit into categories as already conceived, to reproduce what had already been shaped. "It was a bad time to be very young, a bad time to enter the early chapters of your life, a bad time for curiosity or the impulse to explore."[23]

And it was a dissembling time. Sayre maintains that even during the decade's tenure, the 1950s thrived on a cultural narrative of happy talk that was often at odds with everyday experience. The decade's image of itself often derived from cheerful television sitcoms and upbeat ads that did not correspond to lived reality. In order to sustain a self-referential narrative in which all streets led back to Main Street and a glossy wholeness was unmarred by dissent, the decade asked people to lie. It "demanded masks," allowing that duplicitous, dishonest gestures be tolerated if the resultant image was sufficiently pleasing. Consequently, one learned to laugh politely, to behave disingenuously, and to engage in sleight of hand. Hence during her college days, there was far more drinking and carousing than many would dare imagine. She recalls students hiding cans of beer in their dorm rooms, women sliding birth control devices under mattresses or arranging to have abortions while others assumed their inexperience. In order to remain in good graces, one learned to dissemble.

The impetus of many Americans was subsequently to affirm the value of that imagistic paragon so encouraged by the media, to live up to the dream rather than to expose it. For only by perpetuating a totalized look, an image of cohesion endlessly repeated in sitcoms, commercials, billboards, and advertisements, could the mainstream 1950s zeitgeist deny its own internal dissonance. It had to convince people of its totalized truth so that they could in turn reflect that affected truth back to it. "TV shows, paintings, and ads . . . involved their audience in a process of participatory re-creation," writes Marling.[24] Of course, the more serious art and literature of the decade was not singularly affirmative.[25] Yet, according to Sayre, a great deal of media culture treated lighthearted, uncontroversial themes and was never placed in a larger social context. Instead, it remained in an aesthetic sanctuary where it could not comment on social problems but only affirm American success, given that its purpose was largely to entertain.

Other factors having nothing to do with ideology per se had bearing on the discord between the left and the 1950s. Paramount among these is the simple change in America's infrastructure with the decline of the city, for the city had long been the hub of leftist enclaves thanks to its meeting places, its bookstores, and its cafés. The dramatic rise of suburbia that occurred during the 1950s especially contributed to the atrophy of the American city, causing an exodus from established urban limits into expanding, developing environs that were quickly developing a mystique of their own. To be sure, many associate the decade strictly with suburban living: the rows of houses and cars, the backyard barbecues, the cocktail parties at which martinis flowed freely. This draining away of life and livelihood from urban centers caused many American countercultural elements, those elements of artistic and intellectual creativity still resistant to the mainstream, to be evacuated from cities due to rising costs and gentrification. Indeed, the exodus from urban centers and rearranging of urban economies considerably altered our nation's public discourse, precipitating what many regard as an unfortunate decline in the caliber of American intellectual life. Russell Jacoby convincingly argues that America currently suffers from a dearth of what he terms "public intellectuals"—intellectuals who write for a general, nonspecialized public—because of this restructuring in our urban centers. The growth of suburban life so gentrified the cities, he maintains, that renegade communities that previously contributed to public discourse were eventually forced to earn their livings in American universities, the scene of specialized discussions.[26]

The growth of suburbia was necessitated in part by the influx of young men returning from World War II several years earlier. Their military duties behind them, they were now eager to start life over with families and careers. It has been estimated that after the war as many as two million young American newlyweds desired homes of their own, away from the urban enclaves inhabited by relatives.[27] This desire for privacy among the recently married produced a voracious demand for property in locales both amenable to children and not unreasonably far from the cities. Moreover, there was a racial component to the suburbs, for in the days following the Supreme Court's *Brown* (1954) decision, the suburbs were one way white Americans could avoid the mandate of integration and remain, de facto, segregated. "Few blacks bought homes in the new, postwar suburban tracts," write Walter

LaFeber, Richard Polenberg, and Nancy Woloch.[28] In an effort to explain the fact that most blacks migrated from farms to cities rather than to the suburbs, these authors cite real estate brokers who would not show blacks homes, bank officers who would not extend mortgages to blacks, and suburban zoning ordinances that artificially inflated home construction costs to make them unaffordable to blacks.

Thus the sudden explosion in suburban tracts that featured arrays of prim, uniformly shaped domiciles was enjoyed largely by veterans with minimal down payments. Indeed, depending on the property's assessment by the Veterans Administration, sometimes no down payment was required at all.[29] Hence the likes of the northeastern suburb Levittown sprung up around the country, causing a migration of young families away from city dwellings and toward brand-new developments often exhibiting cookie-cutter uniformity. These suburbs were often built in a hurry, sometimes using prefabricated walls and frames that made assembly easy.

Importantly, the proliferation of these residential areas encouraged the growth of American highways.[30] Soon suburban life grew far more rapidly than cities during the 1950s, such that large urban centers experienced an unfortunate population decline while the newly established suburbs were booming. Cleveland's environs grew by 94 percent, Chicago's by 101 percent, and Detroit's by 131 percent.[31] It has been estimated that by the end of the 1950s, one-fourth of America's population had moved to the suburbs, which were fast developing a cachet all their own.[32] Suburban living was soon the sign of success, the hallmark of the American dream come true. And because the suburbs were seen as calm havens, serene but prestigious places that brought one closer to nature, they often developed motifs of secluded quiet and pristine beauty.

Far from Heaven draws deeply on the Edenic attributes of such secluded quiet in its portrayal of a wealthy suburb where, at first blush, life seems picture-perfect. The magnificent panoramic shots of the neighborhood where Cathy Whitaker lives succeed amply in promoting the look of completion so paramount, as I have argued, to 1950s self-understanding. These shots, the filmmakers tell us, deliberately imitate the beautiful 1950s work of director Douglas Sirk, whose signature grandiosity can be seen in such films as *Magnificent Obsession* (1954), *All That Heaven Allows* (1955), *Written on the Wind* (1956), and *Imitation of Life* (1959). The splendid panoramic shots of Cathy Whitaker's neighborhood thus take us directly to the decade's longing to create visual dazzle and so confer the look of integrated wholeness on the culture at large. Yet when this visual sense of totality is combined with the story line's secrets, the society's cultural taboos and transgressions, the film directly confronts the slippage between the historical 1950s and "the fifties" —that is, the fact that the decade's sustained efforts at looking perfect and whole were in reality sullied by its lived experience.

It is the cultural left's antihumanist approach, with its emphasis on non-foundational, performative politics, that is most useful for analyzing the fact that "the fifties" represents a wish that can never come true. This is what grounds the cultural left's critique of American neo-conservatism, upholding its claim that there is no authentic American identity to be revived by looking at the *Saturday Evening Post* and that aggrandizing the spiritual meaning of the Founding is not a solution but a problem. Yet if the cultural left is committed to a position that forever throws open the intellectual ground on which identities claim to stand, if it can only be oppositional and corrosive, does it truly allow for political engagement at all? Can performativity be politically useful if it can only deconstruct existing positions rather than offer any of its own? It would seem that the corrosive irony that always accompanies a performance's self-criticism leads nowhere politically, because it forever undercuts its own strategies by turning back on itself, undermining its claims, making a ruse of its efforts. Indeed, performative politics draws attention to the inauthentic, tenuous standing of all identities. Yet might not the honesty that this demands be troubled by a sense of purposelessness? An aporia thus appears between the postmodern play of the signifier and Benjaminian now-time, the time of a meaningful politics that engages the present by unleashing its potential for change.

The Cultural Left's Critique of "the Fifties"

The act of undermining the claims of identity and its foundational episteme always invokes irony, as it calls into question the very grounds on which the assault itself stands. To critique a stable foundation through a commitment to performativity's logic is thus to assume a position from which to deliver such a critique. And, in assuming this position, it presumably runs the risk of reproducing precisely what it is out to undermine. To undermine hegemony's hold, one must have a platform from which to operate; thus the possibility of an origin, a foundational episteme, again raises its head. Indeed, the cultural left's self-identification as a position committed to unmasking the dissembling quality of all identities is fraught with problems, for it locates itself within the American cultural landscape even as it casts aspersions on such locations' existence. It is itself an identity, albeit one that confronts identity's internal problematic. The irony contained in performative politics thus runs the risk of engaging a cyclical argument hardly conducive to unlocking political potential. Thanks to this cyclical dynamic, we can never be sure that irony is not politically conservative, that its efforts to dismantle a stated position do not turn back on themselves by unveiling the very same properties in itself. "Nothing is ever guaranteed at the politicized scene of irony," writes Linda Hutcheon, who concludes that this form of indirection, insincerity, and cant can never be fully trusted.[33]

Because nothing in its commentary is guaranteed, irony presents itself as a slippery and unfaithful tool, something whose performance remains forever difficult to gauge. Its treacherous nature allows that the hegemonic order putatively being dismantled is in fact being reconstituted by a position that is merely its mirror image. If we claim, for instance, that Superman's immigrant status makes him *authentically* inauthentic, we might just confirm rather than dismantle the complicity of origins to which we object. If we maintain that the man of steel is "so darned American" because he is an immigrant and an orphan, our argument holds the potential to support the very epistemological system it disdains by defining the essential qualities that go into being an American. In Adorno's words, irony is "prisoner of its own form."[34]

Our nation's ideological shift to the right in the late 1970s, a shift claiming to have brought us out of exile and back to Pleasantville, coincided roughly with this changing intellectual paradigm under way in younger academic circles. It is thus significant that Reagan's taking office in 1981 coincided, more or less, with the reception of a philosophical position incredulous vis-à-vis the very idea of home. For by the time neoconservatism assumed a national profile, the influence of a large body of antihumanist texts was widely felt in the American academy. True, some of the most seminal writings of this position had been in print for several decades, and in other countries debates and discussions about poststructuralism and postmodernism had long been under way. And, to my knowledge, the term *performativity* did not enter the discussion until the early 1990s, with the publication of Judith Butler's *Gender Trouble: Feminism and the Subversion of Identity*.[35] Yet the transformative power of antihumanism's philosophical paradigm had seriously affected American academe by the mid- to late 1970s, concurrent with the groundswell of a new conservative voice in this country. By the 1980s, the fundamental tenets of this discourse (e.g., the discursive nature of subjectivity, the death of the author, genealogy, *différance*) had infiltrated numerous fields, making a list of texts and a battery of terms standard fare within disciplinary canons. Indeed, the influence of antihumanism on the American academy today can hardly be overstated.

This more erudite approach to political life, wherein a host of semiological systems take precedence over traditional notions of power and struggle, is precisely what critics such as Todd Gitlin and Richard Rorty lament.[36] They see in this revisioning of the political sphere the very reason the right has captured the American public's heart, for whereas neoconservatives promote family values while excoriating welfare and abortion, the cultural left makes use of French, German, and British philosophical imports to contemplate the cultural sphere in ways that escape the average American. While neoconservatives speak to Americans about everyday concerns, the cultural left speaks to a select few on campuses across the country. "University life could feel like a consolation prize," wrote Gitlin in 1995. "If the Right held political power, what did it matter?"[37] Rorty concurs that the cultural left's focus is misplaced: calling this version of leftist analysis an "unfortunate regression," he argues that it "exaggerates the importance of philosophy for politics, and wastes its energy on sophisticated theoretical analyses."[38]

And to some degree, Gitlin and Rorty are right. The deep insights of theory must have an impact on the larger political structures of a society and not reside in a sanctuary reserved only for those versed in a specific, rarefied discourse. I first became aware of this division between sanctuary and broader political structures during the 1980s, when I was in graduate school, training in the discourse that I now use and teach. Politically, it was an interesting and fractious time on American campuses, for the sea change in American culture had begun to infiltrate the university. In a number of ways, American society was becoming dramatically polarized by the orchestrated backlash against the 1960s and 1970s—against hippie values and feminism and multiculturalism and gay rights—against everything, in other words, since the 1950s. Reagan's mélange of market ideology, technological savvy, and populist sentiment was making its presence felt on American campuses as students veered to the right, while those on the left sought to counter-balance the groundswell. The *Dartmouth Review* had received conservative funding, and all across the country assaults on affirmative action, women's studies, diversity, multiculturalism, and a changed academic curriculum were palpable. While conservative students defended the great books tradition and Allan Bloom, those on the left desired more attention to non-European cultures, a revamping of existing academic boundaries, and a more overt politicization of academic discourse.

The 1987 publication of Allan Bloom's *The Closing of the American Mind* took this debate to an even higher pitch. This was a polemical text that capitalized on the animosities between right and left in American higher education as it offered a stalwart defense of the great books tradition.[39] These polemics of course crystallized around the now hackneyed, exhausted, practically meaningless phrase *political correctness,* which strategically worked to gloss a number of distinct issues often having nothing to do with one another. Neoconservatives argued that the oversensitivities characteristic of this movement had allowed for rampant reverse discrimination in America, that far too many groups were registering their collective grievances against traditional American culture and demanding retribution. They were leveling charges against the canon of classics in American education: against Milton and Shakespeare, Mark Twain and John Steinbeck. They were taking aim at our country's national heroes—Christopher Columbus and the Founding Fathers, Daniel Boone and Davy Crockett—calling them dead white males. They argued that history had not included enough female voices, and that our nation's grounding in classical liberal theory lent itself to a devaluing of women's social status.[40]

Indeed, according to the right, this critique of traditional values and traditional frameworks was an unabashed leftist attack on the very fabric of American culture. Even children's television shows entered the debate when conservative Republicans denounced *Sesame Street*'s Big Bird as an icon of newfangled claptrap. Yet the cultural left insists that its political and intellectual interests have been badly misrepresented by the right, for never was its attention to difference and diversity meant to be cast in such hostile terms. Richard Feldstein offers a leftist critique of the debate's parameters and the strategic misuse of the term *political correctness:*

> Practicing a politics of demonization, the neoconservatives . . . hold a
> worldview haunted by radical monsters (feminists, gay men, lesbians,

and people of color) who have been cast as subhuman miscreants. . . . This backlash has spawned an antagonistic ethnoviolence . . . in a concerted effort to smear the multicultural movement with the broad brush of political correctness. The game is afoot.[41]

Of course, not all students at American universities galvanized around these poles or held strong opinions on these issues. But those who entered the fray tended to see most everything in terms of the right-left division. "What's your excuse for not studying business?" a fellow student asked me one day in an effort to start an argument. It was the early 1980s, and, because he was pursuing an MBA, he felt certain that he carried the future with him. I was studying for an academic degree, which to his mind seemed a waste of time and, more important, money. In a sense, the schools where I studied played out in microcosm some of the ideological rifts that were emerging in the culture at large. One way was through the divestment movement on one campus, which heightened ideological conflict among students and gave them a concrete, pressing political problem to react against. At issue was whether or not our school should rid its portfolio of stock in companies doing business in South Africa, which had yet to lift its apartheid laws. Where one stood with regard to divestment served as a general gauge of where one stood with regard to the Reagan administration in general and its reading of American corporate culture in particular. My cohort was eager to see divestment occur and went to great lengths to hasten its arrival. While I participated in demonstrations and sit-ins, others built imitation shanty towns in the quad, got arrested, and generally went all out for the cause. "If you don't do some fucking divesting right now, you're going to have to carry me out of here on a stretcher!" a friend shouted at a rally.

Yet in addition to such blatant contretemps between divestment advocates and the administration, there were more subtle, insidious battles taking place among the students themselves. Among graduate students, it is always easy to discern individuals' politics based on the professors they rally around, the books they read, and the future careers they have in mind for themselves. Yet on our campus, a host of semiological systems also revealed a student's ideology, and with the added virtue of doing so silently, without confrontation. Facilitating such discernment were a student's hairstyle, hair color, the amount of black in his or her wardrobe, the presence or absence of Doc Martens shoes, and the number of earrings she or he wore. Food was another way to identify student sensibilities: my leftist friends tended toward vegetarianism and generally ate low on the food chain. Conversely, a conservative friend explained that he tried to eat red meat at least once a day.

The strongest identifier, however, was clothing. It was much less draining to impart political statements sartorially than verbally, and thus the vintage clothing we began sporting became a form of critique, an ironic political commentary that in all its muteness proved garrulous. To be sure, vintage clothing, often from the 1950s, became, in that context, a way of countering the preppy look, a way of lambasting the green and pink that Muffy and Buffy had modeled in *The Preppy Handbook* and that now stood in metonymically for the ideology of the right. To counter this statement, we who eschewed the green-and-pink combination wore anachronistic, recycled attire that itself came to metonymically represent the position of the cultural left. We wore vintage clothing not because we were enamored of its retrograde style—the flared skirts, the wide lapels, the cat's-eye glasses with upswept outer edges, the rhinestones. Rather, we wore such items because we longed to parody the swirl of feel-good connotations that they invariably set in motion—namely, the statement about American foundations that they unmistakably imparted due to their alignment with neoconservatism. In short, we wore *literal* 1950s attire in order to counter belief in the *metaphoric* "fifties." Using clothing ironically, we queried the claim that in the 1980s one could ever return to the Edenic foundation that neoconservatism invoked.

Eager to invoke incredulity, then, a number of us shopped at revival stores and built up revival wardrobes. Dressed in flared skirts and cat's-eye glasses, the women didn't really want to *be* June Cleaver. Rather, we wanted to cast aspersions on what June Cleaver had come to represent. The men sported thirty-, sometimes forty-year old oversized jackets, which tended to be double-breasted, along with thick-lensed horn-rim glasses. They didn't want to *be* June's husband, Ward. They wanted to call into question the larger statements about American culture that Ward, and the entire *Leave It to Beaver* series, implied through synecdoche.

For us, vintage clothing (some of which was from the 1940s, and some from the early 1960s) no longer seemed corny; rather it identified a person as incredulous vis-à-vis the neoconservative agenda, not trusting in firm foundations, reliant on pastiche. For in a multicultural, postmodern world, it is pastiche that reigns supreme in the aftermath of Rockwellian meanings. In keeping with the Lacanian critique of language wherein "I am" denotes "I am who am not," or "I am who have lost something," our sporting of vintage attire worked to erode fifties affirmation and to work against the decade's embowered status as the good old days late in the 1990s. It playfully but unambiguously undercut any pretense at America's true foundation, because in wearing vintage attire, we proclaimed: I am (not) a "fifties" person. I (do not) support the Reagan Revolution. The insincerity of simulacrum lingers on once firm foundations have eroded, and we find ourselves in a signifying free fall wherein "the crisis of meaning . . . now appears as the occasion for a good time . . . the comic dance of representations within the exhilarating space that dead meaning has left behind."[42]

Thinking back on my participation in the vintage craze, I am somewhat sympathetic to the criticisms that Gitlin and Rorty register against such forms of cultural critique. Maybe our clothing was a wasted philosophical analysis without any political clout, a sort of sartorial semiotics that went nowhere. Even during my time in graduate school, I shared the feelings of my cohort that our involvement in the divestment movement and general commitment to the cultural left were more important than what we wore. Thus I always admired my friend and roommate, Lisa, who was a leading force behind the divestment movement on our campus. Lisa was involved in nearly every aspect of the movement and sacrificed time and money to make things happen. But, to my knowledge, she never wore vintage clothing. For her politics was about taking action, not shopping for clothes. Furthermore, I am now more aware of the internal problematic that plagues this ironic replaying of 1950s clothing, for the gesture of sporting 1950s garb is perceived as camp only because of its interconnection with the right's political success. It can undermine identity only by assuming an identity and thus repeating the very errors it criticizes.

However, such concerns themselves run the risk of disregarding the full potential of performativity's philosophy. To state that the pastiche of performance and the distance of irony simply allow us to engage in irony fails to understand how committed to a freeing, empowering subversion they in fact are. Indeed, performativity does not stop at its deconstruction of stated origins, but relentlessly orients our attention toward change in the present. What has become increasingly clear to me since graduate school is that, in drawing attention to the tentative, vulnerable nature of articulated positions, an eschewal of ontology asks that the weight of the historical moment be read not as metaphorically absorbed by preexisting categories, but as filled with immediate potential, need, and meaning. As deconstruction draws us away from metaphor's appropriating control, in other words, it leads us into the lived reality of the present in all its idiosyncrasy and need. For if we simply replace one identity with another, allowing the cultural left to be ironically as foundationalist as the right, we fail to see our commitments through to the end. A narcissism takes the place of social engagement, and with the resultant state of apathy, despair, and cynicism, Gitlin and Rorty's worst-case scenarios become reality. This narcissism, a self-absorbed concern with one's own oppositional status and disaffection with the status quo, admittedly tends to plague the left, also keeping it from the needy, imperfect present still filled with potential.

Now-Time and the Imperfections of the Present

Wendy Brown argues that a form of melancholia tends to inhabit the left, one that differs slightly from the theory of melancholia employed here.[43] In making her argument, Brown stays close to Freud's theory of melancholia, and her understanding of this condition thus differs from that of Kristeva and Benjamin. Freud does not argue that the modern imagination longs to furnish itself with a missing substrate even though this act remains impossibile, nor does he purport that an engagement with the present can in any way enliven a buried erotic attachment (as does Kristeva) or unleash an unconscious wish (as does Benjamin). Rather, he maintains that melancholy's dejected state is related to an object loss that remains unconscious; thus the one experiencing melancholia will not always know exactly what about the loved object has been taken away. The loss itself, then, is unavowed. Importantly, the melancholic then transfers the reproach toward the once-loved object onto him or herself and rather than lament the loss of the object in question, heaps on him- or herself countless reproaches and self-incriminations. Unaware of the object loss that has precipitated this state, the melancholic manifests this condition through the expression of self-debasement. In Freud's words, "Melancholia borrows some of its features from mourning, and the other from the process of regression from narcissistic object-choice to narcissism. . . . Where there is a disposition to obsessional neurosis the conflict due to ambivalence gives a pathological cast to mourning and forces it to express itself in the form of self-reproaches."[44]

Brown worries that this form of lamentation, which shifts concern from an object onto oneself in a potentially narcissistic gesture, characterizes the left today. Too often, she asserts, the response of the left to the victories of the right takes the form of commentary about the left's *own* identity and subsequent disaffection with the current state of affairs. The left spends intellectual energy on explaining how its politics and cultural agenda do not match the position promulgated by the right. The effort that the left puts into expressing this disaffection, and perhaps blaming itself for the right's victories, exemplifies Freud's understanding of melancholia. We might then think of the following line from Freud's essay on melancholia in terms of the left's enjoyment of its own political exile: "If the love for the object—a love which can not be given up though the object itself is given up—takes refuge in narcissistic identification, then the hate comes into operation on this substitutive object, abusing it, debasing it, making it suffer and deriving sadistic satisfaction from its suffering."[45] According to Brown, lamenting one's disempowered status thus displays a narcissism that in fact amounts to a form of self-congratulation, as those on the left seem more enamored of proclaiming their renegade status than of addressing problems. For what is most being expressed is the left's inordinate, self-absorbed concern with its *own* identity. Indeed, it seems possible that there is a satisfaction in the state of disaffection, given that it allows the left to constantly use its own identity as the point of analytic reference rather than referring to things in the culture at large where change is needed.

Benjamin himself condemns the subtle fetishism that often pervades left-wing logic, which he describes as a logic overly attached to things and withdrawn from human relations.[46] That thing to which the left has become excessively attached is precisely its own renegade status, its role as outcast, which, at the extreme, it loves more than the world that it professes to want to change. In becoming excessively attached to its own identity, which it currently clarifies in contradistinction to neoconservatism's success, it proves guilty of precisely the kind of static position that typifies the right. "Left-wing melancholy," Brown writes, "is . . . a mournful, conservative, backward-looking attachment to feeling, analysis, or relationship that has been rendered thinglike and frozen in the heart of the putative leftist."[47] Here we see writ large a version of the irony described earlier: namely, a position declaring itself oppositional has in fact become conservative, getting stuck in a fixity even as it presents itself as a progressive movement committed to alternative solutions. For if we stay focused only on our oppositional status

and ostracism from the mainstream, where is our attachment to the
social field? If *our* identity forms the cornerstone of our conversation,
where is the engagement with the world at large that must always
admit the participation of persons who hold different political opinions?

This melancholy disposition to which the left is susceptible, a disposition most reprehensible for its narcissism, clearly does not allow
for the understanding of now-time so crucial to this analysis. There is
no room for the "new" in a position whose self-referencing causes it,
ironically, to be too distanced from the social sphere it says it wants
to change. Hence the left itself, and even the cultural left, runs the risk
of getting caught in the very logic it condemns. For if the status of *being*
the cultural left supersedes all other political considerations, then the
conundrum of being—rather than of *doing*—has again caught it in its
web. Once the cultural left per se becomes our starting point, we find
ourselves again in the complicity of origins that can just as easily lend
this position a mythology of its own. Performativity's mandates are
difficult to live by for any established political platform. Thus identi-
fying oneself in contradistinction to the right's backward-looking orientation may get in the way of the truly practicing performativity's
commitment to the present.

To argue simply that the cultural left risks restating a commitment
to foundations therefore misunderstands the full implications of performativity. For without question, one of the most salient qualities that
advocates of performativity promote is the singularity of each performance and subsequent resistance to any efforts to standardize, reproduce, or contain an individual showing. It upholds an episteme wholly
committed to the uniqueness of a situation, the *doing* of it, and to the
immediate demands of a cultural moment, such that reproduction and
re-presentation are necessarily viewed with suspicion. Thus, as performativity strives to locate the weaknesses in hegemony's hold, it never
promises to replace that hegemony with another, ostensibly "purer,"
more ontologically correct form of politics. Although it does assert that
the eschewal of foundations frees us from melancholia's grasp, there
is no pretense that the subsequent position endorses another foundation. On the contrary, this position recognizes the weaknesses that
plague *all* claims to an identity and, by insisting on action rather than
category, strives always to avoid essentialist claims. Narcissism's powers cannot overshadow a commitment to politics.

Performativity's lesson for cultural studies is thus that excessive
concern over identities obfuscates the purpose of politics. If our focus

shifts from being to doing, from ontology to performance, we can then let go of worries regarding meaning's free fall and focus instead on the demands of the present. The absence of foundations need not delegitimate the mandates of the moment; on the contrary, one of performativity's greatest strengths is the fact that, because it resists absorption into larger philosophical systems or claims to identity, it heightens an awareness of our actions' consequences. If such categories as "being an American," "being a conservative," and "being a left-liberal" are all rendered suspect, what then comes into view is solely what's in front of us. And surely an effort at unpacking the potential of the present in meaningful ways assuages the fears of Rorty and Gitlin by turning cultural critique into something that has a genuine impact on the social sphere. "There is no essential self, no given unity awaiting discovery or realization," writes Bonnie Honig of postmodernity's corrective to standard conceptions of identity politics. "There is no being behind the doing."[48]

To insist that there is no being behind the doing, no ontology to get comfortable in, thus does not deliver the heartless nihilism that many fear and cannot be said to dismiss ethical considerations. I see it instead as entirely ethical, highlighting the need, the potential, and the beauty of the present rather than ignoring these behind a misdirected analysis of what America "is." If we consider David's gesture of reaching out to his mother at the kitchen table and touching her cheek, we see this plainly. Having accepted the imperfections of a mother whose sexual and social roles are essential to the imaginary wholeness that creates desire, David responds by assuring her that the resultant state of fragmentation is acceptable to him. There is no being behind the doing—"It isn't supposed to *be* anything"; she has not disappointed him by not allowing for a firm foundation. Neither Betty nor his real mother has lived up to the standards of June Cleaver, yet it is in realizing and accepting this that he draws closer to his mother. By letting go of the mirage of the Thing, even if he cannot let go of desire's essential structure, David can be awakened to meaningful engagement in the present. His wide eyes that take up the entire screen tell us that this awakening has occurred and that his reliance on a sitcom's imaginary world has ended.

If the cultural left must avoid reproducing the very foundational episteme that it opposes, its understanding of the "new" will parallel David's gesture at the table. Recall that the "new" as understood by both Baudelaire and Benjamin described that time that finally freed itself from the grasp of an anesthetizing system, awakening from a dream-world to a moment in which history would finally stop repeating itself. Thanks to this awakening, the revolutionary potential contained in the present is revealed. Instead of the present being seen as something that repeats incessantly in a weighty, meaningless manner while still search-ing for meaning, it becomes a repository for potential change thanks to the powers of the imagination. In now-time, in other words, the imagination no longer feels that it lacks an antecedent; instead, it has a forward-looking gesture that can accept imperfections without expe-riencing itself as disempowered.

   It is difficult to take seriously the full implications of performativ-ity and to truly act on the conviction that engagement with the world must override the problematic of identity. But the left must let go of its own penchant for narcissistic self-reflection no less than the right, if either identity dwarfs the importance of the social sphere. For those committed to political action, it is difficult to allow that "it isn't sup-posed to *be* anything." Yet David's gesture of touching his aggrieved mother at the kitchen table offers insight into the liberating potential of letting go. Searching for wholeness only got in David's way. Hav-ing given up the search, he can now do something "new" and draw closer to his real mother.

America, a Phoenix Reborn (Again)

ulia Kristeva once referred to the United States as a fundamentally subversive nation, one whose organizing cultural matrix
is, admirably, forever open to reinterpretation.[1] By this, she meant
that ours is a society not founded on any firmly established cultural
practices or sense of inviolable heritage; rather, it remains fluid and
permeable in the deepest sense. The flexibility and freedom she observed
here were very unlike the deeply entrenched cultural norms and values that characterize her European background, such that being American appears synonymous with being in motion, forever in the process
of self-reinvention and reconfiguration. The easy, anticipated morphing of identities that American culture takes for granted makes ours a
nation that "undermines the law without attacking it head-on."[2] This
ever-mutating, "polyvalent" quality imbues American culture with a
uniqueness and a dynamism that, Kristeva asserts, inspires political
life by making it open to change.

Thus, in an interview published in 1977 in the avant-garde literary
journal *Tel Quel*, Kristeva observed that this pronounced restlessness
goes hand in hand with a "passionate" commitment to an enterprising

spirit and a "feeling of discovery."[3] Moreover, the fact that this feeling is shared in the culture at large keeps this restlessness from its potentially harmful extreme—namely, the collective psychosis induced by an absent matrix. Because American polyvalence successfully makes self-reinvention the norm rather than a frightening aberration, a constant undercurrent of change throughout society does not induce the anguish of unclear boundaries. Kristeva could therefore marvel at the hope America offered for a changed reality principle, a reordering of hegemonic rule given the obvious tenuousness of the status quo. For, to her eyes, our country seemed to do things differently in ways that appeared promising for the "new" as defined in this volume: "Although originating in European society and thought, America poses problems for our . . . sense of reason precisely in those areas where we experience our own crises. Perhaps it also gives us some different answers."[4]

Importantly, Kristeva's discussion regarding America's ease with a state of indeterminacy and its potential for delivering different answers made use of the verb *to sublate*. This choice of verb is significant for all that it states and insinuates about the ramifications of experiencing cultural flux. For indeed, the potential psychosis that might set in given the absence of clear cultural norms is transcended, transformed, and held in check in America—in Hegelian fashion, something discarded, something transformed, something retained—Kristeva argued, by the familiarity that Americans display with a constant state of flux. Rather than cower at the frightening implications of a society whose categories and identities are unstable, Americans confront such instability directly and feel at home with the signifying indeterminacy that results. "In fact the American culture that interests me," Kristeva stated, ". . . is the culture that confronts psychosis and sublates it."[5] This explains her observation that the American students attending her seminars apparently held an innate sense of postmodernism's central tenets, for the intellectual shifts being examined seemed to correspond to their lived experience. What had heretofore remained theoretically unexamined in their lives now became explicit in the language of a discourse forged largely by European intellectuals. In surprising ways, then, the postmodern aspects of the contemporary world that Kristeva unpacked for these students in class seemed to correlate with their unspoken experience of life in America. Hence, although the latter were theoretically naive and largely unversed in the philosophy Kristeva taught, their lived experience of the world offered correspondence with the tenets of the avant-garde that she strove to demystify.

To sublate psychosis would be to normalize the absence of foundation that I have described as integral to melancholia. It would be to normalize the impossible structure of desire, which longs to furnish the imagination with a missing substrate, and to transform its debilitating sense of incompletion into an internal struggle to be overcome, surmounted, and survived. The psychic force of a culture whose spiritual foundations remain in flux would not prove debilitating in its potential to overwhelm, but would represent an opening for significant social change. This, of course, would be the best possible response to an awareness of the signifier's open-endedness, for it implies the ability to admit meaning's tenuousness without suffering the debilitating effects of melancholia's tenebrous hold.

In reality, Kristeva's apparent endorsement of the collective American imagination may have been too facile, and she may have been too hasty in her conclusions about the innately postmodern attributes of our culture. She surely received criticism from readers who argued that America is repressive in its own way and that its frenetic motion and empirical orientation are not obvious links to a desirable social structure safeguarded from mental illness. Indeed, critics maintain that America's propensity toward flux, which has only increased since 1977, may itself be symptomatic of an underlying cultural malaise.[6] Nevertheless, her interview testifies to the hope she placed in the United States as a venue for forging a world in which overnaming denotes creative potential and democratic tolerance, and not simply the absurdity of bonds and beings.

Of course, much has changed in America since 1977. Yet Kristeva's argument is still theoretically valuable, given that her reasons for deeming the United States "postmodern" still hold. For instance, our pronounced creative potential to which she refers emanates partly from the fact that American culture is not ensconced in a set of established discourses as are other, older cultures. Unaligned with one given discourse and one cultural lexicon, Americans are not "verbal," not reliant on a single cultural heritage whose narrative is our collective point of reference. Since the late 1970s, the marked heterogeneity of American culture has become even more pronounced given the influx of immigrant populations into the United States from non-European nations. As Andrew Ross notes, migration at that time came to New York City from Asia, the Caribbean, the Middle East, and Latin America, resulting in a multitude of foreign cultures who "had no common Western traditions."[7] The markedly heterogeneous quality of America, coupled with its economic success and great influence in the realm of popular culture, diminishes the roles played by philosophy, language, and literature in our cultural profile. Americans are less beholden to a set of established texts and discourses than are those who live elsewhere, because the cacophony resulting from our diversity makes one unified voice untenable. Subsequently, this inability to arrive at one grand narrative that combines a multitude of voices into one synthesized whole results in Americans' being less invested in discourse. We are, according to Kristeva, a more practical people, defined less by what we think than by what we do. Just before the national groundswell of neoconservative ideology began, then, she pronounced us a nation that gravitates toward performativity.

Indeed, the ideological commitments central to American political thought revolve around being free to *act,* to do, to be enterprising, to practice our revered individualism as we see fit. Ours is an empirically oriented culture that, at the extreme, displays a bottom-line mentality devoted to producing results rather than to synthesizing numerous ideas. "They know what they do," Kristeva states of Americans.[8] "The cultural, technical and religious base is so riotous and multi-faceted that the non-truth that may obtain in a linearizing evolutionism . . . doesn't seem to be able to increase its influence."[9]

Moreover, the logic of postmodernist discourse as it has been received on American soil since 1977 can only be said to encourage the innate postmodernist proclivity that Kristeva identified in American culture at large. Although she claimed to see an ingrained ability to understand the basic tenets of postmodernist discourse among her unassuming American students, the fact that the more fully developed discourse of a polyvalent, densely layered, playful signifier has since been articulated within American intellectual circles only reinforces our culture's tendency toward the "nonverbal." This is not to deny the powerful role played by established leading discourses that of course exert influence over many Americans. Religion, classical liberal theory, and the logic of the free market count among these, and among the more zealous their meanings are far from unstable. Yet the nonverbal quality to which Kristeva alludes, the "riotous" quality of our culture, can be seen as characteristically American if we focus on the frenetic, polyvalent, mutating, and—it is hoped—tolerant aspect of our culture that results from our extreme, at times overwhelming, cultural diversity.

Throughout these pages, I have argued that such a riotous, multifaceted cultural base can be the cause of melancholia. When an overnamed

world too full of signifying potential deprives the imagination of fulfilled desires, it delivers a depleted cultural landscape utterly lacking in
the hopefulness and positive outlook keynoted in Kristeva's 1977 interview. Drawing on Kristeva's later work and the work of Walter Benjamin, I have employed a theory of melancholia and have proposed
that its antidote lies, simply, in the often difficult work of accepting
the reality of an overnamed world. It lies in the recognition that the
postmodern world's swirl of saturated meanings and ambivalent intentions is the state of affairs in the contemporary United States, whose
status as McWorld only heightens the swirl's dizzying effect. Indeed,
in the current setting, our ability to divest ourselves of one identity
and assume another with ease, to mutate deftly in an ever-changing,
ever-adapting manner, is what helps America to meet the demands of
a globalizing economy replete with high-speed connections, shifting cultural boundaries, changing world demographics, and newly emergent
cultural configurations. Our status as McWorld in the globalizing context demands that we assume such internal flexibility, that we accept
the lack of an overarching metanarrative without concluding that life
is a tale told by an idiot.

McWorld insists on the ability to stay loose and to stay fluid in an
interdependent world that can adapt a set of values just as easily as it
can shirk them. It creates a culture whose inner vision rests with the ebbs
and flows of the market and the potential of technology, with commodity culture and the incessant search for new consumers, a cheaper
labor force, faster production, and an increased profit margin. Thus
committed to "progress" as something newer, brighter, and more tech-
nologically advanced, McWorld cannot afford to entrench itself too
deeply in any one cultural configuration given the demands of capital
that drive it. And yet this mobile, mutating quality prone to self-
reinvention is what Kristeva terms "American" when she describes the
nation as postmodern.

I have argued that the vertiginous feel to contemporary life in some
ways encouraged by globalization can, in fact must, be seen as the
abundant potential of America's fundamental fragmentation and lack
of an essential identity. Our immigrant experience and commitment to
multiculturalism, our experience of movements of liberation and the
progressive politics of the 1960s and 1970s, our intellectual (if unconscious) embrace of postmodernist theory—these and other elements
must be read as revealing the fullness of the present moment rather than
the trace of meaning's loss. For if we let go of an essentialist position

wedded to a concept of what America is supposed to be, we can allow a static notion of our identity to yield to whatever is in front of us. Staying with the pain of indeterminacy leads only to a politics of nostalgia for the past and a raging against the present, whereas learning to cope with, and even to enjoy, our nation's open-ended culture might allow us to discover something truly new.

What I wish to highlight is the fact that it is precisely since the late 1970s that an essentialist position has been touted in the United States by neoconservatism, accompanied as it is by an enraged sense that the country has lost its way. This rage, with its longing for retribution, restitution, and a backward-looking cultural agenda, derives from a pronounced *inability* to feel at ease amid the many forms of indeterminacy that inhabit the contemporary cultural scene. It expresses an unwillingness to sublate America's riotous quality and a refusal to allow the subversion of the law that Kristeva identifies as precisely our finest quality. By invoking the pilgrims, the Founding, the glories of the past bound up in the metaphoric "fifties," it displays an unbending quality antithetical to what others marvel at. Viewed in this light, neoconservatism occludes what is best in our culture: the fact that in a multicultural, indeterminate nation like this, even someone from Krypton can assimilate.

Indeed, the invocation of the metaphoric "fifties" conceals an unwillingness to allow our finest qualities to flourish. Because it is refractory to cultural indeterminacy, neoconservatism seeks to harness a regressive impulse that insists that a static American identity exists, against all evidence to the contrary. By freezing a concept of who we are, it puts the emphasis on *being* rather than on *doing* and reaches backward before reaching forward. Conversely, America's postmodern potential locates its creative impulse in the here and now of contemporary society and the current register of time rather than clinging to the annals of history. It allows us, along with David, to escape melancholy's hold and depart TV-land as we reach out to a kinder, gentler nation, right here at the kitchen table.

NOTES

1. "The Fifties," an American Metaphor

1. For authoritative accounts of neoconservatism's rise to national prominence, see Jerome L. Himmelstein, *To the Right: The Transformation of American Conservatism* (Berkeley: University of California Press, 1990); Charles W. Dunn and J. David Woodward, *The Conservative Tradition in America* (Lanham, MD: Rowman & Littlefield, 1996); Sidney Blumenthal, *The Rise of the Counter-establishment* (New York: Times Books, 1986).

2. Ronald Reagan, "Inaugural Speech, January 1981," in *Conservatism in America since 1930,* ed. Gregory L. Schneider (New York: New York University Press, 2003), 344–45.

3. As I will discuss shortly, the right partakes of that American self-understanding that sees our country as the New Jerusalem, the place where the Old World of Europe could start again with a new lease on life. This imbues America with a clear mission, a cairological mission that breaks with the old sense of chronological time and believes in a redemptive social order. See Sacvan Berkovitch, *The American Jeremiad* (Madison: University of Wisconsin Press, 1978); David W. Noble, *The Eternal Adam and the New World Garden* (New York: George Braziller, 1968).

4. A variety of authors have written on this from differing analytic angles. For sociological studies that critique 1950s gender roles and the family, see

especially Stephanie Coontz, *The Way We Never Were: American Families and the Nostalgia Trap* (New York: Basic Books, 1992); Elaine Tyler May, *Homeward Bound: American Families in the Cold War Era* (New York: Basic Books, 1988); and of course Betty Friedan, *The Feminine Mystique* (New York: Dell, 1983). For an analysis of how 1950s nostalgia operated in late-twentieth-century America, see Fredric Jameson, "Nostalgia for the Present," in *Postmodernism, or the Cultural Logic of Late Capitalism* (Durham, NC: Duke University Press, 1992), 279–96; and Arjun Appadurai, *Modernity at Large: Cultural Dimensions of Globalization* (Minneapolis: University of Minnesota Press, 1996).

5. For a full explanation of the pertinence of the Jell-O box to the Rosenberg trial, see Marjorie Garber, "Jell-O," in *Secret Agents: The Rosenberg Case, McCarthyism, and Fifties America*, ed. Marjorie Garber and Rebecca L. Walkowitz (New York: Routledge, 1995), 11–22.

6. David W. Noble's argument is that early American authors such as Cooper and Melville refuted this belief in America's ordained status. As novelists, they could not sustain a belief in the United States as the New Jerusalem outside of chronology's register because, if life is Edenic, there is no need for art. See Noble, *The Eternal Adam*.

7. Quoted in Karal Ann Marling, *Norman Rockwell* (New York: Harry N. Abrams, 1997), 13.

8. Statement made in *Norman Rockwell: Painting America*, broadcast on PBS affiliate station KCET, Los Angeles, November 25, 1999.

9. Newt Gingrich, *To Renew America* (New York: HarperCollins, 1995), 7. Of course, not everyone subscribes to this easy interpretation of Rockwellian charm. Art historian Karal Ann Marling counts among those who have acknowledged the complexities of the artist's portrayal of quotidian America. For instance, in her *Norman Rockwell*, Marling makes mention of the artist's own admission that, despite their meticulous verisimilitude, his paintings expressed a *wish* for American society more than they simply recorded what was in front of him.

10. Maureen Dowd, "From A to Y at Yale," *New York Times*, May 23, 2001, A29.

11. David Savage, "Rehnquist Court Back to the Future," *Los Angeles Times*, September 27, 1999, A1, A16.

12. The war on terrorism in many ways revives a 1950s Cold War mentality. At the very least, George W. Bush's "axis of evil" echoes Reagan's "evil empire."

13. Doyle McManus, "A Week That Could Bolster Bush," *Los Angeles Times*, June 8, 2004, A1.

14. I discuss the manner in which the right views itself as the "remnant" of a much older political tradition in chapter 4.

15. Gingrich, *To Renew America*, 7.

16. Barbara Norfleet, *When We Liked Ike: Looking for Postwar America* (New York: W. W. Norton, 2001), 13.

17. Statement made in *Norman Rockwell: Painting America*.

18. The film's magnificent interiors in fact deliberately imitate the grand style of director Douglas Sirk, whose films, such as *Magnificent Obsession* (1954), *All That Heaven Allows* (1955), *Written on the Wind* (1956), and *Imitation of Life* (1959), give a robust, opulent reading of 1950s America.

19. Jacques Derrida, *Of Grammatology*, trans. Gayatri Chakravorty Spivak (Baltimore: Johns Hopkins University Press, 1976), 92. For an excellent discussion of America's "victory culture" from World War II to the Gulf War, see Tom Engelhardt, *The End of Victory Culture: Cold War America and the Disillusioning of a Generation* (Amherst: University of Massachussetts Press, 1998).

20. See Patrick Lucanio, *Us or Them: Archetypal Interpretations of Fifties Alien Invasion Films* (Bloomington: Indiana University Press, 1987); Thomas M. Disch, *The Dreams Our Stuff Is Made Of: How Science Fiction Conquered the World* (New York: Simon & Schuster, 1998).

21. For an analysis of how these qualities were interpreted as American in postcolonial France, see Kristin Ross's excellent *Fast Cars, Clean Bodies: Decolonization and the Reordering of French Culture* (Cambridge: MIT Press, 1996).

22. John Patrick Diggins, *The Proud Decades: America in War and Peace, 1941–1960* (New York: W. W. Norton, 1989), 180.

23. See Melvyn Dubrofsky and Athan Theoharis, *Imperial Democracy: The United States since 1945* (New York: Prentice Hall, 1988), excerpted in *Taking Sides: Clashing Views on Controversial Issues in American History since 1945*, ed. Larry Madaras (New York: McGraw-Hill, 2001), 102–3.

24. Stephanie Coontz argues that approximately one-fourth of all American families qualified as "poor" during the decade, as did one-third of all American children. Moreover not all families, neither white nor African American, could exist on a single income. See Coontz, *The Way We Never Were*, 29–30.

25. Diggins,*The Proud Decades*, 186.

26. Walter LaFeber, Richard Polenberg, and Nancy Woloch, *The American Century: A History of the United States since 1941*, 5th ed. (Boston: McGraw-Hill, 1998), 324–26.

27. Alice Jardine makes this point in "Flash Back, Flash Forward: The Fifties, the Nineties, and the Transformed Politics of Remote Control," in *Secret Agents*, 107–23. Jardine sees strong parallels between the 1950s and 1990s mainstream cultures' efforts at maintaining control: "From within the contemporary sphere of our American postmodern sense of loss of bearings, the question of control seems to me paramount. If we look back at the early 1950s, control was a major issue then as well" (108).

28. Garry Wills, *Reagan's America* (New York: Penguin, 1987), 5.

29. Nora Sayre, *Previous Convictions: A Journey through the 1950s* (New Brunswick, NJ: Rutgers University Press, 1995), 113.

30. For a firsthand account of the New York art scene during the decade, see John Gruen, *The Party's Over Now: Reminiscences of the Fifties—New York's Artists, Writers, Musicians, and Their Friends* (New York: Viking, 1972).

31. Statement made during the panel discussion "All Shook Up: Lessons and Legacies from the 1950s," sponsored by *The Nation*, 1996 (audiocassette).

32. Wini Breines, "The 'Other' Fifties: Beats and Bad Girls," in *Not June Cleaver: Women and Gender in Postwar America, 1945–1960,* ed. Joanne Meyerowitz (Philadelphia: Temple University Press, 1994), 382–408. For an authoritative account of figurative painting in the fifties, see Paul Schimmel and Judith E. Stein, *The Figurative Fifties: New York Figurative Expressionism* (New York: Rizzoli International, 1988).

33. Breines, "The 'Other' Fifties," 383.

34. Fredric Jameson writes about "the fifties" as expressing a "nostalgia for the present," a nostalgia that shifts the discussion from historical truth to a more mythological register. See Jameson, *Postmodernism*, chap. 9.

35. Ibid., 281.

36. Derrida, *Of Grammatology*, 92.

37. Richard Feldstein, *Political Correctness: A Response from the Cultural Left* (Minneapolis: University of Minnesota Press, 1997).

38. Ibid., 136.

39. Ibid.

40. Kristeva herself acknowledges this overlap in *Black Sun: Depression and Melancholia*, trans. Leon S. Roudiez (New York: Columbia University Press, 1992). As will be made clear, these authors approach this topic from very different angles, for Kristeva's work is grounded in psychoanalysis whereas Benjamin's is more rooted in philosophy and Jewish mysticism. Yet in that both are concerned with the anxieties of the modern imagination structured around a missing substrate, Kristeva is correct in arguing that they share a similar theory of melancholia.

41. Ibid., 171.

42. Ibid.

43. Julia Kristeva, "Women's Time," trans. Leon S. Roudiez, in *The Kristeva Reader,* ed. Toril Moi (New York: Columbia University Press, 1986), 191, 192.

44. Julia Kristeva, "Motherhood According to Bellini," in *Desire in Language: A Semiotic Approach to Literature and Art,* trans. Thomas Gora, Alice Jardine, and Leon S. Roudiez (New York: Columbia University Press, 1980), 241–42.

45. Julia Kristeva, *Powers of Horror: An Essay on Abjection,* trans. Leon S. Roudiez (New York: Columbia University Press, 1982), 6.

46. Sigmund Freud, *Beyond the Pleasure Principle*, trans. James Strachey (New York: W. W. Norton, 1989), 69.

47. Kristeva, *Powers of Horror*, 22.

48. Kristeva, *Black Sun*, 29.

49. Kristeva, *Powers of Horror*, 15.

50. In "Women's Time," Kristeva expounds on how in western culture female subjectivity is more aligned with space rather than with time. Masculine time remains more akin to linearity and "progress," as against the feminine *chora* that "precedes and underlies figuration" (94). "When evoking the name and destiny of women, one thinks more of the *space* generating and forming the human species than of *time,* becoming or history" (190).

51. Gingrich, *To Renew America,* 34.

52. Kristeva, *Black Sun,* 4.

53. Ibid., 53.

54. For an excellent account of Benjamin's understanding of the stored-away wish in the unconscious, see Susan Buck-Morss, *The Dialectics of Seeing: Walter Benjamin and the Arcades Project* (Cambridge: MIT Press, 1989); Kia Lindroos, *Now-Time/Image-Space: Temporalization of Politics in Walter Benjamin's Philosophy of History and Art* (Jyväskylä, Finland: University of Jyväskylä, 1998); David Kaufmann, "Beyond Use, within Reason: Adorno, Benjamin, and the Question of Theology," *New German Critique* 83 (Spring/ Summer 2001): 151–73.

55. David Kaufmann makes it especially clear that Benjamin's use of theology focuses on the present, with theology providing the lens through which to read the fallen, abject state of modernity. This is how both Benjamin and Adorno "can remain fiercely theological without discussing God directly." Kaufmann, "Beyond Use, within Reason," 154.

56. For a discussion of the collective unconscious in Benjamin's works, see Buck-Morss, *The Dialectics of Seeing,* pt. II, especially chap. 5.

57. Walter Benjamin, *The Arcades Project,* trans. Howard Eiland and Kevin McLaughlin (Cambridge, MA: Harvard University Press, 1999), 471.

58. Walter Benjamin, "On Language as Such and on the Language of Man," trans. Edmun Jephcott, in *Walter Benjamin, Selected Writings,* vol. 1, *1913–1926,* ed. Marcus Bullock and Michael W. Jennings (Cambridge, MA: Harvard University Press, 1996), 68.

59. Ibid., 69.

60. Ibid., 65.

61. Ibid., 72.

62. Max Pensky, *Melancholy Dialectics: Walter Benjamin and the Play of Mourning* (Amherst: University of Massachusetts Press, 1993), 51.

63. Benjamin, "On Language as Such," 73.

2. A Vertiginous Languor

1. Paul Vernon, "Chasing the Fado," at http://sunsite.kth.se/feastlib/mrf/ yinyue/texts/fr105fado.html.

2. Quoted in Elaine Sciolino, "Ending His Europe Tour, Clinton Waxes Nostalgic," *International Herald Tribune,* June 8, 2000, 5.

3. Vernon, "Chasing the Fado," 1.

4. Marcel Proust, *Remembrance of Things Past,* trans. C. K. Scott Moncrieff and Terence Kilmartin (New York: Random House, 1981), 48, 51.

5. Max Horkheimer and Theodor Adorno, *Dialectic of Enlightenment,* trans. John Cumming (New York: Continuum, 1972), 4–5.

6. Quoted in Mortimer Chambers, Barbara Hanawalt, Theodore K. Rabb, Isser Woloch, and Raymond Grew, *The Western Experience,* 7th ed. (Boston: McGraw-Hill College, 1999), 663.

7. Peter Gay uses the term *recovery of nerve,* in his *The Enlightenment: An Interpretation/the Science of Freedom* (New York: W. W. Norton, 1977).

8. Not everyone agrees that modernity's epistemological stance is scientistic, that is, basing all its claims on a scientific model to the exclusion of everything else. Here, I am following the lead of Horkheimer and Adorno in an effort to state the most extreme consequences of a disenchanted mind-set as it breeds rupture and fragmentation.

9. It is for this reason that Marshall Berman posits Goethe's Faust as the quintessential modern man, the man whose restlessness and eagerness to move ahead is both his strength and his ruin. Faust, of course, experiences great economic gain and personal growth only when he is willing to make a pact with Mephisto and forgo old world ethical principles. "Mephisto's message is not to blame oneself for the casualties of creation, for that is just the way life is . . . Body and soul are to be exploited for a maximum return—not however, in money, but in experience, intensity, felt life, action, creativity." Marshall Berman, *All That Is Solid Melts into Air: The Experience of Modernity* (New York: Penguin, 1988), 48–49.

10. For a discussion of bourgeois individualism and its anxieties, see Isaac Kramnick, "Equal Opportunity and the 'Race of Life,'" in *Dogmas and Dreams: A Reader in Modern Political Ideologies,* 2nd ed., ed. Nancy S. Love (Chatham, NJ: Chatham House, 1998), 99–112; Erich Fromm, *Escape from Freedom* (New York: Henry Holt, 1994); Herbert Marcuse, "The Origin of Repressive Civilization," in *Eros and Civilization: A Philosophical Inquiry into Freud* (Boston: Beacon, 1974).

11. Kramnick, "Equal Opportunity," 101.

12. Ibid., 107–8.

13. Both Fromm and Marcuse argue that the demands of capitalism answer to the mandates of a patriarchal performance principle, which differs significantly from the maternal attributes of earlier societies based less on performance. See note 10.

14. In *Escape from Freedom,* Fromm argues that bourgeois individualism encouraged the individual's emergence from the dictates of a formerly structured society. Yet this emergence and the freedom that accompanied it were plagued by a fear of life's deeper meaninglessness, an anxiety that, with the disappearance of the older order, there also vanished a clear sense of life's purpose. Fromm writes: "Any understanding of freedom in modern society must

start with that period in which the foundations of modern culture were laid, for this . . . permits us . . . to recognize the ambiguous meaning of freedom which was to operate throughout modern culture: on the one hand the growing independence of man from external authorities, on the other his growing isolation and the resulting feeling of individual insignificance and powerlessness" (36–37).

15. Judith Butler, *Gender Trouble: Feminism and the Subversion of Identity* (London: Routledge, 1990), 6.

16. In Max Pensky's words, the postmodern erosion of stable meaning has "the power to shatter our lives." Max Pensky, *Melancholy Dialectics: Walter Benjamin and the Play of Mourning* (Amherst: University of Massachusetts Press, 1993), 3.

17. Berman, *All That Is Solid,* 121.

18. Quoted in Sciolino, "Ending His Europe Tour," 5.

19. See also Walter Benjamin, "*Trauerspiel* and Tragedy" and "The Role of Language in *Trauerspiel* and Tragedy," trans. Rodney Livingston, both in *Walter Benjamin, Selected Writings,* vol. 1, *1913–1926,* ed. Marcus Bullock and Michael W. Jennings (Cambridge, MA: Harvard University Press, 1997).

20. From *Gaudium et Spes,* quoted in *Catechism of the Catholic Church* (New York: Doubleday, 1995), 520; excerpt from the Catholic confessional prayer often recited collectively at the beginning of a Mass, emphasis added.

21. Thomas Hobbes, *Leviathan,* ed.C. B. Macpherson (New York: Penguin, 1981), 161.

22. Benjamin, "The Role of Language," 60.

23. Walter Benjamin, *The Origins of German Tragic Drama,* trans. John Osborne (New York: Verso, 1998), 234.

24. Benjamin, "*Trauerspiel* and Tragedy," 57.

25. Benjamin, *Origins of German Tragic Drama,* 179.

26. William Shakespeare, *Macbeth, a Tragedy* (London: Cornmarket, 1969), 57.

27. Walter Benjamin, *The Arcades Project,* trans. Howard Eiland and Kevin McLaughlin (Cambridge, MA: Harvard University Press, 1999), 21.

28. Walter Benjamin, "Some Motifs in Baudelaire," in *Charles Baudelaire: A Lyric Poet in the Era of High Capitalism,* trans. Harry Zohn (London: Verso, 1997), 139.

29. On this point, see Berman, *All That Is Solid;* David Gross, *The Past in Ruins: Tradition and the Critique of Modernity* (Amherst: University of Massachusetts Press, 1992), chap. 3.

30. Quoted in Berman, *All That Is Solid,* 133.

31. Baudelaire compared *correspondances* to "universal analogies" in an 1856 letter he wrote to the author Toussenel. See Benjamin, *The Arcades Project,* 241.

32. The phrase "hushed transcendence" comes from Pensky, *Melancholy Dialectics,* 165.

33. Walter Benjamin, "Paris, the Capital of the Nineteenth Century," in *Charles Baudelaire: A Lyric Poet in the Era of High Capitalism,* trans. Harry Zohn (London: Verso, 1997), 170, 171–72.

34. Berman notes that this inclusion of the everyday precludes Baudelaire's being considered a modernist poet, when modernist is understood as formalist. His constant references to mundane realities outside the text prevent his oeuvre from making the self-referential journey inward that typifies other formalist, modernist texts. See Berman, *All That Is Solid,* 142–48.

35. René Galand, "Baudelaire Formulary of True Aesthetics," in *Baudelaire as a Love Poet,* ed. Lois B. Hyslop (University Park: Pennsylvania State University Press, 1969), 61.

36. Benjamin, "Some Motifs in Baudelaire," 141.

37. This translation and all subsequent translations of Baudelaire's poetry are my own.

38. See, for instance, Walter Benjamin, "Baudelaire," in *Walter Benjamin, Selected Writings,* vol. 1, 361–62; Walter Benjamin, *Charles Baudelaire: A Lyric Poet in the Era of High Capitalism,* trans. Harry Zohn (London: NLB, 1973).

39. See Berman, *All That Is Solid,* 131–71.

40. Yet, commensurate with his understanding of the modern poet, Baudelaire holds that not everything about this consciousness, so clearly beset by melancholia as defined here, is to be lamented. The cosmopolitanism of crowded urban spaces makes for a quickness, a mental agility, and a sophistication that serves the demands of the modern intellect. Marshall Berman comments on this nimbleness of the modern mentality, which of course plays into both a sophistication and an open-mindedness that are essential in the secular, disenchanted world. The impact of the crowd can indeed be a refining, enlightening experience, causing one to stretch and adjust intellectually as well as physically. The person on the street "must become adept at *soubresauts* and *mouvements brusques,* at sudden, abrupt, jagged twists and shifts and not only with his legs and his body, but with his mind and his sensibility as well." Ibid., 159.

41. For a discussion of America's absent ancien régime and resultant political culture, see Louis Hartz, *The Liberal Tradition in America* (New York: Harcourt, Brace, 1955).

42. Seymour Martin Lipset, *American Exceptionalism: A Double-Edged Sword* (New York: W. W. Norton, 1996), 31, 32.

3. Overripe America

1. For authoritative discussion of America's religious foundations, see Perry Miller, *The New England Mind: From Colony to Province* (Cambridge, MA: Harvard University Press, 1953); Perry Miller, *Errand into the Wilderness*

(Cambridge, MA: Harvard University Press, 1956). I am grateful to Dan O'Connor for his help on this topic.

2. As David W. Noble, explains, however, early American literature already displays a sense of unease with the idea of an Edenic New Jerusalem. For if literature necessitates tension and the weight of unredeemed chronology, there is no place for it in the place of redemption. Yet the presence of early American authors such as James Fenimore Cooper, Nathaniel Hawthorne, and Herman Melville dispels any pretense that America truly equals a New Jerusalem, for their writings clarify the continuity of European experience on American soil. See David W. Noble, *The Eternal Adam and the New World Garden* (New York: George Braziller, 1968).

3. Sacvan Bercovitch, *The American Jeremiad* (Madison: University of Wisconsin Press, 1978), 8–9.

4. Ibid., 43–44.

5. Alexis de Tocqueville, *Democracy in America,* excerpted in *Ideas and Ideologies: A Reader,* ed. Terence Ball and Richard Dagger (New York: Longman, 2004), 45.

6. Bercovitch, *The American Jeremiad,* 9, emphasis added.

7. Ibid., 7–8.

8. Ibid., 9.

9. For an insightful analysis of the assumption that America holds endless economic opportunities, see Laurence Shames, "The More Factor," in *Signs of Life in the USA: Readings on Popular Culture for Writers,* 4th ed., ed. Sonia Maasik and Jack Solomon (Boston: Bedford/St. Martin's, 2003), 56–63.

10. Ibid., 58.

11. For a discussion of the many cultural meanings contained in the American SUV, see David Goewey, "'Careful, You May Run Out of Planet': SUVs and the Exploitation of the American Myth," in *Signs of Life in the USA: Readings on Popular Culture for Writers,* 4th ed., ed. Sonia Maasik and Jack Solomon (Boston: Bedford/St. Martin's, 2003), 112–22.

12. In "The More Factor," Laurence Shames argues that thanks to the frontier ideology keynoting the American experience, we have come to imagine that there are always great fortunes to be made in the United States. The American mind-set always assumes that there is more to be had: more money, more land, more natural resources, more food. He writes: "There would always be another gold rush, another Homestead Act, another oil strike . . . The habit of more seemed to suggest that there was no such thing as getting wiped out in America" (57).

13. David W. Noble, for instance, argues that American literature has, since 1830, reflected the fact that the premise of American exceptionalism—the belief that American society could honestly occupy a different register of time— creates a tension crucial to the American novel. Noble traces this theme in numerous American novels, from the works of James Fenimore Cooper,

Nathaniel Hawthorne, and Herman Melville to those of Norman Mailer, James Baldwin, and Saul Bellow. Literature must offer insight into the frail, confused, corrupt side of human life, Noble insists, for in the absence of these there is no reason for art. Hence the American novelists "deny that America can become a New World Eden, and they reject the heavenly city on earth as a worthwhile or defensible ideal; they refuse to believe in the perfectability of man." Noble, *The Eternal Adam,* 6.

14. John Adams, "What Is a Republic?" in *Ideals and Ideologies: A Reader,* ed. Terence Ball and Richard Dagger (New York: Longman, 2004), 34.

15. Ibid., 34–35.

16. Newt Gingrich, *To Renew America* (New York: HarperCollins, 1995), 34.

17. Walter Benjamin, *The Arcades Project,* trans. Howard Eiland and Kevin McLaughlin (Cambridge, MA: Harvard University Press, 1999), 4–5.

18. For a discussion of this temporal theme, see Kia Lindroos, *Now-Time/ Image-Space: Temporalization of Politics in Walter Benjamin's Philosophy of History and Art* (Jyävskylä, Finland: University of Jyväskylä, 1998).

19. For a comprehensive discussion of Benjamin's political philosophy, see Uwe Steiner, "The True Politician: Walter Benjamin's Concept of the Political," *New German Critique* 83 (Spring/Summer 2001): 43–88.

20. Benjamin, *The Arcades Project,* 471.

21. David Kaufmann, "Beyond Use, within Reason: Adorno, Benjamin, and the Question of Theology," *New German Critique* 83 (Spring/Summer 2001): 153.

22. Ibid., 161.

23. Benjamin, *The Arcades Project,* 471, emphasis added.

24. See especially Susan Buck-Morss, *The Dialectics of Seeing: Walter Benjamin and the Arcades Project* (Cambridge: MIT Press, 1989); Lindroos, *Now-Time/Image-Space;* Pierre Missac, *Walter Benjamin's Passages,* trans. Shierry Weber Nicholsen, (Cambridge: MIT Press, 1995); *diacritics: a review of contemporary criticism* 22 (Fall/Winter 1992); *New German Critique* 39, (Fall 1986). For more general work on Benjamin, see also Richard Wolin, *Walter Benjamin: An Aesthetic of Redemption* (New York: Columbia University Press, 1982); Terry Eagleton, *Walter Benjamin, or Towards a Revolutionary Criticism* (London: Verso and NLB, 1981); Michael P. Steinberg, ed., *Walter Benjamin and the Demands of History* (Ithaca, NY: Cornell University Press, 1996).

25. Benjamin, *The Arcades Project,* 33; the translations here are mine.

26. Buck-Morss, *The Dialectics of Seeing,* 178. In *The Arcades Project,* Benjamin identifies 1822 as the year of the arcades' inception and explains that they were originally involved in the textile trade.

27. Benjamin, *The Arcades Project,* 872.

28. Ibid., 874.

29. Ibid., 8.

30. Ibid., 7.

31. Karl Marx, "Capital, Volume One," in *The Marx-Engels Reader,* 2nd ed., ed. Robert C. Tucker (New York: W. W. Norton, 1978), 319.

32. "With regard to these reflections," Benjamin writes, "it should be kept in mind that, in the nineteenth century, the number of 'hollowed-out' things increases at a rate and on a scale that was previously unknown." Benjamin, *The Arcades Project,* 466.

33. Ibid., 369.

34. Ibid., 4.

35. Ibid., 4–5.

36. Quoted in ibid., 4.

37. Walter Benjamin, *The Origins of German Tragic Drama,* trans. John Osborne (New York: Verso, 1998), 45.

38. See Walter Benjamin, *Charles Baudelaire: A Lyric Poet in the Era of High Capitalism,* trans. Harry Zohn (London: Verso, 1997), in addition to the essays contained in *The Arcades Project.*

39. Gingrich, *To Renew America,* 38.

4. Making Love with Absence

1. Newt Gingrich, *To Renew America* (New York: HarperCollins, 1995), 5.

2. See Herbert Parmet, *George Bush: The Life of a Lone Star Yankee* (New York: Scribner, 1997), chap. 23.

3. Ibid., 503.

4. Alice Jardine, "Flash Back, Flash Forward: The Fifties, the Nineties, and the Transformed Politics of Remote Control," in *Secret Agents: The Rosenberg Case, McCarthyism, and Fifties America,* ed. Marjorie Garber and Rebecca L. Walkowitz (New York: Routledge, 1995), 112.

5. Statement made in *Norman Rockwell: Painting America,* broadcast on PBS affiliate station KCET, Los Angeles, November 25, 1999.

6. Karal Ann Marling, *Norman Rockwell* (New York: Harry N. Abrams, 1997), 7.

7. Max Pensky, *Melancholy Dialectics: Walter Benjamin and the Play of Mourning* (Amherst: University of Massachusetts Press, 1993), 73.

8. See, for instance, Gingrich's chapter in *To Renew America* on the importance of technology to education as it serves the interests of self-determination.

9. Not all conservatives are critical of government intervention into the economy, however. In fact, some condone such intervention as a form of noblesse oblige, which makes for an interesting combination of Old World sensibility and left-leaning politics.

10. Russell Kirk, "Prescription, Authority, and Ordered Freedom," in *What Is Conservatism?* ed. Frank S. Meyer (New York: Holt, Rinehart & Winston, 1964), 27.

11. Irving Kristol, *Reflections of a Neoconservative: Looking Back, Looking Ahead* (New York: Basic Books, 1983), 49.

12. Allan Bloom, *The Closing of the American Mind: How Higher Education Has Failed Democracy and Impoverished the Souls of Today's Students* (New York: Simon & Schuster, 1987), 322–24.

13. Ibid., 324.

14. Sidney Blumenthal, *The Rise of the Counter-establishment* (New York: Times Books, 1986). Blumenthal argues that both the person and the policies of FDR gave the conservative position something to take aim at, a nemesis against which to marshal its forces. The reasons are obvious, for in many ways FDR's legislative package is anathema to the conservative agenda. The New Deal institutionalized numerous programs and policies, thereby enlarging government, expanding its scope and depth, and sanctioning its increased spheres of influence. It also expanded the role of the presidency, tampering with what many perceive to be the founders' intention that the executive role in national politics be diminutive alongside that of Congress. Indeed, this program's success institutionalized a liberal agenda, ensuring that limited government, unfettered capitalism, and the stalwart individualism that these supposedly breed would long be under siege: Lockean liberalism would have to fight hard to counteract the now deeply entrenched welfare state. So successful were FDR's efforts that, some argue, it is unlikely that his legacy will be dismantled anytime soon.

15. In addition to Blumenthal's book on the rise of neoconservatism, see Jerome L. Himmelstein, *To the Right: The Transformation of American Conservatism* (Berkeley: University of California Press, 1990); Charles W. Dunn and J. David Woodward, *The Conservative Tradition in America* (Lanham, MD: Rowman & Littlefield, 1996).

16. Pat Buchanan, *Conservative Votes, Liberal Victories* (New York: Quadrangle/New York Times Book, 1975), 3.

17. Ibid., 5.

18. David Halberstam, *The Fifties* (New York: Villard, 1993), 5.

19. Dinesh D'Souza, *Illiberal Education: The Politics of Race and Sex on Campus* (New York: Free Press, 1991), 17, 20.

20. This is not to imply that Democrats and other liberals in America never display a populist strain. President Johnson's Texan persona, replete with cowboy hat and boots, certainly cast him in this mold.

21. Gingrich, *To Renew America*, 209–10.

22. Quoted in Susan Jeffords, *Hard Bodies: Hollywood Masculinity in the Reagan Era* (New Brunswick, NJ: Rutgers University Press, 1994), 25–26. Jeffords offers an insightful and entertaining analysis of the manner in which Hollywood icons from the 1980s, such as Rambo and the Terminator, embodied neoconservatism's eagerness to extinguish the image of an American manhood grown soft and sensitive under Carter.

23. See Bruce J. Schulman, *The Seventies: The Great Shift in American Culture, Society, and Politics* (Cambridge, MA: Da Capo, 2002), chap. 5.

24. Andrew Ross, "The Work of the State," in *Secret Agents: The Rosenberg Case, McCarthyism, and Fifties America,* ed. Marjorie Garber and Rebecca L. Walkowitz (New York: Routledge, 1995), 291–99.

25. Ibid., 292. Ross explains that the related anxieties about America's definitions, boundaries, and technology came to the fore during the World Trade Center bombing in 1993 and the subsequent trials of the accused perpetrators, which in many ways paralleled the Rosenberg trial of the early 1950s.

26. See Schulman, *The Seventies.*

27. For an account of the right's organization at the grassroots level in Orange County, California, beginning in the 1960s, see Lisa McGirr, *Suburban Warriors: The Origins of the New American Right* (Princeton, NJ: Princeton University Press, 2001).

28. Edmund Morris, author of the Reagan biography *Dutch: A Ronald Reagan Memoir* (New York: Random House, 1999), explained his decision to introduce himself as a fictional character in the book along these same lines. In an interview on the PBS news program *NewsHour with Jim Lehrer* (October 4, 1999), he said that blurring fact and fiction seemed an appropriate way to tell the story of Reagan's role as an American cultural hero.

29. Garry Wills, *Reagan's America* (New York: Penguin, 1987), 229.

30. See Michael Paul Rogin, *Ronald Reagan, the Movie, and Other Episodes in Political Demonology* (Berkeley: University of California Press, 1987); Jeffords, *Hard Bodies.* Both Rogin and Jeffords discuss the centrality of Hollywood to the Reagan administration in terms of the president's image, his use of a script, and his ability to create narrative featuring himself as the hero.

31. Rogin, *Ronald Reagan,* 6–7.

32. Jeffords, *Hard Bodies,* 4–5. For another in-depth analysis of the overlap between Reagan's career as an actor and his career as a politician, see Rogin, *Ronald Reagan.*

33. Sheldon Wolin, *The Presence of the Past: Essays on the State and the Constitution* (Baltimore: Johns Hopkins University Press, 1989), 18.

34. It is necessary, however, to distinguish different components of the American right today and not speak of the movement as if it were too homogeneous. Specifically, the far right differs considerably from the more moderate conservative contingent, for the valence of political outrage and disaffection with American culture typical of these groups surely differs. Most often, the far right comprises a staunch religious fundamentalism and undying allegiance to the American Founding; it registers nothing short of disgust with modern society and contemporary lifestyles. The moderate right, on the other hand, also expresses loyalty to our tradition, yet it is too aligned with corporate values and the culture of big business, too concerned about America's competitive edge and military muscle, and too committed to our nation's technological

savvy to be truly disaffected with the country at large. The moderate right
surely laments the damage done by liberal administrations, but it hasn't given
up on mainstream America yet, especially given that it argues that its own values match those of most Americans. Hence both strains of conservatism claim
to speak for the real United States, and both engage in an energetic backlash
against the lax liberal lifestyle, but these positions vary in degree and kind
when it comes to the tenor of their discourse, the intensity of their anger, and
the rigor of their fundamentalism.

35. Ronald Reagan, *Speaking My Mind: Selected Speeches* (New York: Simon
& Schuster, 1989), 62, 63.

36. Jeffords, *Hard Bodies,* 25.

37. Reagan, *Speaking My Mind,* 175.

38. Blumenthal calls the Reagan Revolution an effort at "restoration." In
seething invective, he writes: "Reagan's 'crusade' is a mythic battle for a Restoration. . . . We can therefore go back in time to the creation, where we will
recover our 'first principles' and our power. When the Restoration occurs, the
dream of a Conservative Opportunity Society will come true. . . . The Restoration appears like Disneyland, the 'Magic Kingdom,' an amalgam of various
theme parks whose coherence comes from the dreamy sensation they arouse
. . . In the world of community, everyone has come home to stay." Blumenthal, *The Rise of the Counter-establishment,* 256.

39. Pat Buchanan, "A Republic, Not an Empire," in *Conservatism in America since 1930,* ed. Gregory L. Schneider (New York: New York University
Press, 2003), 413.

40. Ibid.

41. Erika Doss argues that Disney's theme park helped assuage anxiety about
the less domesticated, more bizarre elements of 1950s culture. It helped assure
people that mainstream, family-oriented culture could overpower such things
as the surrealism of Salvador Dali. Thus, even as the growth and expansion
of the decade gave expression to things not aligned with family values, Disneyland was there to ensure that imagination itself could be domesticated and
thus remain safe. Erika Doss, "Making Imagination Safe in the 1950s: Disneyland's Fantasy Art and Architecture," in *Designing Disney's Theme Parks:
The Architecture of Reassurance,* ed. Karal Ann Marling (New York: Flam-
marion, 1997), 179–89.

42. Ibid., 180.

43. See Peter Biskind, *Seeing Is Believing: How Hollywood Taught Us to
Stop Worrying and Love the Fifties* (New York: Pantheon, 1983).

44. Rogin writes that an important Hollywood lesson for Reagan lay in how
to "play the heavy" while still seeming innocent, unassuming, and single-
hearted. It was a tribute to him as an actor that he could play such a variety
of roles and still retain the same level of likability. "Throughout his entire
Hollywood career," Rogin writes, "in over fifty films, Ronald Reagan was never

cast as the heavy. Reagan's image was so secure that he could play a foreign spy (Steve Svenko, alias Fred Coe) in *Murder in the Air* or the American turncoat in *Prisoner of War* and still seem Ronald Reagan, the innocent." Rogin, *Ronald Reagan,* 40.

45. Ronald Reagan, with Richard Hubler, *Where's the Rest of Me?* (New York: Dell Sloan & Pearce, 1965), 4.

46. Ibid., 301.

47. Julia Kristeva, *Strangers to Ourselves,* trans. Leon S. Roudiez (New York: Columbia University Press, 1991), 7–10.

5. X-Ray Vision and the Powers of Performance

1. In his later years, Rockwell became more explicitly concerned in his paintings with American social problems such as racial tensions, poverty, labor relations, and social unrest. A *Post* cover from 1961 titled *The Golden Rule,* for instance, is committed to portraying a variety of religious traditions in ways that underscore America's pronounced multiculturalism. People from around the world of all backgrounds, race, economic standings, and ages gather in what appears to be an act of worship, and very few of the faces look American. Although everyone in the picture is praying, this work highlights diversity in ways that clearly portend a changing social fabric. In this, *The Golden Rule* differs radically from earlier Rockwell *Post* covers. Similarly, a *Look* illustration that Rockwell painted in 1967 shows two African American children moving in to a presumably all-white middle-class neighborhood as they are met by three white children who appear to be uncertain of how to greet them. This illustration, titled *New Kids in the Neighborhood,* exemplifies the manner in which Rockwell's later art was no longer cautious about disturbing it audience. Rather, it was the medium for engaging social problems that the earlier Rockwell preferred to overlook in his art.

2. For two accounts of the interconnections between historical narrative and contemporary politics, see Wendy Brown, *Politics out of History* (Princeton, NJ: Princeton University Press, 2001); Melissa M. Matthes, *The Rape of Lucretia and the Founding of Republics* (University Park: Pennsylvania State University Press, 2000). Matthes especially emphasizes how narrative is both foundational and open to interpretation, as constitutive as it is tentative. Citing the rape of Lucretia as a story "on the cusp between myth and history," she writes: "The stories that republics tell are more than literary superstructure; these stories are integral to the construction of the republic's political identity. . . . The stories and their retellings are the creation as well as the remembrance of a shared past" (8).

3. For an authoritative discussion of the relationship between American language policy and identity politics, see Ronald Schmidt, *Language Policy and Identity Politics in the United States* (Philadelphia: Temple University Press, 2000).

4. Gary Engel, "What Makes Superman So Darned American?" in *Signs of Life in the USA: Readings on Popular Culture for Writers*, 4th ed., ed. Sonia Maasik and Jack Solomon (Boston: Bedford/St. Martin's, 2003), 739.

5. See chapter 4 and Andrew Ross, "The Work of the State," in *Secret Agents*, 291–99.

6. Engel, "What Makes Superman So Darned American?" 739.

7. See Wendy Brown, "Resisting Left Melancholy," *Boundary 2* 26, no. 3 (1999): 19–27.

8. Jacques Derrida, *Of Grammatology*, trans. Gayatri Chakravorty Spivak (Baltimore: Johns Hopkins University Press, 1976), 91.

9. Ibid.

10. James M. Glass, *Shattered Selves: Multiple Personality in a Postmodern World* (Ithaca, NY: Cornell University Press, 1995).

11. Peggy Phelan, *Unmarked: The Politics of Performance* (London: Routledge, 1993), 2.

6. The Left Reviews "the Fifties"

1. Benjamin Barber, *Jihad vs. McWorld: Terrorism's Challenge to Democracy* (New York: Ballantine, 2001).

2. According to Barber, "McWorld" encapsulates all that typifies contemporary Western values: hyperindividualism, rampant consumerism, overenthused techno-savvy, a godless secularism. Conversely, "jihad" invokes the array of tribalist, anti-western, anticapitalist values that now prevail in Islamic fundamentalism. And although these opposing forces are in a way diametric opposites, Barber argues that they also prove mutually sustaining: "Jihad not only revolts against but abets McWorld, while McWorld not only imperils but recreates and reinforces Jihad." Ibid., 5.

3. Henry Giroux indicts Disney, Inc., for promoting the conflation of civic virtue and consumerism. He argues that the ideology promoted by Disney, Inc., seeks to persuade consumers that partaking of the many consumer items that Disney promotes is tantamount to endorsing an innocent version of America not unlike the "kinder, gentler" version discussed here. Shopping thus becomes an act of civic virtue, for Disney convinces Americans that owning its products is synonymous with building the safe, law-abiding, family-oriented society that we want. And if corporate culture enjoys a large measure of success, then the academic discipline of cultural studies must retaliate by educating Americans about this and other pernicious aspects of consumer culture. See Henry A. Giroux, *Impure Acts: The Everyday Politics of Cultural Studies* (New York: Routledge, 2000).

4. Barbara Norfleet's *When We Liked Ike: Looking for Postwar America* (New York: W. W. Norton, 2001) offers a large array of photographs portraying the 1950s that indeed correspond to "the fifties." There are pictures

of Tupperware parties, car dealer lots, Burger Queens, Magic Chef showrooms, school yards filled with children hula hooping, and other similar scenes, all suggesting a prosperous, orderly, innocent time unbeset by angst and dissent. Although Norfleet admits that, for the most part, she remembers the decade in this way, she states that these photographs "do not tell the whole truth" (14). Added to this is her realization that "we no longer live with the illusion that any photograph is a simple transcription of a reality" (15).

5. For discussion of poverty in America, see especially Michael Harrington, *The Other America* (New York: Touchstone, 1997); Michael Harrington, *The New American Poverty* (New York: Henry Holt, 1984). See also Stephanie Coontz, *The Way We Never Were: American Families and the Nostalgia Trap* (New York; Basic Books, 1992). For discussion of gender relations during the 1950s, see Joanna Meyerowitz, ed., *Not June Cleaver: Women in Postwar America, 1945–1960* (Philadelphia: Temple University Press, 1994); Betty Friedan, *The Feminine Mystique* (New York: Dell, 1983). For a discussion of racial segregation in the postwar era, see Thomas Borstelman, *The Cold War and the Color Line: American Race Relations in the Global Arena* (Cambridge, MA: Harvard University Press, 2003). For a discussion of class, gender, and race, see Paula S. Rothenberg, *Race, Class, and Gender in the United States: An Integrated Study* (New York: Worth, 2001).

6. Coontz, *The Way We Never Were.*

7. Ibid., 29–30. For a collection of essays about various gender, race, and class issues during the 1950s, see Meyerowitz, *Not June Cleaver.*

8. Paula Giddings, *When and Where I Enter: The Impact of Black Women on Race and Sex in America* (New York: Bantam, 1984), 262.

9. Coontz, *The Way We Never Were,* 30.

10. See Giddings, *When and Where I Enter.*

11. Statement made during the panel discussion "All Shook Up: Lessons and Legacies from the 1950s," sponsored by *The Nation,* 1996 (audiocassette).

12. Elaine Tyler May, *Homeward Bound: American Families in the Cold War Era* (New York: Basic Books, 1988).

13. See Coontz, *The Way We Never Were;* May, *Homeward Bound;* Friedan, *The Feminine Mystique.*

14. May, *Homeward Bound,* 193.

15. Friedan, *The Feminine Mystique,* 31.

16. Herbert Marcuse, *One-Dimensional Man* (Boston: Beacon, 1966), 12.

17. For an analysis of the progression between the Old Left and the New Left, see Maurice Isserman, *If I Had a Hammer: The Death of the Old Left and the Birth of the New Left* (Champaign: University of Illinois Press, 1993).

18. Marcuse, *One-Dimensional Man,* 9.

19. Statements made during "All Shook Up" panel.

20. In 1971, Lardner won an Oscar for his screenplay for *M*A*S*H.*

21. Sobell testified in the Rosenberg trial and was convicted of nonatomic espionage. He spent more than eighteen years in jail.

22. Nora Sayre, *Previous Convictions: A Journey through the 1950s* (New Brunswick, NJ: Rutgers University Press, 1995), 112.

23. Ibid.

24. Karal Ann Marling, *Norman Rockwell* (New York: Harry N. Abrams, 1977), 84.

25. During the "All Shook Up" panel, Sayre discussed several films made in the 1950s that expressed critical distance on the decade's affirmative tendencies. *A Place in the Sun* (1951), *Rebel without a Cause* (1955), and *East of Eden* (1955) explored psychological themes and social dynamics in ways that were not affirmative. And some films probed racial themes in a serious manner. *Giant* (1956), for instance, pursued a dense layering of racial, economic, and sexual matters, all set against the backdrop of wide-open Texan spaces. Indeed, the nexus of erotic desires among the film's central characters cannot be divorced from the socioeconomic dimension of Anglo-American and Mexican identities, for the categories of manhood, womanhood, whiteness, and economic class are tightly interwoven in the film's rough-and-ready frontiersman society organized around cattle ranching and oil drilling. Hence Leslie Benedict (Elizabeth Taylor), wife of the oil-rich landowner Bick Benedict (Rock Hudson), is favorably impressed when a white farmhand, Jett Rink, played by James Dean, serves her tea one afternoon. In all sincerity, she asks him why other poor workers, largely Mexican, cannot improve themselves as he has. He retorts: "I hope you don't go getting me mixed up with none of them. I'm just as much a Texan as Bick Benedict is." Jett's reply, along with his effort to serve tea, clearly lays out the social conflation of manliness, whiteness, and wealth so important to his identity. *Imitation of Life* (1959) pursues similar racial issues in an urban environment. The film was unusual for its time in that it studied racial dynamics and resultant class relations in a sustained, serious manner, never allowing its romantic intrigue to overshadow its somber tone. Throughout the film, Annie Johnson, an African American maid, suffers heartache as her lighter-skinned daughter consistently denies that mother and daughter are related. The latter is often mistaken as Caucasian and would just as soon be thought of as entirely white. Thus when Annie delivers her daughter's rain boots to her at school one day, the teacher explains that she has the wrong classroom, for there are no African American children in her class. Witnessing this exchange, the daughter first sinks down into her seat and then bolts from the classroom.

26. See Russell Jacoby, *The Last Intellectuals: American Culture in the Age of Academe* (New York: Noonday, 1989).

27. John Patrick Diggins, *The Proud Decades: America in War and Peace, 1941–1960* (New York: W. W. Norton, 1989), 181.

28. Walter LaFeber, Richard Polenberg, and Nancy Woloch, *The American*

Century: A History of the United States since 1941, 5th ed. (Boston: McGraw-Hill, 1998), 363. For a detailed analysis of black presence in American suburbs, see Andrew Wiese, *Place of Their Own: African American Suburbanization in the Twentieth Century* (Chicago: University of Chicago Press, 2004).

29. Diggins, *The Proud Decades*, 182.

30. The growth of American suburbia was of course aided by the proliferation of highways and an exponential rise in car sales. The construction of numerous thoroughfares around the country profoundly altered the nation's infrastructure, making access to the suburbs easier and trips to the mall a mainstay. The highway czar who spearheaded this restructuring was Robert Moses, who is sometimes described as the one individual who had the greatest impact on American city life in the twentieth century. Moses oversaw the development of a number of crucial thoroughfares: in New York alone, he undertook the Major Deegan Expressway, the Long Island Expressway, the Harlem River Drive, and numerous bridges. The construction of highways helped change American cities by linking them up with nonurban communities, thus making it easy for suburban commuters to go from home to work and back again in record time. Thanks to the great efforts and enormous success of Moses and others, living outside an urban center became an attractive, even desirable alternative. The suburbs were seen as a haven, an escape from city life into a calm environment that brought one closer to nature.

31. LaFeber et al., *The American Century*, 362.

32. Diggins, *The Proud Decades*, 183.

33. Linda Hutcheon, *Irony's Edge: The Theory and Politics of Irony* (New York: Routledge, 1994), 15.

34. Quoted in ibid., 29.

35. Judith Butler, *Gender Trouble: Feminism and the Subversion of Identity* (London: Routledge, 1990).

36. Both Gitlin and Rorty have argued that excessive attention to the *cultural* implications of politics diverts attention from larger political goals. Thus such fields as cultural studies raise students' awareness of the politics of culture without honing their skills where the culture of politics is concerned. For an excellent discussion of this, see Giroux, *Impure Acts*.

37. Todd Gitlin, *The Twilight of Common Dreams: Why America Is Wracked by Cultural Wars* (New York: Henry Holt, 1995), 152.

38. Richard Rorty, *Achieving Our Country: Leftist Thought in Twentieth-Century America* (Cambridge, MA: Harvard University Press, 1998), 37.

39. Allan Bloom, *The Closing of the American Mind: How Higher Education Has Failed Democracy and Impoverished the Souls of Today's Students* (New York: Simon & Schuster, 1987).

40. On this point, see especially Carole Pateman, *The Sexual Contract* (Stanford, CA: Stanford University Press, 1988); Zillah Eisenstein, *The Radical Future of Liberal Feminism* (Boston: Northeastern University Press, 1986); Linda

Zerilli, *Signifying Woman: Culture and Choas in Rousseau, Burke, and Mill* (Ithaca, NY: Cornell University Press, 1994).

41. Richard Feldstein, *Political Correctness: A Response from the Cultural Left* (Minneapolis: University of Minnesota Press, 1997), 103.

42. Max Pensky, *Melancholy Dialects: Walter Benjamin and the Play of Mourning* (Amherst: University of Massachusetts Press, 1993), 2.

43. Wendy Brown, "Resisting Left Melancholy," *Boundary 2* 26, no. 3 (1999): 19–27.

44. Sigmund Freud, "Mourning and Melancholia," in *The Freud Reader,* ed. Peter Gay (New York: W. W. Norton, 1989), 587.

45. Ibid., 588.

46. See Walter Benjamin, "Left-Wing Melancholy," in *The Weimar Republic Sourcebook,* ed. Anton Kaes, Martin Jay, and Edward Dimenberg (Berkeley: University of California Press, 1994).

47. Brown, "Resisting Left Melancholy," 22.

48. Bonnie Honig, *Political Theory and the Displacement of Politics* (Ithaca, NY: Cornell University Press, 1993), 82.

Conclusion

1. See Julia Kristeva, "Why the United States?" trans. Sean Hand, in *The Kristeva Reader,* ed. Toril Moi (New York: Columbia University Press, 1986), 272–91.

2. Ibid., 274.

3. Ibid., 275.

4. Ibid., 291.

5. Ibid., 276.

6. Specifically, Jacqueline Rose has argued that the "nonverbal" aspect of American society may be symptomatic of America's own special breed of violence and lack of cultural cohesion. See Jacqueline Rose, "Julia Kristeva — Take Two," in *Sexuality in the Field of Vision* (London: Verso, 1988), 141–64.

7. Andrew Ross, "The Work of the State," in *Secret Agents: The Rosenberg Case, McCarthyism, and Fifties America,* ed. Marjorie Garber and Rebecca L. Walkowitz (New York: Routledge, 1995), 292.

8. Kristeva, "Why the United States?" 275.

9. Ibid., 277.

INDEX

abjection. *See* Kristeva, Julia
abstract expressionism during
  1950s, 24
"absurdity of bonds and beings."
  See Kristeva, Julia
acedia: and baroque tragic drama,
  46; and the melancholic outlook,
  71; and the "new," 46; as
  outgrowth of postmodernity, 45;
  as overcome by Jeztzeit, 82. See
  also taedium vitae
Adamic language. *See* Benjamin,
  Walter
Adams, John, 78
Adorno, Theodor: as critical of
  mainstream values, 145; and
  disenchantment of modernity, 39;
  as theorist of irony, 152
Adventures of Superman, The, 126
Aglaia (of The Three Graces), 79

air conditioners: as new consumer
  item during 1950s, 17
Alger, Horatio: as American cultural
  icon, 75
allegory: in Baudelaire's poetry,
  52–69; Benjamin's use of, 83–92;
  connection to Marxist theory,
  87–92; modernity and the
  baroque, 51–92
"All Shook Up: Lessons and Legacies from the 1950s," 145–49
All That Heaven Allows (1955), 150
America: and belief in rags-to-riches,
  75–77, 115; as embodying rupture,
  69–70, 72–96; as Europe's second
  chance, 73–82, 92–96; and
  example of the "new," 164; and
  the frontier, 75–77, 115; as an
  ideological commitment, 123; and
  Iran hostage crisis, 105–7; as

Mary Caputi is professor of political science at California State University in Long Beach.